Y0-CBB-171

TWENTY DAYS

TWENTY

DAYS

A Narrative in Text and Pictures of the Assassination of Abraham Lincoln and the Twenty Days and Nights that followed — The Nation in Mourning, the Long Trip Home to Springfield

BY DOROTHY MESERVE KUNHARDT
AND PHILIP B. KUNHARDT JR.

Foreword by BRUCE CATTON

CASTLE BOOKS

TWENTY DAYS

Printed in the United States of America.

Arrangement has been made to publish this edition by Castle Books, a division of Book Sales, Inc., 110 Enterprise Avenue, Secaucus, NJ 07094 with HarperCollinsPublishers, 10 East 53rd St., New York, NY 10022.

ISBN 1-55521-975-6

Art Director, BRENDAN F. MULVEY

CONTENTS

FOREWORD

Few of the great events in American history have been described as often or in as much detail as the assassination of Abraham Lincoln. Here is one of the pivotal tragedies in our national story, and by now it is so completely familiar that the mere words "Ford's Theatre" or *Our American Cousin* immediately evoke the entire story for every American. If there is one chapter that we think we have by heart it is this one.

Yet there is still something for us to learn about it, and now in this extraordinary book we have the opportunity to do so. The story always leads us, to be sure, to the same haunted, echoing mystery, and it leaves us with the same unwillingness to accept a cruel, seemingly meaningless twist of fate. But perhaps because of that very reluctance it is useful for us to hear the story, not as a tidy and well-arranged narrative but as a tale told by many voices whose conflicting testimony simply emphasizes the shock which the tragedy inflicted at the time.

Of necessity, history is selective. When it deals with an event like this it assembles the pertinent accounts and discards the irrelevant, carefully separates the probably true from the obviously false, pieces stray bits of testimony together, and presents us at last with a coherent story. This is the way history has to be, and if it were not told that way it would be unendurably confusing. Yet we may miss something when we read it that way, and what we miss can be important—the dreadful incoherence which the affair had at the time for the people who were involved in it. History's most compelling moments are not always as orderly as the books make them seem; sometimes they are in the highest degree disorderly, so bewildering that even people who lived through them may have only a shadowy idea of what they themselves saw. There is a confusion of tongues, which may indeed be a deep problem for the historian but which was after all part of the reality at the time. It is no wonder that history's tragedies give birth to myths and legends. Sometimes it seems marvelous that the real truth ever does take shape.

This book, *Twenty Days*, is a good example of what the raw material of history looks like. Never before has the story of the assassination of President Lincoln—from the moment the fatal shot was fired down to the day when Lincoln's body was laid to rest at Springfield, Illinois—been presented in such a wealth of detail. That some of the details, as related at the time, were wrong is precisely the point. Here is everything that happened, and much that was reported and probably did not happen, tied together by what might be called a running text of pictures, and the result is both moving and instructive.

Dorothy Meserve Kunhardt and her son, Philip B. Kunhardt, Jr., have worked in a field made familiar to them and to us by the extensive researches of Mrs. Kunhardt's father, the late Frederick Hill Meserve, who devoted a lifetime to amassing the greatest collection in existence of photographs of Lincoln, his times, and his contemporaries. This magnificent collection was left in Mrs. Kunhardt's care, and she and her son have spent years in an attempt not merely to arrange a selection of pictures that would give a vivid, fresh view of those tragic days, but also to compile a record of the things which scores of people who were immediately involved in those days had to say.

This of course is where the story becomes interesting, because the people who left their stories did not see things the same way. Some of them, apparently, did not see at all what the others saw, so that the testimony is often at odds.

For instance, twenty-five different human beings asserted that they helped carry the body of Abraham Lincoln across the street from the theatre into the little house where he died. It is perfectly clear, to anyone who stops to think, that twenty-five people could not possibly get close enough to one man to join hands and carry him: yet they all said they did, and their stories vary enormously. One man solemnly testifies that the dying President was carried across the street on a shutter, wrenched from a theatre window by ardent onlookers; another man, with equal solemnity, says that the President was carried in the rocking chair he occupied when the fatal bullet was fired; to wind it up, eight different beings insist that they, individually and unaided, held the President's head during the sad journey.

How about the house across the street, where the stricken man died? He was laid on a bed in a suffocatingly small room where four people would make a crowd. According to the testimony, no fewer than eighty-four people were in that room that night, at one time or another. After he died, coins the size of half dollars were laid on his eyelids to hold them down. Each one of three different men, all men of standing whose word there is little reason to doubt, asserts that he and he alone took two silver coins and laid them on those eyelids.

Then there was John Wilkes Booth, who pulled the trigger and, before a theatre full of people, leaped from the presidential box to the stage, shouted something only half-intelligible, then went to the wings and made his exit. How did he do all of this? According to one witness, he made a fifteen-foot leap, ran swiftly off-stage, and vanished. According to another, he slid down a flagpole (which did not actually exist), and more or less crept away. One witness saw him limping painfully across the stage, moaning incoherently; another saw him stalking off calmly, dropping his "Sic semper tyrannis" as a good actor might; another saw him running furiously, saying nothing at all; still another remembered that he went off-stage on his hands and knees, making noises. . . . Apparently he got on-stage and then off, but the testimony about the way he did it is extremely varied.

Now what do we get out of all of this? We get, of course, the essential truth: that this crack-brained actor murdered Abraham Lincoln and then went away; and that the history of the United States thereafter was different from what it might have been if all of this had not happened—and perhaps that is really all we have to know. We have too many witnesses, and they tell too many different stories. Probably all of these people were honest enough; they just saw things differently when a terrible and unexpected catastrophe burst upon their vision. The historians have been working with all of this for generations, and by now they have pretty well agreed on what really happened, so that we have a tolerably clear story. But at the time the whole event was nothing but chaos.

Apparently that is the way events usually are. Maybe eyewitnesses are sometimes the worst witnesses; maybe circumstantial evidence (highly derided in law courts and in mystery novels) is sometimes the only kind that is good. And maybe, too, it is good for us now and then to put ourselves back in the places of the people who had to live through these terrible moments, so that we can understand that history does not usually make real sense until long afterward. . . .

In any case, here it is. It makes a fascinating story in itself, and it also helps us to understand that even the best history is not much better than a mist through which we see shapes dimly moving.

BRUCE CATTON

PREFACE

At about ten-thirty on the black night of April 14, 1865, a man signaled with a lighted candle from the stoop of Petersen's boarding house in Washington, D.C., and shouted four ordinary words, "Bring him in here!" Opposite, across the street, something far out of the ordinary began to move. Monstrous and many-legged like a centipede, it had just squeezed itself out through the doorway of Ford's Theatre and now began to crawl in agonizingly slow motion toward the candle's flame, its many feet moving in weirdly unrelated, out-of-time steps, all struggling for stances in the wheel-rutted and hoof-chopped dirt.

Viewed close up, its true nature became apparent and even more horrifying, for it represented twenty-five soldiers and doctors and bystanders carrying to the nearest bed the body of Abraham Lincoln, sixteenth President of the United States and the first ever to be struck down by an assassin. An officer's sword had opened a path in the crowd that stood transfixed with shock, eyes straining beyond the short flare of three gas jets to glimpse the familiar face. They saw it—wax pale. The President was naked to the waist, but riding lopsidedly on his chest where someone had flung it was his overcoat with its telltale collar, sticky with new blood.

Twice in Mr. Lincoln's journey across Tenth Street there was a halt while the surgeon in charge plucked blood clots from down near the roots of hair at the back of the head, opening the mouth of the wound for free bleeding. Whenever the hole became plugged and the red trickle stopped, so did the breathing—almost.

At last, clumsily inching their way by multiple finicky steps up the Petersen stoop, humping their burden and narrowing file to flow through the tight entrance, the bearers vanished from the view of the crowd.

Even as fifty mud-caked boots moved over oilcloth floor-covering toward the end of the hall where the candle led—entered and filled the modest living quarters of the young soldier who kept them in such apple-pie order—twenty-five stories were born. Twenty-five men would describe and redescribe throughout their days this high point in all their existences—they had helped bear the Union's martyr from the place of assassination to his deathbed. Out of a life's ending came the beginnings of a host of conflicting stories, unimportant but persistent, of remembrances both strange and muddled, and of events impressive and much stranger.

Several weeks before this fateful night Mrs. Lincoln and the President were driving by horse and buggy along the James River in Virginia when they came to an old country graveyard. It was far from the busy world and had tall trees, and on the graves the buds of spring flowers were opening in the sunlight. They both wanted to stop and walk through it and they did. Mr. Lincoln, said his wife, seemed thoughtful and impressed. He said, "Mary, you are younger than I. You will survive me. When I am gone, lay my remains in some quiet place like this."

Twenty days after the shooting at Ford's Theatre the President got his wish. After twelve funerals in twelve cities as he was borne home to his prairie state, his long coffin was placed in a hillside tomb in Oak Ridge Cemetery, Springfield, Illinois—with tender leaves of spring opening on all the trees and a little brook, brimming from April rains, dashing joyfully by.

Long ago in the 1860's there were the people who lived through the Lincoln assassination physically and spiritually. They saw the dead President, and it made them faint and sick. They heard the dirges, and their throats choked up, something electric ran down their spines. They smelled the sweet funeral flowers and it reminded them of all the tender garden moments of their lives. They suffered desolation of heart with the rest of their countrymen that such a thing could happen to such a friendly man they all had known, or felt they had—his talk was so "fireside."

Then, as time passed and memories faded, the shock and grief were forgotten. The Lincoln assassination simply could not be imagined by new generations, the words and the pictures on the pages were not enough. April 14, 1865, was not real and it was impossible to see it real—though the nation grieved over the assassinations of Garfield and McKinley—until November 22, 1963. On that day, and during the weekend that followed, the frightful re-enactment of the awful event ninety-eight years before, so blurred by the paleness of distance, brought the assassination of long ago to life for a whole new generation.

Once again there was the devastating effect on a nation and a world. People walked the streets in shock, the masks that usually guard their feelings stripped away, unconscious of tear-wet cheeks. Once again the churches were filled with believers and unbelievers, kneeling. And the similarities of those four days to the events of the twenty days a century ago were almost uncanny.

The knowledge that he might very easily be assassinated was something Lincoln had lived with for four and a half years before the night he finally was murdered. By the beginning of his second term the threats to his life had increased and so had the warnings from his friends, to be more prudent, not to go about alone.

In 1861 his Secretary of State, Seward, had declared confidently, "Assassination is not an American habit or practice," but with Lee's final defeat he changed his mind, pointed out to Attorney General James Speed that certain individuals among the Southern people would be in a mood of absolute madness and the President might indeed be killed. At that time the Secret Service was not yet responsible for the President's life. There were armed sentries at the White House gates, and the War Department had arranged a detail of soldiers for protecting Lincoln whenever he rode out, but it was a haphazard arrangement. Seward advised Speed to make the trip to City Point where Lincoln was visiting Grant's army, and counsel him to be careful.

When the Attorney General arrived, the President had already walked several miles through the still burning city of Richmond. Its white residents were invisible inside their houses and only a crowd of Negroes followed, trying to kneel in his path and bless him for their emancipation. He made an inviting target for any madman, but no one even called out a bad name.

Lincoln was saying in one breath of his excursion, "I was not scared about myself one bit," and in another that it had occurred to him as he walked that a gun could have been aimed from any window along the route. But then, he had said the same of his daily situation back in Washington. "If anyone wanted to kill me, he could shoot me from a window on Seventh Street any day when I am riding out to the Soldiers' Home. I do not believe it is my fate to die in this way."

Speed tried to talk to the President about Seward's fear for him of assassination but reported, "He stopped me at once, saying he had rather be dead than live in continual dread. Any precautions against assassination would be to him perpetual reminders of danger."

It was not just the Attorney General who warned the President; it was every caller. No one ever let him forget the subject and though the President sometimes met it with light banter, at other times his eyes showed his deep depression and that the continual talk about his possible sudden death had become a torture.

The Secret Service detective La Fayette C. Baker said that whenever he began to bring Lincoln up to date on the latest plots and threats, his manner became playful. "Well, Baker," he would say, "what do they want to kill me for? If they kill me, they will run the risk of getting a worse man."

It was the same with his best friend and bodyguard Ward Hill Lamon. He tried to make Lincoln promise that he would not expose himself in crowds and especially would not go to the theatre while he, Lamon, was away.

The President just laughed and remarked to Secretary of the Interior Usher, "This boy is a monomaniac on the subject of my safety." Lamon was crazy, he said. Lamon wanted Lincoln to sit in his lap all day.

He kept giving people his answers on the touchy subject. "I have received a great many threatening letters but I have no fear of them. . . ." "If they kill me, I shall never die another death. . . ." "I determined when I first came here I should not be dying all the while. . . ." "If anyone is willing to give his life for mine, there is nothing that can prevent it. . . ."

He didn't believe the knife was yet made or the bullet run that would end his life. "I shall live till my work is done and no earthly power can prevent it. And then, it doesn't matter, so that I am ready, and that I ever mean to be."

A black mood could fall upon him without warning and bring, "I shall never live out the four years of my term. When the rebellion is crushed, my work is done."

In a cubby hole of his office desk Lincoln had two letters which he had tied together and labeled "Assassination." One purported to be written to a man who had drawn the lot to kill the "monster" and was meant to bolster the killer's courage. The assassin was to get into the monster's office, "congratulate him, listen to his stories. . . ." "Abe must die and now. You can choose your weapons—the cup, the knife, the bullet."

The President had already barely escaped a bullet. During the summer of 1864, just as he entered the grounds of the Soldiers' Home, riding alone and at night, a hidden marksman had fired at him but the ball had whizzed through his high hat. He asked that no mention of it be made. "It was probably an accident and might worry my family."

There was talk around Washington that the cup had been tried too—that castor oil ordered from a pharmacy had arrived deadly with poison, but had had too queer a taste to be swallowed.

In the same category of whispered rumor was the trunk of old clothes taken from yellow-fever victims in Cuba that had been delivered to the White House on the chance that the Lincolns would come down with the disease, and hopefully it would be fatal. The catch here was that a trunk of second-hand clothing would be the first thing finery-loving Mrs. Lincoln would order burned.

A man kept coming to see the President to say he positively knew that a small square package was being mailed to Mr. Lincoln which would explode when it was unwrapped. Lincoln told him each time, "No package yet, and I promise never to open any small square packages."

Though the mailed bomb proved a myth the President regularly received photographs and drawings of himself spattered suggestively with red ink. Usually there was a rope around his neck, stretching up to the branch of a tree. These he minded chiefly because they upset Mrs. Lincoln. She worried constantly over his safety and he agreed, if it would comfort her, to carry a particularly sturdy cane. But even if he wore a shirt of mail, it would do no good. There were a thousand ways, he remarked, to get at a man if you wanted to assassinate him. He would have to shut himself up in an iron box, if he wanted to be really safe.

Explosives had always been prominent in the Lincoln plot scares. Right now, at the war's end, it was known an infernal machine was ready to be fastened on cross bars under the presidential carriage—the same one in which he rode to Ford's Theatre on the night of the assassination. The train carrying him from Springfield to his first inauguration was to have been blown up as it traveled over a bridge. Then, if Lincoln by any chance was still living, hand grenades would be tossed into his carriage at Baltimore. The President-elect made the last lap of his journey secretly, ahead of schedule, and arrived in Washington safely.

On March fourth came the first swearing-in of an American President under heavy military protection. There were sharpshooters stationed in every window of the two Capitol wings, with their guns trained on the crowd at the foot of the East Front steps. There had been a report that a bomb was set to go off under this platform but a search revealed nothing, and Lincoln rose and made his appeal that the country choose peace instead of war.

All the side streets were full of troops and old General Scott, who had worked out the plan to guard Lincoln, was there a block away as the President took the oath and kissed the Bible. Scott had expressed himself as determined that Abraham Lincoln should live to be inaugurated, and he considered this the most momentous hour of his long career.

Cavalry officers who rode on either side of the carriage taking Lincoln and Buchanan from Willard's Hotel to the Capitol and then after the inauguration to the White House were ordered to spur their animals with pretended clumsiness so that there would be constant, unpredictable movement, and any weapon firing at the head of the new Chief Magistrate would be apt merely to drill a hole in a horse's stomach.

No horse was injured on March 4, 1861, but finally, after four interminable years of threats that would have left most mortals raw-nerved, there had been a hole drilled in the head of the man who was—as he had promised to be—ready.

The story of this book, on this, the one hundredth anniversary of Lincoln's assassination, is the story of the twenty days that began on the fateful night of death a century ago and the mighty effects that event had on the people of the United States as Lincoln was taken back across the land to his final rest. The story is told in photographs and accompanying text. The photographic records of the twelve funerals in twelve cities westward were sought out from the archives and historical collections along the actual funeral route, and the full picture of that incredible trip is shown here for the very first time.

The authors are fortunate in having at their disposal the vast picture collection of the late Frederick Hill Meserve, who made it a special project to assemble the rarities connected with the Lincoln assassination and the trip West, and who was himself born in the momentous year of 1865.

Mr. Meserve, who died at the age of ninety-seven in 1962 after a lifetime of collecting historical photographs, was the father of one of the authors of this book, the grandfather of the other. To him is this work lovingly dedicated.

Frederick Hill Meserve at ninety-one giving his favorite picture of Lincoln to a great-grandson.

PART I

THE ASSASSINATION

The Civil War was over, peace had come at last, and at the moment of his great triumph Abraham Lincoln was struck down.

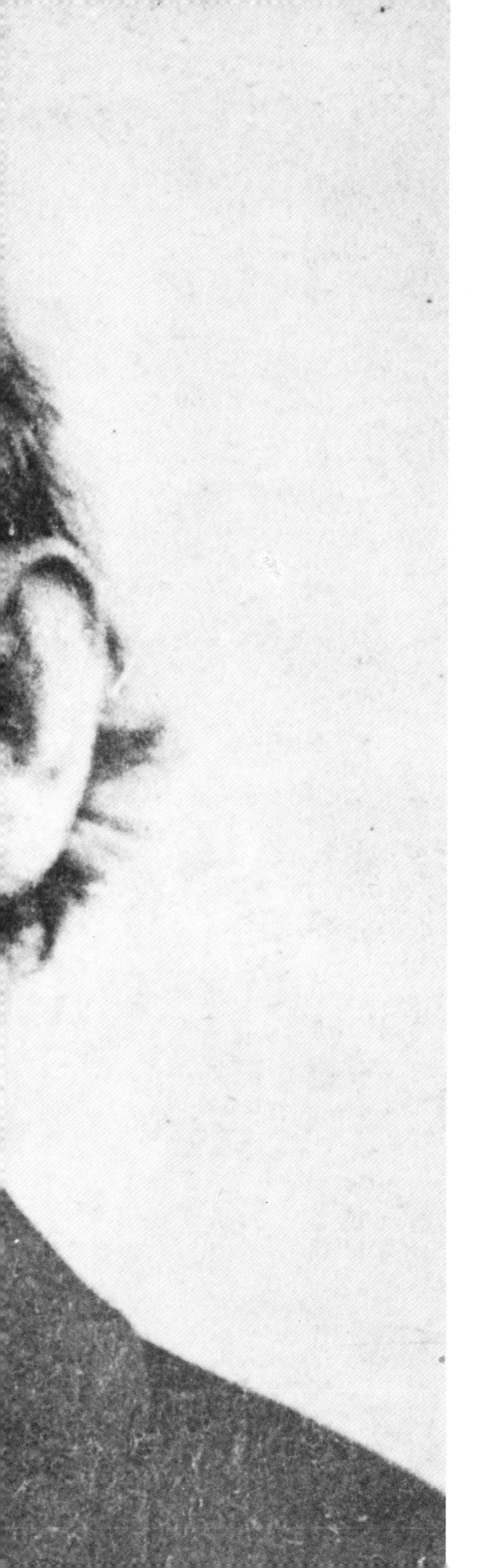

WITH PEACE CAME GLADNESS OF HEART

"I've never been so happy in my life." That's what Abraham Lincoln said over and over in that first week of peacetime after Lee's surrender on April 9, 1865. Long careworn under the burden of the war, suddenly he was erect and buoyant—the President looked grand, absolutely grand, people said. Those who knew him best said that he was not merely happy, he was transfigured with joy over the ending of the war. There were those who looked at Lincoln and looked again and swore they could see a radiance shining from him that was almost physical.

Soon everyone would be able to buy a new picture of the President for their parlor albums that would capture the feeling of great joy and relief. Lincoln heard the news of the war's ending about five hours after it happened, on the evening of Sunday the ninth, at the White House, and the next day he went by appointment to have his photograph taken at Alexander Gardner's studio. Usually when confronted with a camera lens Lincoln became melancholy and stiffened woodenly, but this time he sat before the camera with his soul exposed, captured in a moment of exaltation and thanksgiving. There had been agony for four long, almost sleepless years, and at night when Lincoln did finally fall off to sleep the guard that stood in the hall outside his bedroom heard him moaning. Now all that was over. Now came the glory of peace—and the gratitude, as he would say the next evening to the crowd on the White House lawn, to Him "from Whom all blessings flow."

In Lincoln's view one of the greatest causes for gratitude was the hope of a just and fruitful future which was now open to the Negroes of the country as freedmen. By the Emancipation Proclamation Lincoln had lifted the hearts and passions of the nation, enlisting them not only for the saving of the Union, but also for a

When this photograph was made, Lincoln had four days to live.

higher purpose. He had made the war a crusade to bring to reality American democracy—equality for all men. His steadfast moral courage inspired the nation to fight with new determination now that it was struggling not just to bring back erring sister states to the fold but for great ideals—Justice, Freedom, Right as opposed to Wrong.

For the adult Negro population, unable to read, jobless at the start of its freedom, the future was tragically limited. But it was over the Negro children that the President's heart yearned—he loved all children tenderly—and for these helpless, appealing, small brown sisters and brothers he hoped for education and rich development as human beings. With freedom attained, should not equality follow swiftly? Lincoln was full of hope it would.

That week after the surrender Lincoln asked every band he met parading the avenues to play "Dixie" for him, a wonderful song rightfully captured. And he wrote a formal request to the Secretary of War for some flags which his small son Tad thought he needed to conduct a proper celebration. Now Lincoln could let himself start thinking again of Springfield, of his little brown house out West—there was a good chance he would be going home in four years. There had been times he had been sure he would not live to see the war's end. One of his most hopeless hours had come a few nights before the surrender when he had had that disturbing dream. He believed in dreams—time and again all through the Bible the Lord used dreams to announce coming events. He had gone to sleep and dreamed he woke to the sound of many people weeping in the White House. He made his way to the East Room and there on a catafalque in a coffin lay President Lincoln—he, himself—in his grave clothes, and the people wailed and mourned, "The President is dead."

He had been able to cast off the memory of his dream in his happiness at the coming of peace, but now Mrs. Lincoln said his very happiness frightened her, that the only other time he had said, "I have never been so happy in my life," they lost their three-year-old Eddie the next day. Besides, Mary Lincoln had examined the verses in the Bible which had been used at her husband's swearing-in on March fourth, studied the words at the exact spot where he had kissed the page on taking the oath at his second inauguration. They were clearly a warning of danger—she must be vigilant and on guard to protect the President. And how cruel it was, with all the care she had taken of him, to have this worry her now, in peace time.

The President was anxious for her to get over her nervousness. He felt close involvement in war was probably too great a strain for any woman. "We must both," he told Mary, "be more cheerful in the future—we have both been very miserable."

She would try. She would begin by dwelling on the blessed word *peace*. That Bible warning might have been helpful five weeks ago, but who would want to commit an act of violence now?

This camp boy waited on Grant's officers at City Point.

Many Negroes like these, with hope in their hearts, drifted into the Union lines.

These bright-eyed young slave children were now truly free.

During the war Lincoln's heart was constantly being moved by the youth of so many of the soldiers—"He is very young," he kept writing to the officers. "Let him be sent back to his mother." The President pointed out time and again that it was not fair to condemn a simple country boy to death for desertion and ignore the crafty politician who got him to desert for a share in the illegal bounty he would be paid for a second enlistment. Even Secretary Stanton fought against Lincoln's tender heart and tore up his cards that asked pardons and postponements of execution, and officers said the only way they could maintain discipline in their armies was to shoot the man first and let the Chief Magistrate learn of it afterward.

Though Lincoln did not actually witness executions he imagined them vividly enough to shed actual tears as he discussed them with visitors. "It is shooting day over in Virginia," he would say, weeping and reiterating, "They are so young." The dead on the battlefields of the war he did see, and he walked over a land strewn with newly fallen bodies on his visit to Grant's army just before the surrender.

One of the hardest things the President had to bear, and he bore it in dignity, without denial, was the scurrilous story that he had driven over the battlefield of Antietam and, to distract his mind from the sight of mangled corpses and the heaps of amputated legs and arms where the surgeons had been at work, had asked his friend Hill Lamon to sing one of his amusing little songs. This often-repeated newspaper account hurt Lincoln deeply, but he remained silent, as he had done when called an imbecile, a corrupt despot—and when caricatures of him appeared as a clown telling smutty stories, or a half-man, half-beast with a crown on his head, claws, and a long tail. He was a tortoise too, weak and despicably slow moving. Said the Reverend Wendell Phillips in faint praise—"No one cares whether a tortoise is honest."

But it was the charge that he was oblivious of the sacrifice of "him who shall have borne the battle" and those "who gave the last full measure of devotion" that cut most cruelly.

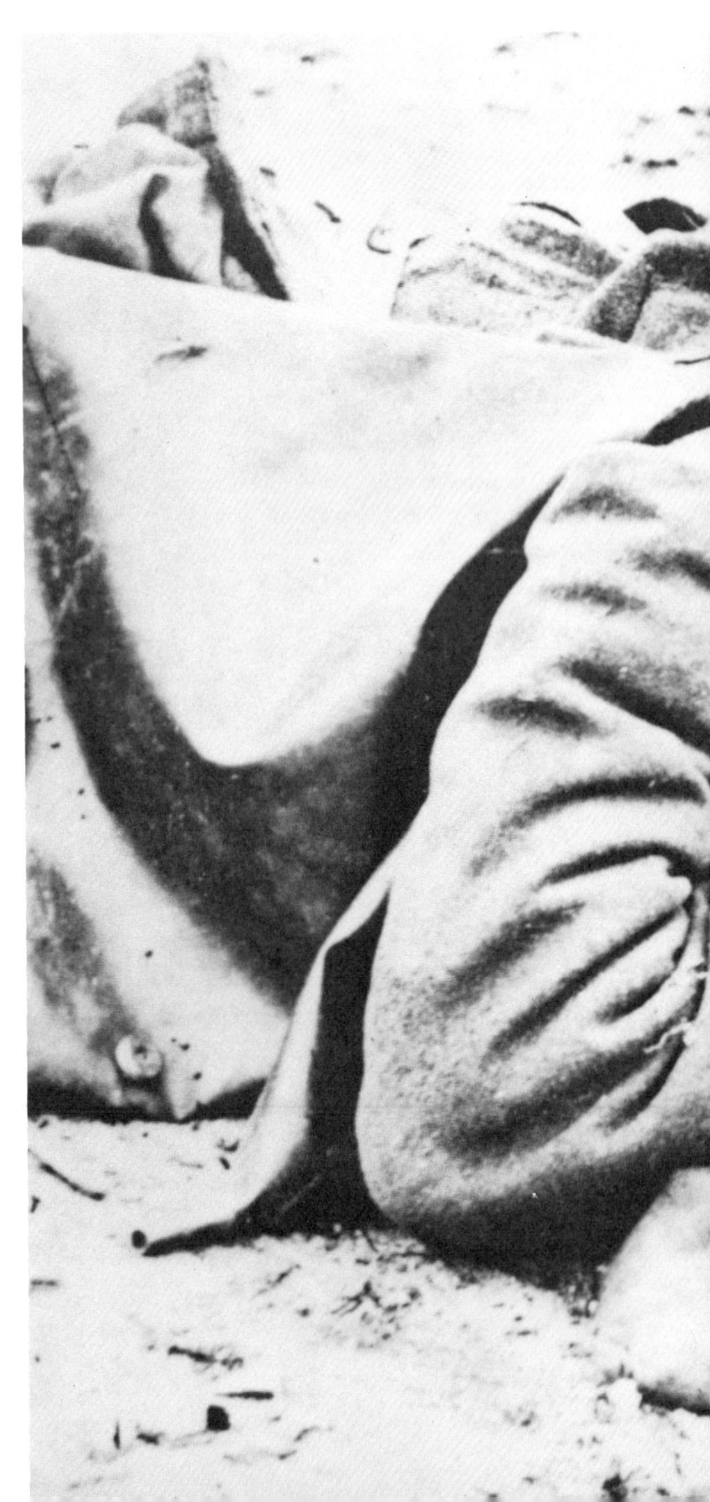

Now the young would not have to die.

Union drummer boys, the sort Lincoln wanted sent home to their mothers.

"The last full measure." Lincoln grieved that a boy like this young Southerner could never go home.

Now no one
would starve in prison
any more
and
men could play again.

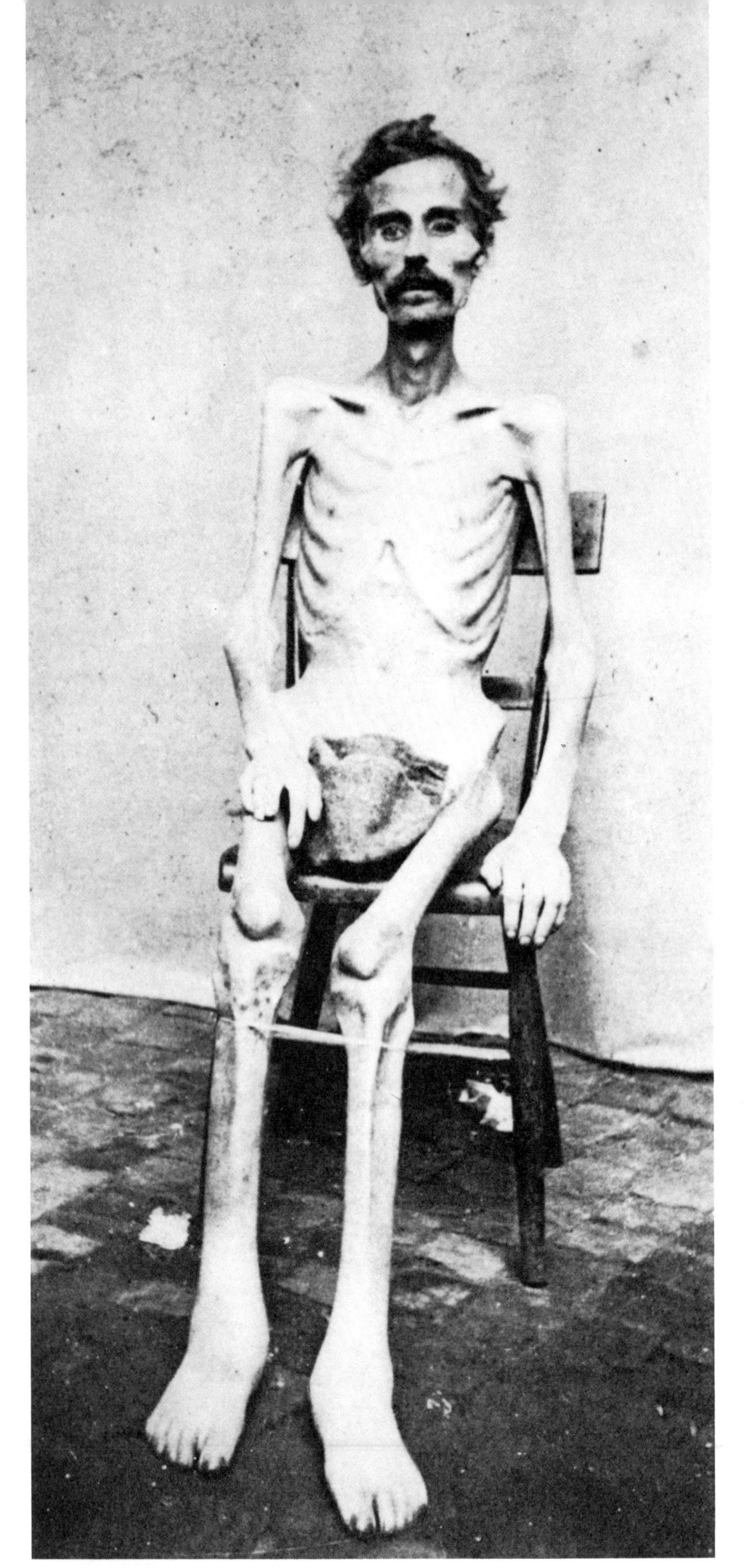

A barely living testament to war's brutality.

Wartime clowning typifies the country's mood as it celebrates peace.

No one could restore to life the thousands of Union prisoners in Southern hell holes and desolate weather-exposed pens who had traveled too far to the edge of death. Even with peace throughout "our common country," as Lincoln had persisted in calling it to the rebels, many like Philip Hattel of Pennsylvania, who had been imprisoned at Andersonville, Georgia, were too weak from starvation to be saved. The Federal authorities were almost incredulous, but they wanted proof for the record, and they photographed Philip sitting naked in a chair, with his knees tied together by a piece of string as he was too weak to hold them in position. This prisoner died less than two months after Lee's surrender, but his image remained—a graphic explanation of that lighted look of thanksgiving in the President's eyes at Gardner's studio on the first day of peace.

In the five days of the week of peace, the President relaxed and watched the shooting fireworks and laughed when mischievous Tad took time out to wave a rebel flag behind his father's back. He was the cordial host at meals in the White House to guests whom Mrs. Lincoln delighted to summon with her meticulously written invitations. Rejoicing at the White House was restrained and prim, but everywhere else in the city the population was reacting with uninhibited zest. Even staid officers clowned and played with one another like boys.

A circumspect ordained minister, the Reverend George Buzelle from Bangor, Maine, summed up everyone's feelings when he wrote his family a letter postmarked City Point, Virginia, April 9, 1865.

Evening—

Great News!! Lee's army of Northern Virginia is surrendered—Lee has surrendered—so goes the news. Guns—drums—yells—cheers—shaking hands, general confusion and wildness—hip! hip! hurrah! Bully! Yi! Ge whoop! Keee-ih!! Then—just then—our dog Jack came into the tent and I told him to "holler" but he wouldn't and I grabbed him by the throat and choked him until he gave a half strangled "Yakerwakrrr" and I threw him off and knocked the table and upset the lamp and smashed the chimney and set the table in a blaze—whowray!! Yi keeoo Yeep! Keweew!!

Good! Well good night and thank God.

George

On the Fifth Day of Peace Lincoln asks his son

This unpublished ambrotype (*left*) shows Lincoln's eldest son, Robert, as a student at Phillips Exeter Academy in New Hampshire. Five years later Robert Lincoln had grown his first mustache and gone off to war.

That first week of rejoicing was drawing to a close when on Friday morning, April fourteenth, Lincoln's eldest son, twenty-two-year-old Robert Todd Lincoln, arrived home from the last campaign of the war in time to breakfast with his father and spend a whole hour talking to him. He had only been a soldier for three months and had been placed with the rank of captain on Grant's staff when Lincoln wrote the General asking him as a favor to make Robert a member of his personal family. Mrs. Lincoln had insisted that Robert should remain at *to join the theatre party.*

Harvard and graduate, which he did in June of 1864, but there was so much criticism of the President for allowing other families' sons to fight for the country while his own remained safe at home that Robert got his uniform and set out for the front in February. It was what he had begged to be allowed to do all along.

Mr. Lincoln questioned Robert closely in that breakfast hour on what he knew about the surrender and Robert was proud to give his father a first-hand report. As a member of Grant's staff he had been present when General Lee rode up in his impressive uniform, wearing his sword and a bright red sash, on his famous gray horse Traveller. Robert stayed outside on the porch of Mr. McLean's house on the main street of Appomattox Courthouse, Virginia, with the other young officers, and could not hear the sound of Grant's and Lee's voices inside, discussing the terms of the surrender. He was called in with the rest of the younger men to be presented to Lee when all was over—but still did not hear his voice as Lee merely bowed. Then his friends picked up a rag doll that lay on the floor of the surrender room, forgotten in her haste by little Lula McLean, and outside on the porch again and in the yard the young officers tossed the doll back and forth to each other, calling her the Silent Witness and wishing in their hearts they could have been as fortunate as the doll. Lee came out, mounted Traveller and rode away, and an officer on Sheridan's staff appropriated the rag doll and rode away with her as a singular treasure. Robert showed his father a *carte de visite* of Lee and Lincoln studied it gravely. He said, "It is a good face. It is the face of a noble, brave man. I am glad the war is over at last."

Even at breakfast, Robert was so sleepy he could barely keep his eyes open. He had not slept in a bed since February and had eaten too many beans and too much hard tack. He was planning to take a dose of medicine before he climbed into his own comfortable bed that night. He did not go with his parents and Tad when they drove that afternoon to the Navy Yard and went all over the battered ironclad warship, the *Montauk*, but he did have dinner alone with his family, and then went straight to his room. There his father sought him out and said the few words he would never forget all his life.

"Son," he said, "we want for you to come to the theatre with us tonight."

Robert explained he was too sleepy, was longing to lie down in a real bed between sheets.

"All right, son," said the President, "run along to bed."

This rag doll was present in the room where Lee surrendered to Grant, but Robert Lincoln had to wait outside on the porch with the other young officers.

Also on the Fifth Day of Peace

As the President's Friday morning Cabinet meeting was drawing to a close, far to the south a ceremony Lincoln cared very much about was getting under way. On February 18, 1865, Union troops had occupied Charleston, South Carolina. The war was drawing to an end and by early March President Lincoln had decided to have the old starry flag which had been driven out of Fort Sumter on April 14, 1861, raised again in that fort exactly four years later. Henry Ward Beecher, minister of Plymouth Church in Brooklyn, was to make the oration. A good many prominent men were invited to be present, sailing from New York on the steamer *Arago* which left New York on April eighth under the charge of Major-General E. D. Townsend. There was quite a rivalry between the passengers of the *Arago,* who had their whole trip paid for, and those of the steamship *Oceanus,* which was chartered by about one hundred and eighty people who were not invited officially and who paid $100 apiece for the trip. Townsend wrote that certain people on the *Oceanus* were hoping to take part in the ceremonies but they would have to content themselves with "swelling the grand chorus to 'The Star-Spangled Banner' and joining in the doxology, to the tune of 'Old Hundred.' "

General Anderson knelt at the crowd's center, wept as he said, "I restore to its proper place this dear flag."

Townsend described the scene: "The fort was found to be a perfect mass of ruins. Hardly any trace of its character, except broken gabions and shattered casements, was to be seen. A large platform, covered with myrtle, evergreens, and flowers, had been erected in the center of the parade ground, with an arched canopy overhead, draped with the American flag, and intermingled with beautiful wreaths of evergreens and flowers. . . . The flagstaff, about one hundred and fifty feet high, had been erected in the center of the parade ground. . . . At the proper time Major Anderson received the old flag, packed in the Fort Sumter mail bag, from Sergeant Hart, the soldier of Anderson's command who had hauled down the flag. Together they opened the flag and adjusted the halyards. Anderson fastened a wreath of roses to the top of the flag. As soon as he could control his emotion he said that he was here 'to fulfill the cherished wish of my heart for four long years of bloody war and restore to its proper place this dear flag . . .' Anderson then seized the halyards, Sergeant Hart also passing them through his own hands, while the General's young son Robert held on to the ends. Anderson knelt to do his part of the raising and refused everyone's help, wanting the flag to go up by his strength alone." Then there were tremendous cheers and shouts, the booming of cannon from the surrounding forts, the firing of guns from Admiral John A. Dahlgren's fleet, which lay at anchor in the waters surrounding the fort, and the playing of several bands, all at once.

Henry Ward Beecher made his long, carefully prepared address, which he read with great difficulty in the high wind as he was trying to hold his hat and manage the fluttering pages of his speech. "We lift to the breeze our fathers' flag . . . with starry eyes it looks all over the bay for the banner that supplanted it and sees it not. . . . We offer to the President of the United States our solemn congratulations that God has sustained his life. . . ."

Beyond the battered walls of the fort, flag-draped Union ships ride at anchor, ready to fire off their guns when the old banner is raised.

Henry Ward Beecher made the main address—emotional, tiresome, wordy. Secretly he was contemptuous of Lincoln for being too forgiving.

Four years ago General Anderson (shown here with his son) marched his almost suffocated men out of the burning fort, with permission from the rebels to salute the union flag.

Lincoln's frail private secretary, John Nicolay, had come from a few days' rest in Cuba to represent the President at the flag-raising.

GOOD FRIDAY IN WASHINGTON

Ford's Theatre Prepares for the President

At eleven-thirty that Good Friday morning of April 14, 1865, less than eight hours before curtain time, a White House messenger arrived at Ford's Theatre with the welcome news that the President accepted the management's invitation to attend that evening's performance of *Our American Cousin.* Ever since John Ford had bought the old First Baptist Church of Washington in 1859 and turned it into a theatre, it had been a focal point in the city. When the building burned to the ground on December 30, 1862, Ford built an even finer brick theatre, at which he presented the best actors and actresses of the time. Lincoln attended plays there often, finding rest and distraction in watching such noted actors as Edwin Forrest, James H. Hackett and Edwin Booth. He liked Shakespeare, but remarked dryly that Shakespeare's characters did talk a great deal while they were dying. Sometimes he was so weary, as he was on April 14, that just getting to the theatre seemed too great an effort. As he said after seeing Edwin Booth in *The Merchant of Venice,* "I had a thousand times rather read it at home if it were not for Booth's playing."

Now Ford was away on a trip to Richmond and the news of Lincoln's attendance that evening was received by his brother James, business manager of the theatre. A third brother, twenty-one-year-old Harry, realizing that a presidential visit during the week of national victory was an occasion, personally set about furnishing and decorating the ample space provided by throwing boxes Numbers Seven and Eight together. He used a sofa,

Twelve feet above the stage which is set for Act III, Scene 2 of *Our American Cousin* is the flag-draped Lincoln box. In this photograph, taken a few days later by Mathew Brady, the Treasury Guard's flag hangs furled on a staff against the center pillar of the President's box. On the night of the assassination the flag was staffless and was draped across the outside of the box just below the two American flags, displaying its great handpainted eagle.

flags, a framed engraving of George Washington, two stuffed chairs on casters, and a rocking chair, which he thought the President would find comfortable, and six straight-legged chairs for possible guests. The rocking chair was part of a Victorian set, and it was such a comfortable chair that when it had been stored downstairs the ushers had lounged in it and their hair had made a greasy spot on the figured dark-red satin with which the chair was upholstered. So the spot would not get worse Harry had kept it upstairs in his own room. Now, feeling that the disfigurement would not be noticed in the few rays of gaslight which would penetrate the presidential box with its double curtaining of lace and satin, he got a theatre errand boy to carry it on his head to the dress circle. Harry then placed the chair where its long rockers exactly fitted, in the left-hand corner.

This is the bar of wood

This is the peephole Booth bored in the inner door to Lincoln's box in the theatre.

At eleven-thirty that morning John Wilkes Booth, the actor—he was Edwin's younger brother—had arrived at the theatre to pick up his mail, a privilege he had been given by his close friend, John Ford. There he learned of the President's visit. He seemed casual as he sat down on the theatre steps to read his letter but everyone who saw him from that moment on noticed he was deathly pale—thought he looked sick. He left soon to begin a day of frenzied preparation. No one has ever pinpointed the hour at which Booth stole back into the theatre, made a hole in the wall for a bar to jam the door of the box, and bored a peephole in the door, grinding through the wood with a large iron-handled gimlet, then carving it out to the size of a finger with a penknife. Through it he had a dead-eye view of the back of the rocking chair.

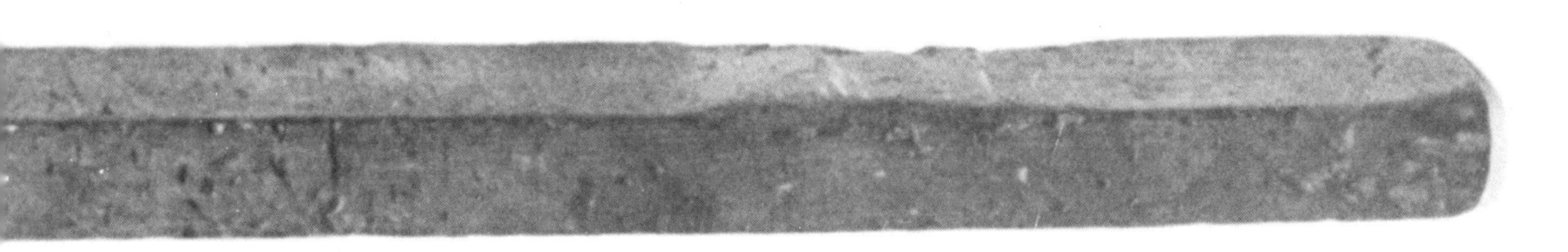

Booth used to jam the outer door by bracing it between the door and a mortise he gouged in the plaster wall.

Lincoln's three companions in the theatre box:

The President and Mrs. Lincoln had had a hard time assembling guests for their theatre party. Besides their son Robert they had invited twelve people to go with them and at the end had had just two acceptances.

Even though it had been announced in the papers that General and Mrs. Grant would be in the theatre box that evening with the President and his lady, as the afternoon began Mrs. Grant did her best to release herself from the prospect of an unpleasant three hours. At City Point, a few days before, Mrs. Lincoln had refused to step on shore until the Grants' boat was swung out from the dock and the Lincoln vessel maneuvered into the place of honor—she would not set foot on the Grants' deck. And when the General's wife sat down on a coil of ropes on board a war vessel she had been asked, "How dare you sit in the presence of the wife of the President of the United States?"

General Grant finally told Mr. Lincoln with apologies that he and Mrs. Grant were so longing to see their daughter, at school in New Jersey, that they could not wait until the next day but would leave by train immediately.

Mrs. Stanton, wife of the Secretary of War, also took every opportunity to avoid the First Lady—as she put it, succinctly and coldly, "I do not call on Mrs. Lincoln." Mr. Stanton declined for himself and his wife, though he gave as his reason his strong disapproval of the President's risking his life by appearing in a public place at a time when passions ran high.

The Lincolns had picked up their last-minute substitute guests, Major Henry Reed Rathbone and his stepsister and fiancée, Clara Harris, at the Harris home and driven them in their carriage to the theatre—with Edward Burke, their coachman, in livery up on the box and Charles Forbes, the President's personal attendant, beside him. It was just a month since the Lincolns had last invited Clara to go with them to the theatre, and Mrs. Lincoln seemed to have forgiven her father, Ira Harris, a prominent lawyer of Albany who had been elected to the Senate in 1861, for asking the blunt question one day in the White House—"Why isn't Robert in the army?"

Major Rathbone was twenty-eight years old and had only recently been appointed by the President as Assistant Adjutant General of Volunteers. Obviously he had not had it impressed upon him that he was to watch out for the President's safety that evening, for he sat on the sofa in the far front of the box slightly behind Clara but nowhere near the President. A seat behind Lincoln would have placed him in the path of the box door by which Booth was to enter.

HENRY REED RATHBONE, a young major, was one of the Lincolns' two last-minute substitute guests.

CLARA HARRIS, the pretty young daughter of a New York Senator, was engaged to Rathbone.

MARY TODD LINCOLN laughed delightedly during the play at the old-chestnut jokes, rested her hand on Lincoln's knee and joshed her husband.

The last words Lincoln heard were "you sockdologizing old mantrap"

LAURA KEENE, an Englishwoman in her forties, was the play's star.

The presidential party was so late that evening that the curtain had to go up without the Lincolns and their guests. In about half an hour they were seen in the dress circle approaching their box, and the play stopped, the audience rose and applauded and the orchestra struck up "Hail to the Chief." The First Lady was all smiles, but Mr. Lincoln seemed weary and his face was serious. The audience had settled down for an evening of laughter at a silly play, and now the President's melancholy mood would be a poor match for the high spirits of the crowd.

It was true that Lincoln had experienced one of his swift changes from confident hope to depression. Late that afternoon he had walked to the War Department with his guard, William Crook, as he had done so many times before, and had said something that he had never said before.

"Crook, do you know," he said, "I believe there are men who want to take my life." Then he lowered his voice, as though talking to himself. "And I have no doubt they will do it."

"Why do you think so, Mr. President?" asked Crook.

"Other men have been assassinated," Lincoln answered. "I know no one could do it and escape alive. But if it is to be done, it is impossible to prevent it."

And a little later when he left for the theatre in his carriage, for the first time, the guard remembered later, Lincoln said, "Good-by, Crook," instead of the usual "Good night." The newly hired White House guard, John Parker, who was a patrolman on the Metropolitan Police Force, had been charged with Lincoln's protection for the evening. Parker had gone on ahead to the theatre—there was no official protection for the President throughout the short drive.

On the night of April 14 Laura Keene was playing the part of the young girl Florence Trenchard in *Our American Cousin* for more than the thousandth time. By her grace and natural style of acting in an age when many characters were played in a stylized manner, she managed to give a pleasing illusion of youth. Laura Keene had shiny auburn curls, a creamy complexion, and dark brown eyes which were a little on the beady side. When she first presented *Our American Cousin* in New York in 1858 at the Olympic Theatre she had the benefit of being supported by the famous actors E. A. Sothern, as Lord Dundreary, and Joseph Jefferson, as Asa Trenchard. But now, on tour, Harry Hawk was proving a very well-received Asa, the comically eccentric backwoodsman.

Harry Hawk was a permanent member of Laura

Keene's company and toured with her as her manager as well as principal comedian in the plays she presented. During this Good Friday performance both Laura Keene and Harry Hawk as well as the Ford's Theatre orchestra leader, William Withers, could see the Lincoln party up in the box enjoying the play. While Mrs. Lincoln laughed openly and heartily at every joke, her husband frequently leaned forward and rested his chin in one hand, seemed to be thinking of something not present. There were people in the audience who watched, guessing that he was pondering his greatest problem, how to welcome back the Southern states and make them feel at home in the Union, from which he held they had never been absent. His own instruction to his officers, given only a few days before, was still his consuming wish: "Let 'em down easy."

The First Lady was oblivious of the fact that the President's thoughts were straying from the performance. She was to be questioned closely as to what Mr. Lincoln's exact last words had been, and she would ultimately take refuge in remembering two completely opposite versions, which she told alternately.

First, she recalled that her hand had been on Mr. Lincoln's knee and she had been leaning across the arm of his chair, over very close to him, so close that she had asked rather apologetically, with a look at the engaged couple in the front of the box, "What will Miss Harris think of my hanging on to you so?" The last words were the pronouncement, "She won't think anything about it."

But then later Mrs. Lincoln was sure the President had turned to her just before Booth's shot and remarked earnestly, "How I should like to visit Jerusalem sometime!" This was an odd sequence of thought as the play had been following a less than spiritual course and convulsing the audience as a wildly caricatured American backwoodsman arrived to visit his English cousins. The Lincolns had heard Binny the butler ask Asa Trenchard if he would like to have a "baath," heard Asa tell Binny to "absquatulate—vamose!"—that he was a "tarnal fat critter—swelling out his bosom like an old turkey cock in laying time," had heard the butler's answer, "I suppose I shall be a hox next, or perhaps an 'ogg." Down in the drawing room Our American Cousin offered to mix a drink for a young lady invalid and promised his concoction "would make a sick girl squirm like an eel in a mud bank." Two minutes before Booth's shot sounded in the box Asa warned the girl who was flirting with him, thinking him a rich catch, "Don't look at me that way . . . if you do I'll bust. I'm biling over with affections which I'm ready to pour all over you like apple sass over roast pork." The actual last speech before the assassination was by the American Cousin in answer to the scheming mother who had just found out he was not rich and called out angrily that Asa did not know the manners of good society. Asa was alone on the stage and for the final time Abraham Lincoln heard the sound of a human voice. "Don't know the manners of good society, eh? Well, I guess I know enough to turn you inside out, old gal—you sockdologizing old mantrap."

WILLIAM WITHERS, the orchestra leader, and HARRY HAWK, the comic lead in *Our American Cousin*, were minor players in Lincoln's last hours.

THE ASSASSIN AND HIS CONSPIRATORS

JOHN WILKES BOOTH had said a year earlier, "What a glorious opportunity there is for a man to immortalize himself by killing Lincoln."

If Abraham Lincoln had been given time to turn around in his rocking chair that night in the theatre, he would have instantly recognized his assassin. Twenty-six-year-old John Wilkes Booth was one of the country's promising actors though no one expected him to come near the genius of his father, Junius Brutus Booth, or his incomparable brother, Edwin Booth. Lincoln had seen him perform, seen that handsome pale face, the thick, raven hair, the deep-set eyes, black as ink and filled with a strange, wild fire. Only a few months before, the President had been at Ford's Theatre in his usual box watching Booth play the part of a villain, and whenever the Maryland actor had anything ugly and threatening to say he had stepped up near the presidential box and shaken his finger toward Lincoln and said the lines directly to him. "He looks as if he meant that for you," the President's companion said, and Lincoln replied, "Well, he does look pretty sharp at me, doesn't he?"

For six months Booth had been working on plans to kidnap Lincoln, meeting regularly with the band of conspirators he had gathered together—among them a Maryland coach painter and blockade runner, an unstable twenty-three-year-old drug store clerk with a mind ten years younger, and a former Confederate soldier. At first they had planned to spirit Lincoln away to Richmond and demand that all Southern prisoners be freed and the war ended. One scheme was to throw the President from his theatre box to the stage below, rush him out the back door and drive him away, tied up, before the audience knew what happened. On the fourth of March, as shown by the extraordinary photograph on the following two pages and the extreme enlargements taken from it, Booth and his men had had a perfect opportunity to strike during Lincoln's second inauguration. Later in March the conspirators had surrounded and stopped the President's carriage, only to find another man, not Lincoln, inside. By April, Booth had decided that kidnaping would not do, that Lincoln must die. "Our country owed all her troubles to him, and God simply made me the instrument of His punishment," Booth wrote in his diary.

After learning that Lincoln would be in the audience on Good Friday night, Booth, dressed in high silk hat and dark suit, went straight from Ford's Theatre to Pumphrey's Livery Stable. There he hired a swift little bay mare, with a white star on her forehead and black tail and mane, saying he would call for her about four. At

Here, in this astonishing photograph, are the men who conspired with Booth to murder President Lincoln and Secretary of State Seward.

This is the remarkably revealing photograph from which the detail of the conspirators on the preceding page was taken. It is an over-all scene of Lincoln's second inauguration. The famous Washington photographer Alexander Gardner made several exposures of the great spectacle that took place on March 4, 1865, on the steps of the Capitol. One shows Lincoln seated in his chair before rising to deliver the address; in another the President is standing and reading. Still another exposure did not show Lincoln at all because a careless fingerprint on the emulsion of the still wet negative blotted him out as he stood at the speaker's stand. What this third picture did show, though, was something that neither of the other two did. Up behind the railing of the right-hand buttress, peering almost directly down on Lincoln from underneath his fashionable stovepipe hat, is the handsome, inscrutable face of the man who forty-one days later would drill a bullet through Abraham Lincoln's head. And equally astonishing, just beneath the speaker's stand, only a few feet away from the President, are five of the men who were part of the assassination plot.

the appointed time Booth returned, now wearing a soft dark hat and high riding boots. Pumphrey warned him not to tie the mare if he left her—he must get someone to hold her. She was high spirited and would break her halter. Booth mentioned that he was going to Grover's Theatre to write a letter, that he intended stopping for a drink somewhere, and indicated that he might take a pleasure ride.

Instead of going to Grover's, Booth went to the National Hotel, where he was staying, to do his writing, walked into the office there, looking for privacy, it seemed. He appeared dazed and asked the clerk in charge, Mr. Merrick, what year it was. Merrick said surely he was joking and Booth said no, he wasn't. On Pennsylvania Avenue at about four-thirty Booth met John Matthews, a fellow actor who was playing the part of an attorney in *Our American Cousin,* handed Matthews the letter he had just written and asked him to give it the following day to the editor of the *National Intelligencer.* Ten minutes later he spotted a carriage taking General

PICTURE PROOF THAT BOOTH AND THE CONSPIRATORS WERE THERE.

At the right is an enlargement of that portion of Gardner's fingerprint-marred exposure which includes both Booth above the speaker's stand and the conspirators below. It is history that Booth attended this ceremony as the invited guest of his fiancée, Lucy Hale, daughter of the New Hampshire Senator. But before this print was discovered in the Meserve Collection a few years ago no one knew his exact vantage point. It is pinpointed now, as can be seen even more clearly in the extreme blowup at the left, showing Booth in his high hat beneath the massive marble pioneer wresting a tomahawk from an attacking Indian just to the right of the head of the pioneer wife (separated by one person). Booth later said, half regretfully, "What an excellent chance I had to kill the President if I had wished, on inauguration day."

Below is a row of portraits of the conspirators and directly underneath each one is the corresponding enlargement from the Gardner picture.

LEWIS T. POWELL alias LEWIS PAINE — GEORGE A. ATZERODT — DAVID E. HEROLD — JOHN SURRATT — EDWARD SPANGLER

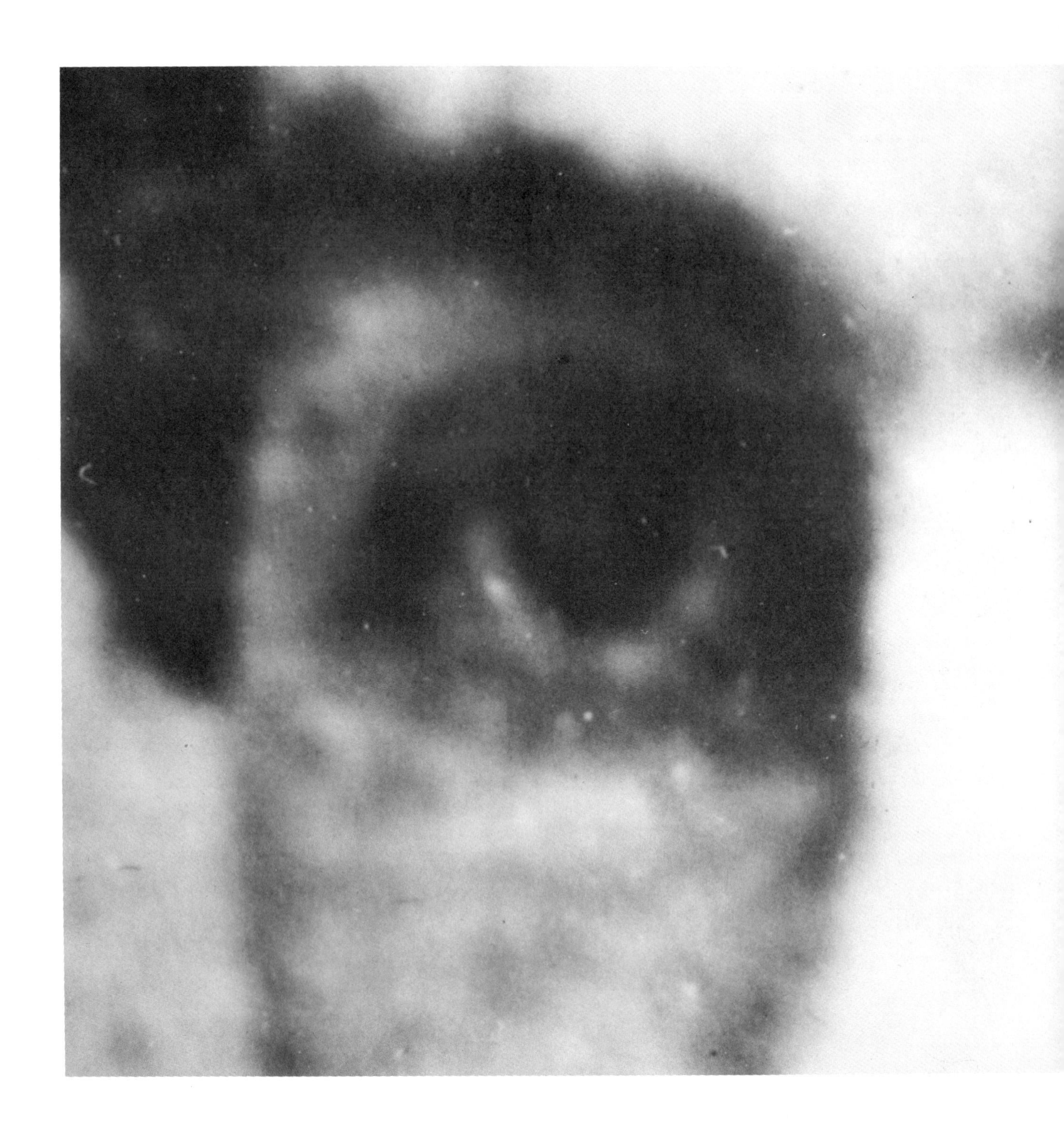

and Mrs. Grant to the station on their way to New Jersey. Booth galloped after the carriage and made them uncomfortable by peering closely into it.

Sometime that afternoon—the clerk did not remember exactly when—Booth appeared at the desk of the Kirkwood House with a card, addressed to no one, on which was written, "Don't wish to disturb you. Are you at home? J. Wilkes Booth." The clerk thought he heard Booth say the name Johnson and he put the card into the box of Vice-President Andrew Johnson's private secretary.

At six-thirty that evening Booth had supper at the National Hotel. At about eight o'clock he met his accomplices at the Herndon House and went over the plans to kill Secretary of State Seward at the same moment that he himself planned to shoot Abraham Lincoln.

It was about nine-thirty when Booth rode into the alley behind Ford's Theatre. With Peanuts, a messenger boy, holding his mare's bridle and the horse already stamping in protest, he entered the back door and asked if he could cross the stage, was told no, the dairy scene was playing, which took the full depth. In a few moments he went down under the stage and through a special stage

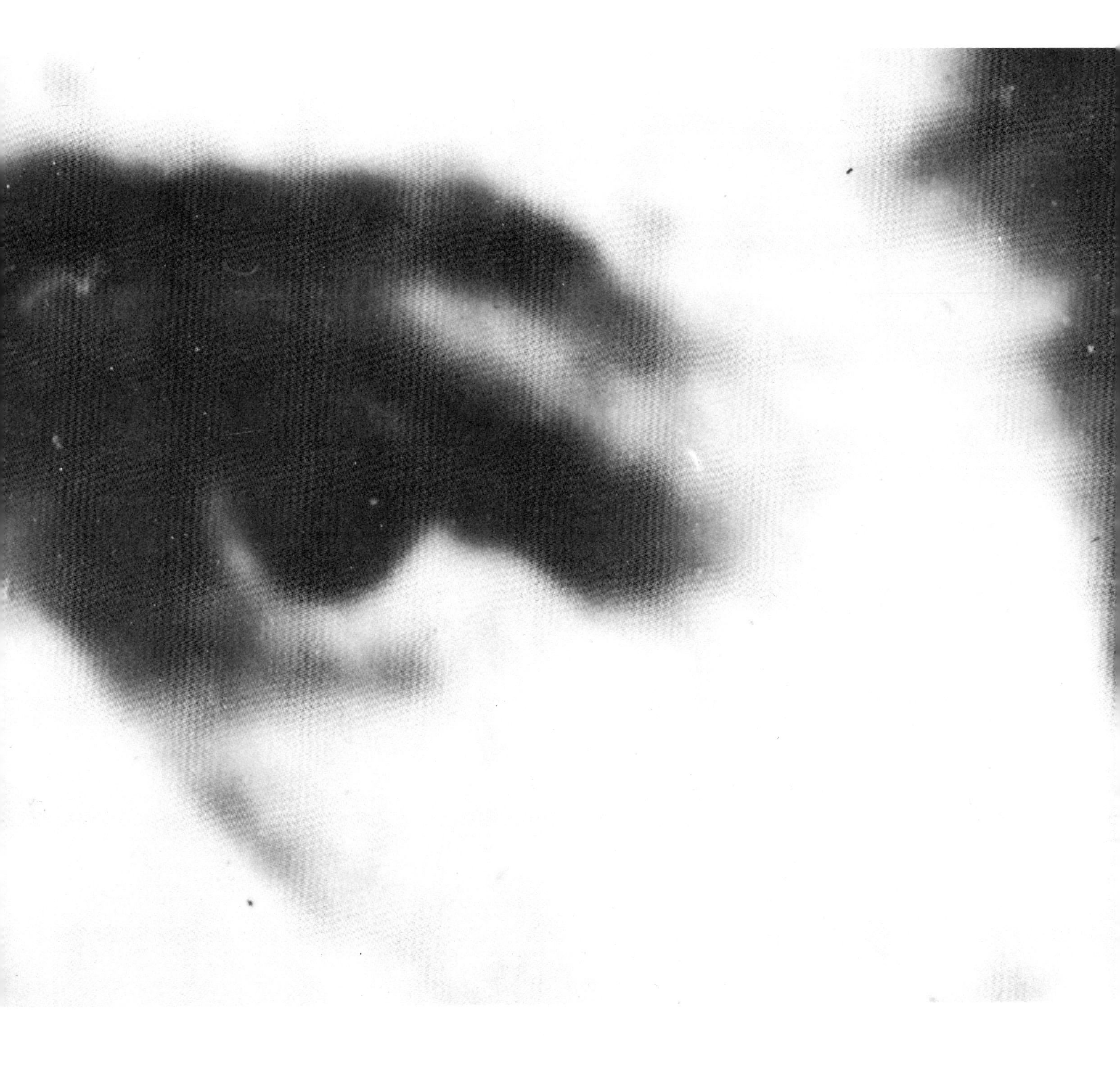

door to another alley that led to the front of the theatre. The ticket seller, John Buckingham, saw him leaving and entering the theatre lobby five times. Booth seemed very nervous. He took hold of two of Buckingham's fingers and asked him the time. Buckingham told him there was a clock in the lobby. It was after ten o'clock. When Buckingham went into the saloon next door for a drink, Booth was there drinking brandy. About ten-fifteen Booth went into the back of the house and stood looking at the audience. Then he walked up the stairs leading to the dress circle, humming a tune. He was still wearing his dark slouch hat and riding clothes—high boots and spurs. He approached the special policeman who was supposed to be sitting outside the door of the President's box but who had gone down into one of the dress circle seats to watch the play. Booth tapped a card out from his card case, showed it to the man, and a moment later entered the door of the little hall leading to the presidential box, closed and barred it behind him. Now in the darkness immediately to his left was the door to the box. A tiny gleam of light shone through the hole he had drilled. Booth drew his pistol, his left hand felt for and turned the knob. Then he stepped into the box directly behind President Lincoln.

THE MOMENT OF ASSASSINATION

It was an instant in history the world would never forget. Lincoln was leaning forward, looking over the rail down into the audience, when the tiny pistol was fired just behind his head. The enormous handmade leaden bullet struck the President behind the left ear, flattened out as it drove through his skull, tunneled into the brain, and came to rest behind the right eye.

For a split moment no one spoke—no one moved. Mrs. Lincoln and Clara Harris sat frozen in their seats. A dense smoke enveloped the President and curled upward, and suddenly the assassin appeared within the smoke, as though materialized by some demon magician.

President Lincoln threw up his right arm at the impact of the shot and Mrs. Lincoln instinctively caught him around the neck and struggled to keep him upright. Now Rathbone lunged out of his seat and grabbed at Booth's arm. Booth had dropped the pistol and was brandishing a dagger, which he tried to plunge into Rathbone's chest. The major knocked the knife upward with his arm, and received a two-inch-deep slash just above the elbow.

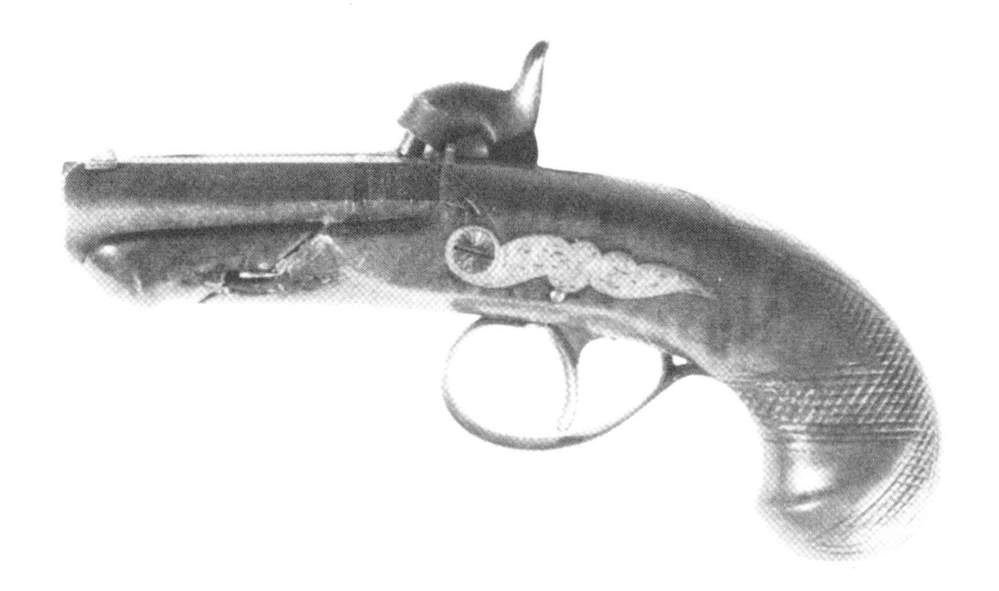

The actual derringer pistol that killed Lincoln is used here with this tilted profile of the President to show the exact angle and the extremely close range at which he was hit.

Now as Booth vaulted over the railing of the box Rathbone clutched at him again, felt cloth tear as Booth wrenched himself free and leaped the twelve feet down to the stage. As he dropped, his spur caught in the Treasury flag draped on the railing of the box and the off-balance landing shattered a small bone above his left ankle. "Stop that man!" Rathbone cried. Clara Harris screamed, "Stop that man, won't somebody stop that man!" Then Mrs. Lincoln was leaning over the box and shrieking "Help! Help! Help!" followed by a series of words that made no sense at all—gibberish, insane sounds that filled the stunned theatre. Standing on the stage all alone Harry Hawk saw Booth coming for him, brandishing a large knife, calling out, "Sic Semper Tyrannis"—thus shall it ever be for tyrants. Hawk turned and fled terrified into the wings and up a flight of stairs. Booth charged backstage and toward

the back door. There was orchestra leader Withers and Booth slashed out at him and cut his coat below the collar. A moment later he was outside, knocking over Peanuts, who was still patiently holding the reins of his horse, kicking the boy to the ground, clumsily throwing himself onto his horse, which for a moment circled crazily in the alleyway, and then set off at a gallop into the night.

"Hang him!" The shouts began from the audience. "Hang him!" Up in the box Clara Harris was screaming down for someone to bring water, and now there was pounding on the outer door that Booth had barred shut. Rathbone, dripping blood from his arm, rushed to open it, to admit the world to the tragedy.

CHARLES AUGUSTUS LEALE The first doctor to reach Lincoln, twenty-three-year-old Leale had only two months before been graduated from Bellevue Hospital Medical College, was now chief surgeon in command of the officers' ward in the United States General Army Hospital on Armory Square in Washington. Leale's special major studies had been the heart, the lungs, and, in surgery, gunshot wounds—all of which knowledge served him well that night.

CHARLES SABIN TAFT Doctor Taft had come to the theatre that night especially to see the President, whom he admired greatly. From his orchestra seat he could see Lincoln plainly during the play. He reached the box a few moments after Leale. Here, in this detail from a rare picture, Charlie Taft poses at the Signal Corps Camp of Instruction at Red Hill, Georgetown, where he was surgeon in charge.

Two doctors were the first to reach the dying President.

Dr. Charles Augustus Leale was seated in the dress circle only forty feet away from the President's box. For a moment after the shot he sat transfixed as a man jumped from the box onto the stage, the knife in his hand shining like a diamond in the gaslight. Then, gathering his wits, Leale hurtled over the seats and got to the door of the box where people were pounding just as the bar was being removed inside by the terrified Rathbone, who showed Leale his bleeding arm and begged for help. The doctor quickly saw that the real help was needed by the President. He was being supported now in his chair by Mrs. Lincoln, who cried, "Oh, Doctor, do what you can for my dear husband! Is he dead? Can he recover?" The President was indeed almost dead—he was paralyzed; there was no pulse in his wrists and he drew breaths only at long intervals. Leale laid the President on the floor and with a penknife cut his collar and coat away around the shoulders and neck. He ran his fingers through the hair until he came upon a clot of blood behind the left ear. He removed the clot and inserted the little finger of his left hand into the smooth opening as far as it would go. With the hole open for blood to ooze from, the breathing became better.

At this moment, a second doctor, Charles Sabin Taft, also twenty-three years old, arrived. Through the confusion that reigned in the theatre—the cries of "Kill him!" "Lynch him!" "Water!" "A surgeon!"—Taft had bounded out of his seat in the orchestra, leaped onto the stage and half scrambled, half was lifted up over the railing into the box, where he joined Leale. Realizing he had perhaps only seconds now, in desperation Dr. Leale straddled the spare body, his knees on the floor on each side of the hips. He bent forward, opened the mouth, firmly pressed down and forward the back of the tongue, which was acting as a stopper to the windpipe. He directed Dr. Taft to raise and lower the arms and he himself pushed with his hands up against the diaphragm, then put all the strength of his fingers into massaging the section above the silent heart. There was a sucking-in of air, three gulps, then stillness again. Now Dr. Leale leaned down with his face pressed against the President's, sealed lip to lip. He drew in his own breath to the bursting point and forced it with all his might again and again down into the paralyzed lungs. After mouth to mouth, he breathed mouth to nostrils, and working on like a straining athlete, aching and stubborn, once more mouth to mouth. All at once he realized Mr. Lincoln was inhaling by himself. The heart was stirring, just barely, but there was a faint, irregular flutter.

Leale stood up. "His wound is mortal," he said. "It is impossible for him to recover."

Here is the rocking chair in which Lincoln was slumped and senseless when Dr. Leale reached the box.

Across muddy Tenth Street . . .

"We must get him to the nearest bed," said Dr. Leale. Now, before the move was attempted, a diluted spoonful of brandy was poured between the President's lips and it was swallowed. This would be done three times more during the evening, so thus it happened that the last sustenance that passed into Lincoln's stomach was alcohol, which he had avoided all his life, saying it made him feel flabby and undone. He was beyond any feelings now nor could he see or hear in the slightest degree as Laura Keene arrived in the box with a pitcher of water and begged emotionally to be allowed to hold the President's head in her lap and bathe his temples. Mrs. Lincoln, who was usually so jealous of other women that she disliked seeing one engage her husband in conversation, was now so absorbed in her loud sobs that she made no objection. The actress sat on the floor, bending

LINCOLN'S LAST LIVING JOURNEY made in the arms of young doctors and others from the audience, began at the theatre box (*left*), passed the seats of the dress circle, where the soldier (blurred) stands guard, wound down the stairs and out the furthest high-arched entranceway (*center*), across Tenth Street, then up the stairs of the boarding house opposite the theatre (*right*).

close to Lincoln's upturned face as she tenderly and uselessly sprinkled and patted and the red stains slowly spread on the skirt of her elaborate satin dress.

Two other doctors had been in the audience and had joined Leale and Taft in the box. They were Dr. Africanus F. A. King, twenty-four, so named because of his father's admiration for the Dark Continent, and Dr. Charles A. Gatch, who had served through the war with the armies of General Rosecrans. Now Dr. Leale directed Dr. King to lift the President's left shoulder, others raised the rest of the body, and Leale himself supported the head. Thus Abraham Lincoln began his final journey in life. Slowly, struggling, the group edged out of the never-to-be-forgotten box, the floor of which was lined with a deep red Turkey carpet, the wallpaper a deep crimson also. Past the dress circle, down the stairs, into the lobby of the theatre, out onto Tenth Street the procession went. Now a passage through the stunned and staring crowd was being cleared by soldiers.

"Bring him in here!"
were the words he realized his own voice was crying.

Young Henry Safford had been out celebrating the war's end for five wild nights in a row and tonight he was tired enough to stay home and doze in his stuffed chair over a good book. He had snake-danced down Pennsylvania Avenue and labored at keeping the victory bonfires blazing all over the city of Washington until dawn this morning and it just suited him to be alone in the boarding house and rest his aching bones. The landlord William Petersen, the German tailor, and the four other gentleman boarders were still at it. They had all walked spryly down the front steps and been swallowed up again in the whirl of excitement. From Henry's second-story front window the crowds didn't seem to have quieted down a speck, even if it was Good Friday.

Sitting there with his head back, on the edge of sleep, he caught through the cracks of his eyes an impression of the White House carriage and pair of horses and coachman waiting in front of Ford's Theatre across the street. Well, he would just have to miss the President and First Lady when they came out at the play's end. There would be plenty of other chances.

The nap turned out to be a short one.

At about ten-thirty a sudden noisiness across the street exploded into the angry yells of a riot. Jolted awake, Safford saw people streaming from the theatre doors and it seemed to him they were acting peculiarly, hitting and even kicking each other. "Are they all mad?" was his reaction. He threw open his window. His shouted "What's the matter?" got an immediate answer, "The President has been shot."

Safford hurled himself down the narrow stairway, lighted a candle and went to the front doorway. Halfway across the street a knot of men moved directly toward him. He heard a voice, "Where shall we take him?" and then what he realized was his own voice crying, "Bring him in here!"

Suddenly he was both frightened at taking the responsibility and proud that he was inviting Mr. Lincoln into a house that was one hundred per cent loyal to the Union. He had heard things were different in the dwellings on either side.

He watched the crowd's struggle to negotiate the stoop's abrupt right angle by giving the President a

quick hoist to a higher level. The man in the lead climbed backward, reaching out with both hands to grasp his particular share of the attenuated, endlessly mounting figure—the head, it proved to be, by the candle's flicker. Obviously in authority, this first hunched climber gave the command, "Take me to your best room!" and Henry Safford led the way to a small sleeping apartment straight back at the end of the first-floor hall and stood holding his candle up near the ceiling.

The candle's flame fanned to a mere pinpoint of fire in the breeze made by the throng of bearers who were settling Abraham Lincoln's mortally wounded body on the bed. It would be much harder in the dark, trying not to let the President's arms dangle, not to land him with a bump, fumbling and feeling with so many fingers to get the overcoat spread quilted-satin side down over the bare chest.

Somehow, Henry's tiny glow held and he used it to light the single gas jet which was to provide not only the greenish illumination which intensified every horror of the night, but for good measure a furious hissing, maddening in its persistence.

The best room was a sort of shed-like extension with a roof that sloped from a high right-hand wall to a low window on the left. It was shabby but Safford knew the carpet was swept and there were clean sheets on the low walnut cottage bed, though right now all that showed was the Irish worsted coverlet, woven in red, white, and blue, with its militant eagles in each corner. The young boarder, William T. Clark, who occupied this modest space, was meticulous in the care of his few possessions and it was neater here than in the rooms upstairs where Henry lodged with a group of friends who were passionate naturalists by night, after their daytime jobs. They were usually home in the evenings, studying their books on beetles and toads and turtles and working on their specimens, but tonight fate had planned that they be part of the rejoicing city of Washington, just as it had planned for Henry Safford of Springfield, Massachusetts, in charge of the property returns division in the War Department, that he stay home that evening and lead the President to his death bed.

The four doctors in the room dismissed the other twenty-one bearers and, led again by Safford, the men left with their lungs full of air almost druggingly sweet from lilacs blooming in the yard outside the window, looking back with eyes that ranged hurriedly from crocheted pincushions on a bureau to pictures of fat farm horses, framed against the brownish wallpaper.

Once again Dr. Leale, the young surgeon who had carried Mr. Lincoln's head, spoke urgently to Safford, telling him to get washboilers of water boiling on the cookstove in the Petersen House kitchen and to search for bottles—any kind of bottles he could find—whisky bottles, medicine bottles, that could be filled with hot water and put next to the President's legs.

The doctors now stood helpless beside the rumpled figure on the bed, gaining time to think by murmuring that they must let the President rest after the exertion of being carried across the street. They knew he had lost

This artist's sketch of Lincoln's feet protruding from the coverlet at the end of the bed was drawn from a description given artist Albert Berghaus by observant young Willie Clark.

HENRY SAFFORD was the young boarder across the street from Ford's Theatre who guided Lincoln to the room where he died.

both blood and brain matter on the way; how much could never be measured, for the red dribble had been churned into the Tenth Street mud batter by the half-hundred boots of his bearers. Their patient lay so ominously still and out of kilter, exactly as he had been set down, knees bent and the soles of his high boots pressing hard against the footboard. Nothing was going to do any good, but it was unthinkable to do nothing, even while waiting for the messengers sent earlier from the theatre by horseback and by foot to nearby hospitals for mustard plasters, hot water bottles, army blankets, and brandy.

Suddenly Dr. Leale had an unreasonable desire. He was a high-strung young man, who by virtue of having been the first to enter the theatre box after John Wilkes Booth's shot could give the orders now. He had just had the sickening experience of wiping from his palms and fingers the blood and seeping brain matter that his hands had received as they carried Lincoln's head, with its bullet wound down behind the left ear, in the interminable street crossing. Now, though he knew the patient was totally unconscious, like a fussy nurse he wanted to make everything nice, to get him in a comfortable position lying exactly in the middle of the mattress, under sheets with no wrinkles. "Break off the end of that bed," he ordered and the other doctors wrestled with the sturdily built spool-turned rungs, but the walnut held like cast iron. The only alternative was to arrange the six-foot-four-inch body diagonally, with its feet sticking out over near the wall. The head was moved over next to the door and settled on two overhanging pillows, which would soak up blood for several hours at least before they could take no more. Then the red puddle would begin to form on the worn Brussels carpet below, but right now the room was still immaculate.

HENRY ULKE, a talented painter, and his brother were by far the most distinguished boarders at the Petersen House.

JULIUS ULKE was a portrait photographer and along with Henry ran a flourishing photographic studio on Pennsylvania Avenue.

The next step was obvious. Perhaps there was a stab wound somewhere on Mr. Lincoln's body, in addition to the hole made by the bullet. Everyone in the theatre had seen the shining dagger that Booth flourished back there on the stage. It was imperative that they make an examination, immediately. But the four men seemed suggestible to the paralysis of their charge. They moved with such sluggish deliberation that they were still agreeing that they must act quickly when there was a burst of excitement at the front of the house.

Mrs. Lincoln was making the journey across Tenth Street, almost unrecognizable as the First Lady who had curtsied so happily two hours before at her husband's side, when the audience rose, cheering and waving handkerchiefs, to the thrilling sound of "Hail to the Chief." All her delicate Southern belle femininity gone, she dug the heels of her evening slippers into the manure-spattered soil in exaggerated paces, whirled and pulled along her escort, Major Rathbone, as though he were weightless.

Once in the hallway she flounced away from hands outstretched to help her as if she were being manacled and cried wildly, "Where is my dear husband? Where is he?" She walked past two locked rooms on the left to the bed where she saw him lying with his boots still on, but the doctors asked her to leave while they made an examination and she allowed herself to be led back toward the entrance.

Young red-haired Major Rathbone was unexpectedly taking up most of the hallway space, extended full length on the floor and unconscious from loss of blood. The messy wound in his left arm, a jab and a two-inch upward slit by Booth's dagger, had bled in livelier spurts after the punishment of his being wrenched this way and that during the street crossing with Mrs. Lincoln. While Clara Harris made arrangements for a carriage to be brought through the crowd to drive her betrothed back to the Harris home, strenuous efforts were made to find somewhere for the First Lady to sit down.

There was no time to search for keys to the locked rooms so their doors were broken open with heavy kicks and an onslaught of ramming shoulders that just happened to be available in the clogged passageway. The front one that looked across at the theatre was chosen as Mary Lincoln's refuge during the long night. It was an exceptionally prim parlor, furnished with black horsehair-covered chairs and sofa—a slippery, unyielding sofa on which the wife—and when morning came the widow—lay and gave herself up to spasms of sobbing that reverted unpredictably to deafening, high-register screams.

In about twenty minutes now the Lincoln family doctor and the Surgeon General of the United States, as well as members of the Cabinet, who were being sought out all over the city of Washington, would arrive. Soon after, there would come tiptoeing into that nine-by-seventeen-foot space more doctors, making sixteen in all, and a changing parade of not only the chiefs of departments but senators, congressmen, army officers, personal friends, the four other Peterson House boarders and their landlord, Mr. Lincoln's son Robert and his mother's circle of comforters, actors from the interrupted *Our American Cousin*, and just plain people who had slipped in somehow to watch Abraham Lincoln die. More than ninety individuals would pass in and out of the death room during the night, filling it to the choking point, pressing against the bed, weeping, kneeling to pray. Uncounted others, nameless, would slip into the confusion of the hallway like restless sleepwalkers, every so often escaping the delirium to let those keeping vigil out on Tenth Street know it would not be long now.

This was all in the future, as, in comparative peace in the cramped space provided—with only Mrs. Lincoln's lamentations in the front room and the snoring, jerky breathing of the patient to unnerve them—the four medical men began their futile ritual.

They undressed the President, beginning by pulling off his sixteen-inch-high, partygoing boots, size fourteen, made of black French kid with a surprising gay band of maroon goat skin at their tops. They had been a comfortable exact fit, for Mr. Lincoln had stood on a piece of wrapping paper and himself drawn with a pencil around his own toes, insteps, and heels. He had then shipped the amusing result off to the master bootmaker, Dr. Peter Kahler in New York, who encouraged the trade of customers with unmatched, interesting feet and advertised that his handiwork contained a hidden, unique invention to avoid squeaking.

Since winter was over, there was no longer the jolly sight of long red flannel underwear under the baggy trousers, and the four men solemnly folded together the little bundle of clothing. The shirt had been slashed into strips of white cotton and the shirt's collar was hacked away completely. There was a cuff button bearing the graven letter "L." Its link had been broken, as the button was wrenched with urgency from its lost mate.

A search of the overcoat turned up two pairs of white kid gloves. The President's good-natured efforts to avoid wearing gloves in the face of Mrs. Lincoln's insistence that he cover his hands like a gentleman were public knowledge, and he sometimes had eight pairs stuffed in one pocket, where he had got rid of them as soon as "Mother's" back was turned.

When Mr. Lincoln lay naked on the bed, the physicians jointly examined every inch of him. There was one old scar on his left thumb, two small scars in his scalp well hidden among the black locks. As to anything new, he was unharmed except for that brutal thrust through his head.

There would be disagreements among the four doctors as to the right treatment to pursue and their versions of what happened on the death night would vary startlingly. There was total agreement always on the astonishment they all felt at that first sight of Mr. Lincoln's extraordinary physique.

They were familiar with the dark-brown face, weather-worn and criss-crossed with lines, and they knew as much as that Old Abe's neck too was leathery and wrinkled and that the "old" in his nickname was apt.

The stunning surprise was that the President's body was the body of a much younger man and was unbelievably perfect. The beautiful proportions, the magnificent muscular development, and the clear, firm flesh were all the more astounding because the visible man had given no clue. Charlie Taft pointed out that there was not one ounce of fat on the entire frame. Charles Leale was something of a student of classical sculpture, and he remarked immediately that the President could have been the model for Michelangelo's Moses; he had the same massive grandeur.

WILLIAM T. CLARK, a Massachusetts soldier who worked for the Quartermaster's Department, returned to his boarding-house room that night to find the dying President in his bed.

A hospital steward arrived with the bottles from the hospitals filled with hot water downstairs, and the mustard plasters, and Henry Safford trudged up from the basement kitchen with his collection of bottles. Safford had been delayed in his bottle hunt through having been dispatched to a pharmacy for spirits of camphor to restore Mrs. Lincoln, who lay in a sudden fainting spell in the front parlor. He had wedged his way back through Tenth Street, looked up in astonishment to see the gleam of bayonets as soldiers patrolled the Petersen House roof, and the military on guard at the front door had proved hard to convince that though he was panting and almost incoherently insistent upon entering he was not an assassin.

The hot water bottles were laid along the sides of the President's legs, which had grown cold to a point above the knees. Outsized mustard plasters were placed like clammy pies solidly over the entire upper surface of the body, from ankles to neck. When in a few minutes Dr. Leale raised the corner of a sinapism—he disliked the layman's term, plaster—and saw no slightest pink tinge in the parchment skin, he ordered a stronger paste of mustard and flour mixed up downstairs, and the heating of a supply of army blankets brought from the hospitals. Soon Mr. Lincoln lay between walls of bottles and under steaming layers of wool, and clinging to him as though a death mold were being made of his form was that hot yellow dough, enfolded in an assortment of cloths. There was no reaching the cold within him, though, just as he had always said during the war years there was no way of reaching the tired spot that was inside.

William Henry Seward and his daughter, Fanny.

The Secretary of State lay in a pool of blood, almost murdered too.

In that dark and shaken city of Washington, in another house, in another bedroom, the second most important official of the United States also lay close to death. For at almost the same moment Booth had fired his fatal shot in Ford's Theatre, an accomplice—the huge, handsome, bull-strong Lewis Paine—had attacked Lincoln's Secretary of State, William Henry Seward, viciously slashing his throat as he lay helpless in his bed.

Almost five years earlier Seward, Senator from New York and leader of the antislavery faction, had lost the Republican nomination to Lincoln, and it had been a terrible, bitter blow to him—completely unexpected. He had been sitting on the porch of his Auburn home waiting for the victory telegram from Chicago. A cannon had been brought to the yard and friends hovered over it ready to light the fuse. When the horseman finally galloped up with the telegram that read "Lincoln nominated," Seward had turned ashen pale. In moments the victory cannon was rolled away, flags were collected and furled, and the groups of tearful, unbelieving neighbors vanished. The chair on the porch was empty.

Although Seward had later campaigned for Lincoln strenuously, underneath he thought of the Republican choice as a "prairie politician," and he only accepted the job of Secretary of State Lincoln offered him because he felt he could not "leave the country to chance." At first the two men seemed to share little beyond their mutual love for cats—new kittens in the White House always sent Lincoln's spirits soaring, and Mr. Seward would sit at his desk through a day's work with his cat purring on his shoulder. Feeling that the new President had been underprivileged socially and knowing his schooling had been a matter of months, the new Secretary started out with extensive suggestions on the phrasing and content of Lincoln's messages and letters, told him how to stand at receptions, and exactly what to say to visiting foreign dignitaries. Still, by the end of the war there was a good working relationship and real affection between the President and his sallow, hollow-chested Secretary, whose eyes, with their indirect, subtle expression, always gave the impression that he was thinking something secret and mysterious. He dressed fashionably, continually smoked expensive cigars, loved being with people and relating his important experiences endlessly, philosophizing, making predictions, arguing, always courteously and urbanely, with a curious elegance in his harsh, guttural voice.

A few weeks before the fateful night of April fourteenth Seward received a letter from the U.S. Consul in Paris dated March twelfth saying that three days before two desperate characters had left by fast steamer and were being paid $5,000 apiece, one to go south to kill General Sherman, the other to go to Washington and murder Seward. Seward did not change his way of life at all after this letter, and on April fifth it was still unanswered. It was on this day, when the mysterious assassin from abroad had had plenty of time to reach Washington and when there had also come a letter to the government warning that assassination could be effected by a "hired domestic," that Secretary Seward almost lost his life. His coachman, who had come to pick him up at his home, had just opened the door for the Secretary with his right hand, holding the reins in his left, and Seward had just climbed inside the carriage when suddenly, inexplicably, the horses bolted. The unguided carriage careened wildly across the entire city of Washington before Seward made a desperate leap from it, falling heavily to the ground and breaking his right arm close to the shoulder and fracturing his jaw. He was carried home and his family doctor, Tullio Suzzaro Verdi, a homeopathic practitioner, set the arm and encased his lower jaw and neck in an elastic wire bandage which supported his head rigidly. The threat of a murderer who was in town to kill him for $5,000 was forgotten, and the Secretary lapsed into half consciousness. Whenever he came to he was in agony, and the family was grateful when he could drift off again.

Lincoln had been away from the capital at the time of Seward's accident, visiting General Grant's army at City Point with his son, Tad, but as soon as he arrived back in the city, at sundown on April ninth, he went straight to Seward's house to visit with him in his sickroom. It was dark, the gaslights were low, and Lincoln

LEWIS PAINE, Booth's tall and immensely strong accomplice, almost succeeded in killing the Secretary of State.

This contemporary woodcut shows the violent bedroom attack Lewis Paine made on Seward.
Robinson, the nurse, grapples with Paine as the Secretary's daughter Fanny throws up her arms, screaming "Murder! Murder!"

This is the Seward home opposite Lafayette Park. After the attack Paine fled out the front door, galloped into the night.

stretched himself out across the bed and leaned on his elbow to talk with the Secretary. Seward could not make answers to what Lincoln told him, but the two men were alone more than an hour while the President described his visit to the front and to Richmond and said, "I think we are near the end at last."

Five days later, on Good Friday morning, Seward's barber, named Wood, came up to his third-floor-front room to shave him and went back immediately to his barber shop near Grover's Theatre to take care of an actor named John Wilkes Booth. That night at nine o'clock Dr. Verdi visited Seward and found him much improved. Everything was planned in that big comfortable house for a good night's rest for the sufferer. Seward's son Frederick, who was Assistant Secretary of State, was close by. His other son, Major Augustus Seward, had gone to bed in his room on that same third floor at the early hour of seven-thirty so that he could be called at eleven to take his turn watching over his father. The first watch of the evening was being kept by young

Fanny Seward and a recovering invalid soldier in the Eighth Maine Volunteers, George T. Robinson, who had been injured in the leg some months before and was now assigned to nursing duty.

A little after ten Robinson heard someone coming up the stairs, stepping heavily, and he said to Miss Fanny, "Wouldn't you think that person would be more quiet coming up to a sickroom?" Frederick Seward heard the noise, too, and when he stepped to the top of the stairs to see who it was, he was met by a great muscular giant of a man in a light overcoat, dark pants, and a slouch hat, carrying an exceedingly small package. It was Lewis Paine. He was delivering medicine from Dr. Verdi, he told Frederick, and he insisted the doctor had said he must give it to Mr. Seward personally. The two men argued, Frederick repeatedly telling Paine that his father was sleeping and he was too ill to accept packages anyway. Suddenly Paine drew a large pistol, pointed it directly at Frederick's head and pulled the trigger. There was only a click, the gun failed to fire. Now Paine leapt forward and hammered Frederick's head with the pistol in a succession of vicious blows, leaving young Seward with blood streaming down his face and with two gaping cracks in the back of his skull. Paine drew his knife and stumbled into the sickroom where the gas jet was turned very low. Robinson saw the flash of a knife before he was cut in the forehead and knocked to the floor. The assassin punched Fanny out of the way and jumped onto the bed. With his left hand pushing down on Mr. Seward's chest, he began slashing savagely with his huge knife, cutting both sides of Seward's neck above the protecting metal bandage, and slicing open his right cheek so violently that one could look directly through a gaping hole at the bloody tongue.

Seward now slid off the bed onto the floor, pulling his sheet after him, and Paine turned around to fight off Robinson, who had jumped on the bed too. The knife cut into Robinson's neck and plunged into his shoulder, striking the bone. The two men rolled to the floor and wrestled and tumbled out onto the brightly lit landing. At this moment Major Augustus Seward came out of his room where he had been sleeping. He was only half awake and was under the impression that the soldier nurse had become demented and was attacking his father, so he grabbed Robinson to subdue him. Robinson shouted "For God's sake, Major, let go of me and take the knife out of his hand and cut his throat." Paine struck at Augustus' forehead and his hand with his knife, broke away from the nurse and bounded down the stairs, pounding with heavy, noisy new boots. Still using his knife wildly, he slashed a messenger for the State Department as he passed him. "I am mad! I am mad!" he yelled and disappeared out the front door into the night. Back in the Secretary's room Augustus Seward, who was the least badly wounded of the five persons attacked, helped the nurse to pull off his father's bloody clothes, and Robinson listened for a heartbeat. All of a sudden, Mr. Seward opened his eyes and said, "I am not dead, send for a surgeon, send for the police, close the house."

Frederick Seward, whose father had been criticized for making him Assistant Secretary of State, was one of the five bloody victims of the Paine attack.

These two profiles, the first taken in 1861, the second five years later, show how the night of horror turned Seward into an old sickly and sour-faced man. In his few remaining years of life he would not allow the right side of his face with its ugly knife scar to be photographed.

The Secretary of War assumes charge of the nation.

Through that night of shock and panic the government was driven and directed by one man—Lincoln's dynamic, unpredictable, and emotionally unstable Secretary of War, Edwin McMasters Stanton. Stanton had just begun to undress for bed when downstairs a frantic voice shouted the incredible—Secretary of State Seward had been murdered. "Humbug!" Stanton grunted. Hadn't he just left Seward a few minutes ago? But soon the night outside was filled with the terrible news and Stanton was dressing and rushing across the square to Seward's house. The Secretary of State was indeed lying pale and ghastly looking on a wildly disordered bed, while a doctor held pieces of ice against severely bleeding gashes in his neck and cheek. The President, they were saying, had been murdered, too, and who knew how many others. Now, through all the floundering and confusion and pain, Stanton assumed total power, rushing by hack to the Peterson House and setting up an office in the room next to where Lincoln lay. Along with his Assistant Secretary of War, Charles A. Dana, Stanton began dictating orders and telegrams. The country had to be alerted, witnesses questioned, the assassins identified and captured. Roadblocks were to be set up in Maryland; all passenger trains and Potomac ships heading south were to be stopped; the whole countryside round about the city was to be patrolled. The orders to all commanders—find a man named John Wilkes Booth, "twenty-five years old [sic], five feet eight inches tall, dark hair and mustache. Use all efforts to secure him."

CHARLES A. DANA, *Assistant Secretary of War*
Helping Stanton through the night was the former managing editor of the New York *Tribune*, whose job during the war had been to keep Washington in close touch with Lincoln's often uncommunicative generals.

It was a frenzied night for Stanton, a pudgy, nearsighted man with such chronic asthma that twice during the war years he was found unconscious in his office, seemingly suffocated by his attacks; a curt, rude, disobliging man who worked with a kind of demon energy all day long and far into the nights in the crumbling old War Department building, just a short walk for Lincoln across the White House lawn. When Lincoln made Stanton Secretary of War the department was in a hopeless condition, ridden with graft, and Lincoln needed a man whom he knew to be absolutely honest and fearless, a man like himself obsessed with the conception of an indivisible Union and a tireless leader who would drive others as he drove himself. Stanton had been Attorney General in Buchanan's administration. When Lincoln became President, he buried all remembrance of their first meeting in Cincinnati, when both had been lawyers on the same case. Stanton, secure in his reputation as one of the well-known, competent lawyers from the East, had seen to it that the minor advocate from Springfield was made something of an outcast. He was given no chance to present the brief on which he had worked so hard, and Stanton added ridicule to humiliation, remarking, "Where did that long-armed creature come from?" and "Du Chaillu was a fool to go all the way to Africa—he could have found the original gorilla in Springfield, Illinois."

It was only by a superhuman effort that Stanton controlled himself that night as Lincoln lay dying in the next room. For Stanton had an unreasoning, morbid fear of death. He had always reacted peculiarly when death came near him in the past. In 1833 when a young girl in the boarding house where he was living died of cholera and was buried instantly, he went that evening to dig her up—he could not believe she was really dead, as she had served him lunch that very day. In 1841 when his little daughter Lucy died he had her body exhumed and kept the coffin in his own room for two years. When his wife died in 1844 he dressed and re-dressed her in her bridal clothes—putting jewels and letters beside her, which friends kept removing—and after she was buried he walked about the house at night asking, "Where is Mary?" When his brother committed suicide, cutting his throat, Stanton had run wildly through dark woods and had to be overtaken and led home.

Though he was obviously trying to hold his emotions in iron rein as he ran the country through the night of the assassination, Stanton did a strange thing later. He ordered the rocking chair in which Lincoln had been shot carried to his office and kept it there for a year, where his eyes would fall upon it daily.

EDWIN M. STANTON, *Secretary of War*
Stanton took over the reins of government throughout the death watch, set up an emergency office in the Petersen House, conducted the first hurried investigations.

These four men helped Stanton through the long night.

As Stanton and Dana worked through the night in the back parlor of the Petersen House, four men helped carry out their orders. Lincoln himself had touched upon the lives of two of these men in very personal ways. The other two had never met their President in life, but the memory of his death would be indelibly stamped on them, as it was on all who entered the Petersen House that night.

Thomas Thompson Eckert was chief of the Military Telegraph under the War Department during the Civil War and at one time had been in deep trouble with Stanton. Obeying a previous order which should have been canceled but never was, Eckert had sent all incoming telegrams to General George McClellan instead of straight to Stanton. Stanton was furious because direct news from the front was not reaching him, and he wrote out an order to have Eckert dismissed from the army. Eckert with great difficulty secured an appointment to speak in person to Stanton. Stanton kept Eckert standing in front of him for ten minutes before he looked up from his writing, then accused Eckert angrily. Before Eckert could speak he felt an arm on his shoulder. It was Lincoln who had come in and heard the whole thing. He said to Stanton that there must be some mistake, that he had called daily at McClellan's headquarters, where Eckert had been working, and whether it was early in the morning or midday or late at night he had always found Eckert at his post. Stanton instantaneously had one of his irrational and strange changes from intense bad humor to an almost fawning good humor.

THOMAS THOMPSON ECKERT, whom Lincoln had asked to the theatre that night, was a forty-four-year-old major who could break iron pokers.

JAMES TANNER, an obscure little man who had had his legs amputated during the war, suddenly became famous for his small role during the long night.

LOUIS HENRY PELOUZE, a distinguished twenty-four-year-old soldier, helped take testimony from Ford's Theatre eyewitnesses.

He tore up Eckert's dismissal from the army, scattered the pieces on the floor and said he was immediately promoting Eckert from captain to major. To seal his apology, he would make further acknowledgment soon. The further acknowledgment proved to be a fine horse and carriage, available night and day to Major Eckert.

Eckert had been one of the twelve people invited to be Lincoln's theatre guests who had one by one, almost unbelievably, declined. He would reproach himself for the rest of his life for it, for with his strength he could have easily knocked aside that one-bullet tiny pistol and overcome the assassin had he seen Booth in time. He would have been alert, too, for his job at the War Department kept him closely informed on the latest assassination threats. He even had heard that John Wilkes Booth had been working to kidnap the President for months, and although the War Department had not taken the rumor seriously, still the presence of the actor anywhere near Mr. Lincoln tonight would have, to the competent Eckert, immediately signaled danger.

That afternoon at the War Department Lincoln had gone first to Stanton. He had decided, he told the Secretary, that it would be sensible to accept protection this evening, and he knew how strong Eckert was. He reminded Stanton of the time a new lot of pokers had been ordered for the fireplaces in his building and Eckert maintained the iron used was poor quality. When he whacked five of them across the muscle of his left arm to prove it, all five had broken. "I am thinking he would be the kind of man to go with me tonight," said Lincoln. "May I take him?" Stanton refused, saying he had important work for Eckert, late into the night. The

Secretary of War had already expressed himself violently to Eckert, saying that the best way to discourage Lincoln's exposing himself to danger in a public place was to refuse to go with him. And so Tom Eckert did not go.

David Cartter was a large man with black hair that seemed charged with electricity, huge glistening eyes and a dreadfully pockmarked face that almost amounted to disfigurement. He also had a very distressing stutter. At the time of Lincoln's nomination Cartter was a delegate from Ohio and had the honor on the third ballot in the Wigwam in Chicago to rise and say, "I rise—stutter—Mr. Chairman, stutter, to announce the change of four votes of Ohio from Mr. Chase to Mr. Lincoln." There was a moment's silence, wrote a reporter, "as a deep breath of relief was taken, then a noise in the Wigwam like the rush of a great wind in the face of a storm—thousands cheering with the energy of insanity."

Lincoln had appointed Cartter Minister to Bolivia in 1861 and two years later made him Chief Justice of the District of Columbia. On the night of April fourteenth Cartter was playing whist with Surgeon General Joseph Barnes at the Cartter house just around the corner from Secretary Seward's. When the news reached them of the attack on Seward, the two men hurried to the Secretary's house, where Barnes worked over the terrible gashes in the wounded man's face and neck. A colored driver pulled his hack to a stop in front of Seward's house and rang the bell urgently. Cartter went down to the door and heard what had happened to the President. Leaving Seward with Dr. Verdi, his own physician, Barnes and Cartter rushed down the stairs, ordered the hackman to drive them to the Petersen House. The terrified Negro insisted he was too frightened to drive, whereupon Cartter pushed him into the hack alongside Barnes, slammed the door shut, swung himself up into the box and drove the horses at a gallop through Washington, by some miracle arriving at the Petersen House without killing a pedestrian. Forever after Cartter described this ride as one of the most thrilling events of his life.

Louis Pelouze graduated from West Point in 1853. He fought all through the war and was severely wounded in the battle of Cedar Mountain in Virginia on August 9, 1862. It took him until November to recover, and then he was put to work as Assistant Adjutant General of Volunteers with the rank of Lieutenant Colonel. When Pelouze heard that Lincoln had been shot he raced to the War Department, ordered the guards there to go immediately to the front door of Ford's Theatre. When they arrived, a huge crowd had already gathered. The guards reversed their muskets, used the butts to make a path to the door, the dense mass of people closing in solidly behind them. When the bearers appeared with the President, they opened a new path across the street so that Lincoln could be carried to the Petersen House. Afterward Pelouze stayed in the back parlor through the night, helping Stanton take testimony from witnesses.

The last of the four was James Tanner, a twenty-one-year-old corporal who had been so badly wounded in the second battle of Bull Run that he had to have both his legs amputated just below the knees. He got around with strapped-on peg legs, studied shorthand, and was given a position in the Ordinance Bureau of the War Department. On April fourteenth he was boarding in a house on Tenth Street next door to William Petersen. He was a loyal Union man in a dwelling that was suspect in the mind of his neighbor Henry Safford.

On the night of the fourteenth Tanner took the horsecar to Grover's Theatre, and it was there he heard of the shooting. Tanner made his way home, was allowed to push through the crowd and go up to his two rooms overlooking the street. At about midnight General Augur, in charge of all the troops in Washington, came out on the steps of the Petersen House and called for someone who could write shorthand. In a couple of minutes Tanner was seated in the back parlor at a table opposite Stanton, and he took down the testimony of a succession of witnesses until half past four in the morning. "In fifteen minutes," he wrote later, "I had testimony enough down to hang Wilkes Booth, the assassin, higher than ever Haman hung."

DAVID KELLOGG CARTTER also assisted Stanton in taking testimony, after driving the Surgeon General of the Army to the scene in a wild night ride.

He took a nap as Lincoln died.

JOHN PALMER USHER, the Secretary of the Interior, was forty-nine years old in 1865, a pink-skinned, blue-eyed man with fair hair and a portly figure—an affable, easy-going man who was nevertheless a very diligent worker in running his department. He thought highly of Lincoln—if anything the President was too good, too kind-hearted. He said it was strange—Lincoln got along without ever hurting people's feelings and he could refuse their requests and still send them away in good humor.

On April fourteenth Usher dined out with friends, then went home to his hotel, where he was chatting in a darkened sitting room when he heard people saying the President had been shot. As quickly as he could he joined the group around the bed, which was formed of the Cabinet and other people he already knew. Each visit Mrs. Lincoln made to the room during the night "beggars description," he later said. She implored her husband to speak to her but he never opened his eyes or said a word all night. Mrs. Lincoln called for Tad to be fetched, saying his father would surely speak to him—he loved him so.

Usher seems to have been the only person in that crowded house of death that night who managed to catch forty winks. Secretary of the Navy Gideon Welles felt a little faint from the stuffiness of the room at 6:00 A.M., walked outdoors for fifteen minutes and came in again to find Usher asleep on the unmade bed in the back parlor.

He comforted Lincoln's son.

CHARLES SUMNER, Senator from Massachusetts, probably provided the greatest contrast to Lincoln of anyone in the government. He was a Boston Brahmin, born to position and wealth, and he prided himself on his classical education, his knowledge of Europe and its languages, his tall figure and handsome features, and the image he had of himself as a crusader for the rights of Negroes—though people said he never spoke with or became a friend of any individual Negro. He was a passionate, impatient abolitionist and was a thorn in the President's side all during the war, pushing him relentlessly to declare the slaves free, while Lincoln was feeling out the temper of the nation, really caring most about preserving the Union, but ready to issue an emancipation proclamation if that should prove militarily advantageous, which it seemed to him it was in September 1862.

Gracious-living Senator Sumner had just sat down to a bottle of after-dinner wine when the door to his house was thrown open by a man with the dreadful news. Sumner did not believe him but he went straight to the Executive Mansion. Together he and Robert Lincoln hurried to the Petersen House. Sumner sat down at the head of the bed and took Lincoln's hand. A doctor said, "It's no use, Mr. Sumner. He can't hear you. He is dead." "No, he isn't dead," replied Sumner. "Look at his face, he's breathing." "It will never be anything more than this," came the answer. Then Robert broke down in tears and Sumner put his arm around Lincoln's eldest son and held him close during much of the night and tried to comfort him.

He screened the bedside visitors.

MONTGOMERY MEIGS
with renditions of his engineering projects.

Montgomery Meigs had been Quartermaster General of the Union armies since 1861 and had spent, with scrupulous honesty, just under two billion dollars in feeding, clothing and moving to different places by rail and water an army of between five hundred thousand and a million men. Toward the end he was spending more than two hundred and fifty million a year, replacing dead horses and mules alone at the rate of five hundred a day. For the first six or seven years before the war, Meigs had been the engineer in charge of building the great aqueduct that brought water from the Great Falls of the Potomac River into the city of Washington—a tremendously complicated and successful engineering job for which two great bridges had to be built to conduct the giant pipes. Meigs was also the engineer in charge of building the new Capitol wings and the new iron dome.

When Meigs was commissioned Quartermaster General in 1861, he had to leave his engineering projects to others. But knowing of Lincoln's great interest in the aqueduct, he took the President on a drive westward to see it. The picture at the left is believed to be of Lincoln on that inspection trip on May 19, 1861. It was taken by the son of a man who supervised one of Meigs's engineering jobs. Lincoln wore a short-coated suit very similar to this one in Springfield in the summer of 1860, and though he wore much longer coats as President, it is probable that he would have put on an old suit to make an inspection which might involve dust and rust.

Meigs was a man of fiery temper, utter integrity, and passionate devotion to the Union. Then, too, he was rather self-righteous—he knew he was brilliant and honest and he resented criticism. His son, John Meigs, who was with Sheridan on a scouting party on October 3, 1864, had been caught by Southern troops and had surrendered but still he was shot down in cold blood. Sheridan ordered the burning of every home within five miles of the body but that did not comfort his father. After the war Meigs never forgave the men he considered had been traitors to the old flag. Several Southerners who had been his warm friends before the war tried to see him again and renew friendship, but he told them coldly there could never be anything more between them.

On April fourteenth, Meigs, who was deeply religious, went to a Good Friday service at St. John's Church on Lafayette Square opposite the White House—he would not have dreamed of going to the theatre that day as the President did. That night he was sitting at home with his wife, Louisa, when a messenger banged on the door with the news about Seward. Meigs hurried the three blocks to Seward's house, found the Secretary in a pool of blood on the floor, his daughter Fanny unconscious, his son Frederick incoherent from terrible blows on the head which smashed his skull, and the family doctor getting to work in dazed unbelief. Secretary Stanton and Gideon Welles arrived and the three hurried to the Petersen House. Through most of the night Meigs took charge of the front door, tried to let in only the people who had a real right to be there.

Important people arrive . . .

RICHARD JAMES OGLESBY

"If I had been in the box I would have grabbed the assassin by the neck and choked him to death." Like Lincoln, the rough, blunt, newly-elected governor of Illinois was carrying a bullet in his body right at that moment, there in the death room. He had been shot through the left lung in the battle of Corinth and given up for dead. He recovered, but the doctors never dared go after the ounce ball. It was partly due to Oglesby's imagination and strategy that Lincoln was elected President. Trying to think of a way to dramatize and symbolize his candidacy, he brought into the convention hall actual rails that Lincoln had split. The "Rail-Splitter Candidate" caught fire.

JOHN BLAIR SMITH TODD

Into the crowded house came John Todd, first cousin of Mary Lincoln and a frequent visitor at the White House. Born in Kentucky in 1814, four years earlier than Mary Todd, John moved to Springfield, Illinois, when he was thirteen years old. After graduating from West Point, he fought in the Florida and Mexican wars, became an Indian trader in Dakota, was Brigadier-General of Volunteers at the beginning of the war and in 1865 was serving for the second time as a delegate to Congress from Dakota. Through the night he stayed with his cousin Mary in the front room. He could see that the shock to her was terrible, and he regarded her as "poor heart—bowed to the very dust under the weight of her bereavement."

JAMES SPEED

As morning came James Speed, the Attorney General of the United States, sat down in the back parlor and wrote the official letter to Vice-President Johnson informing him that he should prepare himself to take the oath as the new President in a matter of hours. James was the younger brother of Joshua Speed, Lincoln's closest friend and roommate in his early Springfield days. Born to a fine and well-to-do Kentucky family, the Speed brothers kept close to Lincoln through the war and it was a great deal due to their efforts that Kentucky did not go over to the Southern side.

WILLIAM PITT FESSENDEN

Standing the death watch, the spare, dry, severe scholar of economics, William Fessenden, who had recently resigned as Secretary of the Treasury to begin his third term as Senator from Maine, must have recalled his change of heart about Lincoln. In Lincoln's first term Fessenden had said, "The simple truth is that never before was such a shambling, half and half set of incapables collected in one government, since the world began." But toward the end he recognized Lincoln's wisdom and he told him, "Mr. President, the people of the United States are praying that God will spare your life to see the end of the rebellion."

HENRY WAGER HALLECK

Standing at Lincoln's death bed General Halleck, Chief of Staff and the President's personal military adviser, must have felt he was losing his only defender. For the current opinion of Halleck was that he had no nerve or pluck, he was by nature a behind-the-scenes planner and a most timid doer. No one understood why Lincoln kept watery-eyed "Old Brains" on. John Hay thought he was "little more than a first-rate clerk," and Gideon Welles found him a "military imbecile." Yet to everyone's bewilderment Lincoln was loyal to Halleck to the end.

. . . on into the night.

SCHUYLER COLFAX

Elected Speaker of the House of Representatives in 1863, Schuyler Colfax was a slight, short man with light hair and blue eyes who smiled constantly, so that he was given the nickname of "The Smiler." He spoke so fast as he presided over the House that he was likened more to an auctioneer than a speaker. On Lincoln's last day Colfax was the first visitor to the White House, arriving while the President was at breakfast to ask whether Lincoln was going to call a special session of Congress during the summer (the answer was no). He was also the last visitor of the day. He came this time to receive a long message from Lincoln to the miners of the West. Lincoln asked him to go to the theatre with him but Colfax said no, he wanted to get to bed early as he was leaving the next day for California. He said the last good-by to Lincoln as the President drove off in his carriage to Ford's Theatre. He hurried to the deathbed several hours later in an agony of self-accusation at not having been at his friend's side "to give my life for his."

"Damn the Rebels, this is their work."

This unpublished Brady photograph of Gideon Welles was judged unworthy by the photographer. He scraped a cross on the glass plate and discarded it.

One of the many contemporary drawings of the

Gideon Welles, Lincoln's efficient, garrulous Secretary of the Navy, had attended the Cabinet meeting on the morning of the President's last day. Along with the other Cabinet members he had heard the President tell of his strange dream of the night before, the dream he always had before some important event—of being in a strange vessel, sailing rapidly toward a shadowy shore. Mr. Lincoln turned to Welles and remarked of his dream, "It has to do with your element, Mr. Welles, the water."

That evening Mrs. Welles—Mary Jane—one of Mrs. Lincoln's few intimate friends—went to bed early because she had been in the house for a week with a bad cold and cough. Gideon went up to bed about ten-thirty and soon afterward a Navy Department messenger called up to the window the news about Lincoln and Seward. While Welles was dressing, he did the unprecedented thing of swearing in front of Mary Jane: "Damn the Rebels, this is their work!"

Through the night Welles sat quietly beside Lincoln's bed. This shy, dignified man, who wore a huge wig which did not match his beard, described the scene in his extraordinary diary.

> *The giant sufferer lay extended diagonally across the bed,* Welles began. *He had been stripped of his clothes. His large arms, which were occasionally exposed, were of a size which one would scarce have expected from his spare appearance. His*

death scene, this one is less idealized than most. shows Gideon Welles sitting calmly amidst the confusion of the room.

slow, full respiration lifted the clothes with each breath that he took. His features were calm and striking. I had never seen them appear to better advantage than for the first hour, perhaps, that I was there. After that, his right eye began to swell and that part of his face became discolored.

Welles had been a newspaperman for thirty years, editor of the Hartford *Times* in Connecticut. His great interest was the skillful use of words. With an inborn intuition of which he was proud, he sought to describe the men and events of his time. The name of Welles was one of the first Lincoln put down for membership in his Cabinet the very night of his election, and Welles, in turn, had been one of the very first to feel Lincoln's greatness. Before he was nominated for the Presidency Lincoln had come to Hartford after his Cooper Union address and Welles had heard him speak.

This orator and lawyer has been caricatured, Welles wrote in his diary. *He is not Apollo, but he is not Caliban. He was made where the material for strong men is plenty; and his loose, tall frame is loosely thrown together. He is in every way large—brain included—and his countenance shows intellect, generosity, great good nature, and keen discrimination.*

Mrs. Lincoln disliked these men and it was mutual.

ANDREW JOHNSON *of Tennessee,*
newly elected Vice-President for Lincoln's second term of office.

Washington was filled with people Mary Lincoln hated and more often than not the feeling was mutual. One of her greatest "enemies" was Vice-President Andrew Johnson. On the night of the assassination Johnson was staying at the Kirkwood House, and in the middle of the night Stanton sent for him because he thought the Vice-President should make an appearance at the dying President's bedside. Johnson had only been there a very few minutes when word came from the front room that Mrs. Lincoln wanted to pay another visit to her husband. It was quickly agreed that Johnson must be got rid of first as Mrs. Lincoln despised him so. The Vice-President spent the rest of the night excitedly walking up and down his hotel room saying, "They shall suffer for this! They shall suffer for this!" Mrs. Lincoln never stopped believing Johnson was somehow mixed up in the assassination plot. A year later she wrote in one of her violent letters, ". . . that miserable inebriate Johnson . . . He never wrote me a line of condolence and behaved in the most brutal way. . . . As sure as you and I live, Johnson had some hand in all this."

Lincoln's gay, witty, assistant private secretary, John Hay, was another of Mary Lincoln's pet dislikes. Once she had questioned the cost of the grain that Lincoln's secretaries' horses were eating in the White House stables, and when she economized by getting rid of an

BENJAMIN B. FRENCH, *Commissioner of Public Buildings, a poet at heart.*

JOHN HAY, *Lincoln's assistant private secretary, brought from Springfield by the President.*

employee she wanted Hay to turn over to her for her personal use the money the employee would have been paid. "The Hell-cat," Hay described her, "is getting more Hell-cattical day by day." Hay spent the early part of the assassination evening with his great friend Robert Lincoln, and the two young men gossiped, studied Spanish together, and talked about Robert's impressions of General Lee, at the surrender.

Benjamin B. French, the Commissioner of Public Buildings, first incurred Mrs. Lincoln's wrath on the same subject over which she had fought with Hay—money! He refused to manipulate the White House expense account and cover up for her when she overran her decorating allowance by thousands of dollars. "Old French," she wrote, "has feathered his nest at my expense $83,500, besides $30,000 more. . . . He is a smooth-faced, avaricious villain and he got up the story of losses for his own particular benefit!" At the Petersen House French controlled his true feelings, sought out Mrs. Lincoln in the front room and took her hand. But privately, in his diary, he set down in verse what he really thought of her. She

> "moved in all the insolence of pride
> as if the world beneath her feet she trod;
> Her vulgar bearing, jewels could not hide,
> And gold's base glitter was her only god!"

They were absent for good reason

It was almost midnight when General and Mrs. Grant and their small son Jesse arrived by carriage from the Broad Street Station in Philadelphia at Bloodgood's Hotel near the ferry that would take them across the Delaware River to Camden. Then it was only an hour's more journey to Burlington, New Jersey, where the Grants' two other sons and their daughter, Nellie, were at school. They planned a short rest, with a bite to eat at Bloodgood's. But there was to be no rest. A messenger from the Philadelphia office of the American Telegraph Company was waiting in front of the hotel with the heartbreaking news from Washington. The young man saw the glow of Grant's cigar inside the hack as it drew up but he let the family make its way to the supper room before he delivered the telegram.

Mrs. Grant was taking off her bonnet as the General stood reading the dispatch without changing his expression in the slightest. "President Lincoln was assassinated at Ford's Theatre this evening and an attempt was made on the life of Secretary Seward. It is supposed that there is a plot to assassinate all men prominent in the Government. Be careful who comes near you on the boat or train."

Grant handed the sheet to Julia and at the first words her crossed eyes, which the General would not let her have corrected because he adored her as she was, brimmed with tears. She buried her face in her hands and sobbed.

Salmon P. Chase, newly appointed Chief Justice of the Supreme Court, had not forgiven Lincoln for "shelving him"—he had been actively plotting to have himself elected President. He alone, of all the important men who were notified of the assassination, made no effort to go to his chief's side. He was wakened, remarked that he could do no good and would probably be in the way. Just before Lincoln's death the next morning he walked across the street from the Petersen House and was told the President still lived. He kept on walking, his eyes bloodshot and his features twisted in a strange contortion. He soon was caught up with and received an eye-witness account from the man who had been the first to arrive in the Petersen House and the last to leave—Maunsell B. Field, who would never forget the sight of Mrs. Lincoln standing rigid as in a seizure, shouting "Why didn't he shoot me? Why didn't he shoot me?"

Field was a pet of Chase's in the political world who had been the actual cause of Chase's sudden exit from Lincoln's Cabinet. Chase insisted to the President that Field be made an assistant secretary of the Treasury. Lincoln said no. He knew Field as a man who had become intoxicated at a social affair with ladies present and kicked his stovepipe hat to the ceiling. Lincoln remarked that he preferred not to appoint a man of that caliber and seized this latest disagreement with his Secretary of the Treasury to accept his latest resignation. No one was more surprised than Chase, who found his new position as Chief Justice burdensome and no fun—he now had no patronage to distribute.

After hearing Field's description of the death room, the Chief Justice walked on. Half an hour later at the Kirkwood House, where Andrew Johnson was staying, Chase appeared—his formal, composed, and impressive self again. He then swore in the new President of the United States.

JULIA DENT GRANT SALMON P. CHA

Lincoln's close friend and bodyguard was in Richmond.

Ward Hill Lamon never forgave himself for being away in Richmond, shown at the left at war's end, still smoldering, in this never before published Brady photograph. Lamon always insisted that if he had been with Lincoln at the theater Booth would not have fired off his shot. And he probably was right. For this six-foot-two, handsome "Virginia Cavalier" was Lincoln's self-appointed bodyguard. He had been Lincoln's law partner in Danville, Illinois, and he had hoped to be made Minister to France, but the President-elect had said, "I need you, Hill," and named him Marshal of the District of Columbia. Lincoln laughed at Lamon's agonized warnings to be cautious, looked pensive when Lamon pointed out that he went frequently to the theatre with only Senator Summer as a companion, who gave him no more protection than a woman could. Often Lamon rolled up in a blanket and slept on the floor by the President's door at the White House and he had wrathfully threatened to submit his resignation if Lincoln did not obey him.

One time Lamon had almost killed a man in a street-corner illegal assembly. "Hereafter," said Lincoln, "when you have occasion to strike a man, don't hit him with your fist; strike him with a club or crowbar or something that won't kill him!"

Richmond with Brady's stereoscopic camera in foreground.

WARD HILL LAMON posed for Brady in this photograph, which is published here for the first time.

PHINEAS DENSMORE GURLEY, pastor of the New York Avenue Presbyterian Church in Washington, stayed with Mrs. Lincoln through the night and tried to console her.

JOSEPH K. BARNES, Surgeon General of the United States, took over from the younger doctors, probed the wound and found it fatal.

A minister, a surgeon, and a best friend

Early in the night Surgeon General Joseph Barnes sent word to Mrs. Lincoln in the front room that the wound could only result in death. So the waiting was a waiting without hope. In her hours of desperation the friend Mrs. Lincoln called for over and over and wanted most by her side was her devoted dressmaker, Lizzie Keckley. Mrs. Keckley had been a slave who with her own earnings from making dresses had bought both her freedom and that of her only son—for twelve hundred dollars. The son had enlisted in the Union army as "white." He could—he had inherited his white father's color. The boy was killed in a battle at the end of the first summer of the war, and both Lizzie and Mary Lincoln were heartbroken. Then a few months later they had gone through Willie Lincoln's death together, and it was Lizzie Keckley who washed and dressed the body of Lincoln's son and sat upstairs with the distracted mother when she could not face coming down to the East Room funeral. But tonight none of the messengers sent to find Mrs. Keckley could discover her whereabouts. She had left her boardinghouse to visit friends. Phineas Gurley, pastor of the Washington church the Lincolns attended, tried to console Mary Lincoln with no success, by stating his own belief that the Lord had allowed the President to be shot for some very good purpose. Lincoln had chosen Gurley's church because he heard that this minister inserted no politics into his sermons—he said he got enough politics during the week. All during the time he knew the President, Dr. Gurley kept notes on the little human things about him—that, for instance, he was fond of pears—and that after the second inauguration Lincoln had blisters on all four fingers of his right hand from having it squeezed by so many people—that he once popped the question at a wounded soldier who was applying for help without any papers to prove his record: "How do I know you did not lose your leg in a trap in somebody's orchard?" And that one morning Lincoln asked him to come to the White House and talk to him an hour before breakfast—Lincoln said the only time he had to think was at night when other people were sleeping. That morning Lincoln had wanted to talk to Gurley about the state of the soul after death. He wanted, with pathetic earnestness, to be given an affirmative answer to whether he would be able to see and talk with his son Willie in heaven.

LIZZIE KECKLEY, Mrs. Lincoln's dressmaker and close friend, was sent for over and over, but it was not until eleven o'clock Saturday morning that she finally came to the White House, took Mary Lincoln in her arms and quieted her sobs with loving words.

A mourning band circling his hat, Tad Lincoln tensely sits for his portrait soon after his father's death.

The Tyrant of the White House was at another theatre.

While *Our American Cousin* was being performed at Ford's, a gala production of *Aladdin! or His Wonderful Lamp* was under way a few blocks away at Grover's Theatre. Just before a moment in the Aladdin extravaganza where a man was supposed to tumble to the stage from a balloon, the manager stepped to the footlights to announce that President Lincoln had been shot. For a moment there was silence, then a voice called out that it was a trick of pickpockets to set the audience in a panic. But suddenly a boy sprang from his seat and went shrieking "like a wounded deer," the papers later said, to the theatre's door and out.

Twelve-year-old Tad Lincoln had been taken to the theatre that evening by White House doorkeeper Alphonso Donn, a great favorite with the Lincoln family. Now he was driven home where his other doorman friend, Tom Pendel, tried to calm his fears and comfort him. About midnight Pendel got Tad up to his father's room, undressed him, and lay down on the trundle bed beside him till he dropped off to sleep.

Abraham and Mary Lincoln had hoped Tad would be a girl, but when he arrived on April 4, 1853, they had a fourth son. Their second child, Eddie, had died at the age of three and Willie, their third, had been less than a year younger than Eddie. Tad was a squirming little baby with a big head and Mr. Lincoln nicknamed him Tadpole along with his given name of Thomas, for the child's grandfather who had died in 1851. Tad was going to be harder to take care of than the other boys because he was born with a cleft palate, and already when he tried to drink milk it dribbled out of his mouth. There would be a speech difficulty, making his words sound queer, breathy, nasal, almost another language. When Tad tried to say "Papa's shot" that night, it came out "Papa's tot."

By the time Tad came East to live in the White House in February, 1861, he had turned out to be the exact opposite of obedient, studious Willie. Tad was mercurial like his mother—mischievous, fun-loving, work-hating, destructive, and behind his parents' backs was awarded the summing-up of—spoiled brat. But Tad's naughtiness was ignored by his parents. Back in Springfield when friends came for an evening's festivity, he got out of bed and joined them in his red flannel nightshirt—and was welcome. When the Lincolns went out to dinner down the street, he followed and was allowed to stay. When the painter Mr. Hicks arrived from the East to do Mr. Lincoln's portrait, both Tad and Willie squeezed his tubes of color against the wall and made streaks with the palms of their hands. Mr. Lincoln beamed fondly.

One time Judge Treat was playing chess with Lincoln in the State House and Tad was sent by his mother to say dinner was ready. When his father went on making moves, Tad kicked the board from underneath right off both the men's laps. The Judge was wordless, but Lincoln said mildly, "Come, Tad," and they walked away together.

At the White House Tad had a happy first year along with Willie, riding ponies and watching regiments of soldiers drill. After Willie died in the winter of 1862 Tad became even more tightly glued to the President's side. He seemed like a normal, merry boy until Willie's name was mentioned, and then he would throw himself on the floor and kick and scream as he had seen his mother do.

He was the tyrant of the White House. He turned the hose on Secretary Stanton, interrupted important state meetings with his three quick raps on the door followed by two slow bangs. His father inevitably let him in—"I promised never to go back on the code."

When a huge turkey was sent to the President in October 1864 for the family's Thanksgiving dinner, Tad begged hard for the turkey's life to be spared, and, when it was, led him about the Executive Mansion grounds on a string, calling him Jack. It was just before the November eighth balloting which would decide whether Lincoln or McClellan should be president from 1864 on, and the President called down to Tad from his office window, asking if Jack was planning to vote. Like a flash Tad answered, "He isn't of age," and the proud father repeated the story to every visitor he had for the next week.

Tad's mind teemed with plans and his body never rested. He whittled the elegant carved rosewood furniture in the White House into designs he liked better. He drove his team of goats through the East Room, riding on a kitchen chair behind them. If he saw his father walking down the hall, he would race to him and give him a tight, fierce hug "like a thunderbolt" and dash away again. While Lincoln worked in his office until midnight, Tad would fall asleep on the floor under the President's table, and when the last paper was signed Lincoln would carry the boy down the hall to his room and lay him down on the low trundle bed and climb wearily into his own great bed.

Tad was allowed to run wild and just grow. "Let him run," said Lincoln. "There's time enough for him to learn his letters and get pokey." Tad never did become pokey. He broke the tall mirror in the White House vestibule with his ball. His father invited him to walk to the telegraph office in the War Department, where he dipped his fingers in a bottle of ink and drew them in lines along a marble tabletop. The officers in the room looked at the President indignantly. "Come, Tad," said Lincoln, with a pleasant smile. When Tad locked the door of the room in which photographers had set up their apparatus to develop pictures of his father, for once Lincoln was smileless. "Tad," he said, "do you know you are making your father a great deal of trouble?"

Tad immediately surrendered the key and burst into violent tears.

Tad was fascinated by money and hoarded it, though at the age of ten he still could not understand that a small gold dollar was the same in value as a handful of larger coins. He wanted the money that was big, and "a lot." His indulgent father often bribed his son, whom his mother called "my troublesome little sunshine," to make him be still and not break in on conversations with Cabinet members or generals.

Tad was given an actual colonel's commission by Stanton, and a real uniform with a real sword was made for him.

Tad was not particular about how he made his money. Ralph Waldo Emerson was visiting the White House and heard Tad bet Secretary Seward a quarter that he could not guess what new animal he and Willie had. Seward guessed a rabbit, Tad shook his head, pocketed the quarter and left in a hurry. Willie remarked gravely to the Secretary that it had indeed been a rabbit.

On several occasions when Tad wanted to fill his pockets to bursting quickly, he bought out the supply of gingerbread and apples of an old woman who kept a stand a few blocks from the Executive Mansion and set up business beneath the big columns at the entrance to the White House, where he could put pressure on the multitude of visitors to buy his wares. His father laughed and thought Tad was clever and enterprising, just as he laughed fondly when Tad, in anticipation of a National Fast Day, hid a succulent supply of goodies from the family kitchen in the coachhouse—where he could retire and munch while the nation went hungry. "If Tad lives to be a man," said the President, "he will be what all women love—a good provider."

In addition to being a trifle sharp about money matters, Tad was tender-hearted. When a widow came to the upstairs waiting room of the White House to beg that her husband be let out of prison—her children were cold and starving she told Tad—the boy went weeping to his father, put his arms around Lincoln's knees and implored him to save the children. And within a few minutes Tad had them saved. Another time he led into his father's office a delegation that Mr. Lincoln had been trying for days to avoid seeing because he felt he could not grant their request. Afterward, when Lincoln said, "Why, Tad, did you do that?" he answered, "I thought they were your friends, and they looked so sorry." "That's right, my son," said Lincoln. "I would have the whole human race your friends and mine, if that were possible."

Sometimes Lincoln tried to get Tad to leave his office and play outside. "Tad, my dear son, go to your mother. You must be tired here."

"No, no, Papa," Tad would say, "I want to stay and see the people."

He would listen eagerly as his father talked to army officers, laughing whenever his father laughed. He was an annoyance to some of the men, who got tired of never being able to see the President alone. Some even kept back important information when they did happen to find Lincoln without his son. The feeling was, "He can't keep a secret. He would tell Tad."

Tad made full use of the tiny white cards on which his father wrote succinct messages to people in pen and ink, signing them "A. Lincoln." He got a pardon for his Zouave doll whom he had condemned to death for sleeping on picket duty. The President wrote as carefully as though he were addressing a Cabinet officer, "The Doll Jack is pardoned. A. Lincoln."

Sitting on the captured beautiful little pacer, Little Jeff, Tad is shown here at City Point visiting Grant's army with his father just before the surrender.

"Tad wants some flags. Can he be accommodated? A. Lincoln" served Tad's purpose perfectly, and "Captain Dahlgren may let Tad have the little gun that he cannot hurt himself with. A. Lincoln" brought him a miniature brass model on which he doted.

In the last weeks of the war the President took Tad with him to Grant's camp at City Point, Virginia. It was the first time in many months that Lincoln had left his desk, and here the boy and his father had almost a vacation together. They rode—Tad was a daring rider—but he rode in the form most comfortable to himself, with his legs in very little relation to the horse's sides. Father and son rode happily over the countryside together on horses lent them by General Grant. Lincoln rode Cincinnati and Tad Little Jeff, the blooded, smooth-paced little horse the General had captured from Mrs. Jefferson Davis in Vicksburg.

Lincoln and Tad visited the surrendered cities of Petersburg and Richmond together. They walked hand in hand through the still-smoking capital, from the waterfront to Jefferson Davis's house, where Lincoln sank into a chair and asked for a glass of water. He must have been nervous, though he never said so, at bringing his son to this most rebel of all rebel cities, but nothing happened and the two went back up the river, looking at the floating torpedoes in the water as they passed and the jumble of wood and metal obstructions and dead horses floating.

On the night of April eleventh, as the President stood in the candle-lighted window above the White House portico, ready to deliver his last speech, someone in the crowd cried out, "What shall we do with the Rebels?" A voice answered, "Hang them!" and Tad said quickly, "Oh, no, we must hang on to them." "That's right, Tad," said his father proudly, "we must hang on to them."

Finally dawn came

All night long people moved endlessly in and out of the tiny room, only the most important of whom were recorded in the many refined drawings of the scene which were later published. Some of the sketches inaccurately included people who were not there—like young Tad Lincoln, Chief Justice Chase, and Vice-President Johnson, who is shown here close to the moment of death, although he had visited the room for only a few minutes many hours earlier. None of the sketches captured the frantic fight of the doctors to do something, anything—probing the wound to keep it bleeding, trying to warm the President's cold body, trying to remember to put clean towels over the blood-soaked pillows whenever Mrs. Lincoln appeared, to save her the horror that transfixed everyone else. At 11:30 P.M. a great protrusion of the President's right eye was noted, and for the next twenty minutes there was twitching on the left side of Lincoln's face. At five minutes before one o'clock he began making a struggling motion with his arms. His chest muscles stiffened, his breath held, and then finally exhaled as the spasm passed. Twice during the night Dr. Gurley prayed, and everyone in the room got down on his knees. At a quarter of two, and again at three o'clock, Mrs. Lincoln made her last two visits to the bedside. She

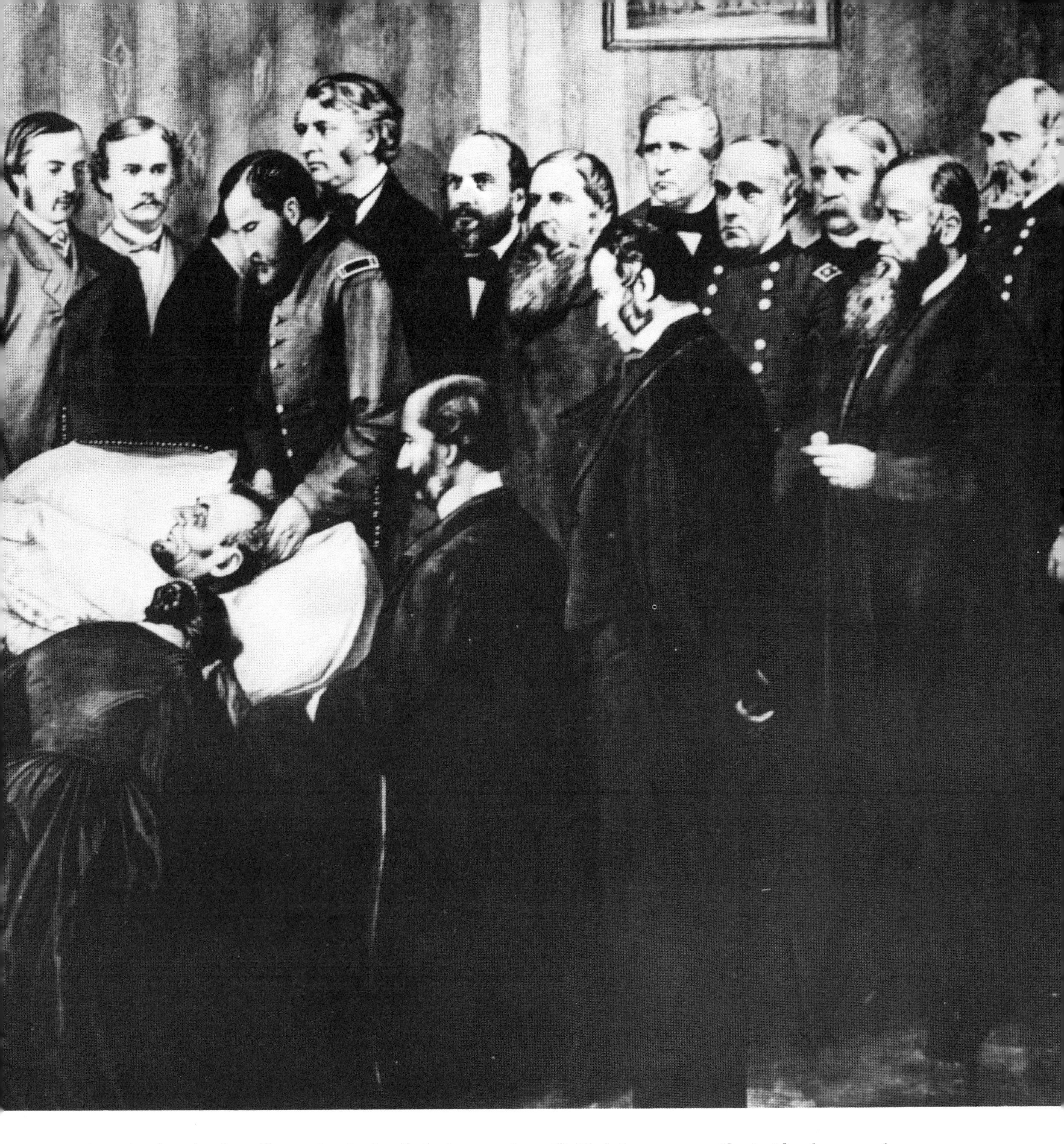

wept piteously, throwing herself upon her husband's body, begging the doctors to kill her and let her join him. Putting her face close to Lincoln's she pleaded, "Love, live but one moment to speak to our children—Oh, oh, that my little Taddy might see his father before he dies." A spell of loud rattling breathing by the President frightened her, and with a piercing shriek she fell fainting to the floor. Stanton ordered: "Take that woman out and do not let her in again!" As she was led down the hall, Mrs. Lincoln cried, "My God and have I given my husband to die!" It was the last time she would see Lincoln alive.

Finally dawn came. It was Saturday morning, the fifteenth of April. A cold rain drenched the silent crowd that still filled the street outside. Inside, the men of government, the men of medicine, the family, the friends whispered and waited. As the end drew near Dr. Africanus King, the obstetrician member of the task force of surgeons —a young Englishman with a flair for telling words—made notes. At 6:25 Lincoln's breaths were "jerking." At 6:40 "the expirations prolonged and groaning—a deep, softly sonorous cooing sound at the end of each expiration." At 6:45 "respiration uneasy and grunting, lower jaw relaxed." Then "a minute without breath—face growing dark." At seven "still breathing at long pauses." Now Dr. Gurley left Mrs. Lincoln in the front parlor and entered the death room to be present at the end.

"HE IS GONE: HE IS DEAD."

At twenty-two minutes past seven o'clock Dr. Taft's hand, pressed upon Abraham Lincoln's chest, felt that great heart throb one last time and then go still. Dr. Barnes, touching the carotid artery, felt the last thrust of blood, as did Dr. Leale, who held the right wrist pulse. All night long Leale had held Lincoln's hand "so that in his darkness he would know he had a friend." Now the darkness was absolute.

The fullest account of that terribly sad, historic moment was made by James Tanner, the wooden-legged corporal who took down testimony through the night for Stanton. "His stertorous breathing subsided a couple of minutes after seven o'clock. From then till the end only the gentle rise and fall of his bosom gave indication that life remained. The Surgeon General was near the head of the bed, sometimes sitting on the edge, his finger on the pulse of the dying man. Occasionally he put his ear down to catch the lessening beats of his heart. Mr. Lincoln's pastor, the Reverend Dr. Gurley, stood a little to the left of the bed. Mr. Stanton sat in a chair near the foot on the left. . . . I stood quite near the head of the bed and from that position had full view of Mr. Stanton across the President's body. At my right Robert Lincoln sobbed on the shoulder of Charles Sumner. Stanton's gaze was fixed intently on the countenance of his dying chief. The first indication that the dreaded end had come was at twenty-two minutes past seven, when the surgeon general gently crossed the pulseless hands of Lincoln across the motionless breast and rose to his feet. The Reverend Dr. Gurley stepped forward and lifting his hands began 'Our Father and our God' and I snatched pencil and notebook from my pocket, but my haste defeated my purpose. My pencil point (I had but one) caught in my coat and broke, and the world lost the prayer, a prayer that was only interrupted by the sobs of Stanton as he buried his face in the bedclothes. As 'Thy will be done, Amen' in subdued and tremulous tones floated through the little chamber, Mr. Stanton raised his head, the tears streaming down his face. A more agonized expression I never saw on a human countenance as he sobbed out the words: 'He belongs to the angels now.' "

Later, others in the room recalled Stanton's remark as loftier—"Now he belongs to the ages."

Dr. Gurley remembered the physician saying, "He is gone; he is dead," then four or five minutes of absolute silence before anyone stirred. Gurley could hear the watches in all the men's pockets around the bed ticking loudly. "At length the Secretary of War, who was standing at my left, broke the silence and said, 'Doctor, will you say anything?' I replied, 'I will speak to God—' said he, 'do it just now.' And there, by the side of our fallen chief, God put into my heart to utter this petition, that from that hour, we and the whole nation might become more than ever united in our devotion to the cause of our beloved, imperiled country. When I ceased, there arose from the lips of the entire company, a fervid and spontaneous 'Amen.' "

The mask of Lincoln's face shown here was made two months before his death. It was the work of the sculptor Clark Mills, who had had remarkable success in making life masks. In February he had come to the White House, covered the President's face with sweet oil, slathered on plaster, stuck straws into Lincoln's nostrils so that he could breath during the hardening process. In the working off of the plaster it broke into bits, but Mills artfully fitted the pieces into a whole.

It was difficult ever after for people to accept the fact that this life mask was not really a death mask, so sad and worn were the features. John Hay said that on that face of this mask was "the peace that passeth understanding." Curiously, those who watched Lincoln die noted a few minutes later a faintly happy expression appear around his mouth. They said it resembled "an effort of life," as though he had found peace.

Lincoln died here two hours ago.

Here is the evidence of that agonizing night of dying one hundred years ago. This historic photograph—fading, torn at the edges—unpublished and unknown for ninety-six long years—reveals death's course in shocking detail. Just a few minutes before it was taken Lincoln lay diagonally across this rumpled bed, having bled all night from his head onto this pillow. Another blood-soaked pillow was lying on the ground in the yard outside the death room. William Petersen, the proprietor of the boarding house, angry at the condition of his house after a night of being used as a makeshift hospital, had snatched the other pillow while the dead President was still lying there, and hurled it out the window.

As soon as the last visitor had left, the upstairs boarder Julius Ulke brought out his cherished camera, a great unwieldy wooden box with its powerful lenses set in shining brass. All night long the Ulke brothers had helped carry hot water upstairs from the kitchen to Willie Clark's room where Lincoln lay. Now that the room was empty Julius persuaded Clark not to move anything, even by a quarter of an inch, until he set up his camera and adjusted it on its stand at the far end of the room. During the night the bed had been pulled out from the wall so that the doctors could encircle Lincoln. Now Ulke and Clark pushed it back to its original position. The trays and bottles were ready. The long exposure of the sticky, collodion-coated glass negative was made, and, as it had to be, immediately developed. Five minutes later Ulke held it up to the light. There on his piece of glass was the humble room, there the morning light streaming in through the front door past the stairway banisters, there the pillows with their dark evidence, there the chair in which Mrs. Lincoln had sat as she begged, "Oh, shoot me, Doctor, why don't you shoot me, too?"

The torn and faded evidence of the tragic night.

PART II

WASHINGTON KEEPS LINCOLN SIX DAYS

All over the country the people put on their badges of mourning. But the first six days after the President died he belonged to the city of Washington, and it was there in the nation's capital that the first of Abraham Lincoln's incredible twelve funerals was held.

This is Abe's stepmother, Sarah Bush Lincoln.

"I KNOWED THEY'D KILL HIM."

The news that President Lincoln was dead spread like prairie fire from the Washington telegraph office across the nation. The people heard the news and the people were stunned, and each in his own heart suffered alone and in his own way. The mantle of grief was like a bond, so that all of a sudden friends felt a terrible closeness and strangers passing in the street knew what was in each other's eyes and hearts and were brothers.

Dennis Hanks, the cousin who had lived with Abe in

the Indiana cabin, took the news out to an old woman on the Illinois prairie. This was Sarah Bush Lincoln, Abe's stepmother, born December 13, 1788. No one knew the origins and the yearnings of the boy from the wilderness the way Sarah did. And no one was more responsible for the paths he had taken. First Sarah had been married to a county jailer in Kentucky. He died in 1816 and left her almost destitute. She bought a cabin for twenty-five dollars and began to raise her three children. Abe's father, Thomas Lincoln, remembered Sarah well. Thomas had married Nancy Hanks in 1806, and moved from Kentucky to Indiana. He built a cabin, and all was going well until October, 1818, when Nancy died of the "milksick"—drinking milk from cows that had eaten poison snakeroot. Abe was nine then and his sister Sarah was eleven. After a year and two months of desperate loneliness, Thomas Lincoln set off for Kentucky, leaving his two children alone in the cabin with young Dennis, who was ten years older than Abe and had been the first person, after the baby's father, to touch little Abraham on the day he was born. It was a custom in Kentucky to "run and greet the newborn babe," Dennis remembered. "I tuk and run the hull two miles to see my new cousin. Nancy was laying thar in a pole bed lookin' purty happy. Tom'd built up a good fire and throw'd a b'ar skin over the kivers to keep 'em warm. . . . You bet I was tickled to death. Babies wasn't as plentiful as blackberries in the woods o' Kentucky."

When Tom Lincoln got back to Kentucky, he asked the widow, Sarah Bush Johnston, to marry him. She said she had debts to pay first, he paid them, they were married and they started for Indiana in a covered wagon along with her three children. Thomas was forty-one, his bride ten years younger.

When Sarah arrived at the cabin the Lincoln children liked her immediately. She was tall, slim, curly-haired, she had lovely white skin, blue-gray eyes and a beautiful nature. She scrubbed Abe and his sister, made one family of all five children, cooked the good game with which the forest was filled, and made Thomas clear more land and raise vegetables. She got him to put a wood floor in the cabin and stop the roof from leaking. The leak had been so bad that snow had drifted in on the boys sleeping up above the one room where she, Thomas, and the three little girls slept. Although she could not read or even sign her own name, Sarah brought with her three books—*Webster's Speller*, *Robinson Crusoe* and *The Arabian Nights*. Abe already owned *Aesop's Fables* and *Pilgrim's Progress*—and there was the family Bible which his own mother had read daily to him. The boy "raised to farmwork," as he said of himself, spent long hours reading, borrowing books from every neighbor within walking distance. Sarah's greatest contribution to her stepson's life was convincing her husband that it was important not to disturb this reading time and force Abe to turn wholly to physical labor. She had felt an immediate kinship with this boy. "His mind and mine," she said proudly, "what little I had, seemed to run together, move in the same channel."

Later when Thomas and Sarah lived in their cabin in Illinois, Lincoln came as often as he could when he was practicing law in Springfield or riding the circuit. Mary Lincoln never went the seventy miles to see her husband's parents, nor did she ever invite Sarah to Springfield or allow her three sons to meet such humble relatives. A few days before he went East to be inaugurated President of the United States, Lincoln made the trip once more to see the woman he wrote and spoke to as "Mother." He brought her a woolen shawl and a black wool dress. He took her in his arms and she cried over him. She told him she would never see him again and that he would be killed.

So when Dennis Hanks set out for Sarah's cabin with the dread news, the old lady knew before he spoke. "Aunt Sairy," Dennis said, "Abe's dead."

"Yes, I know, Denny, I knowed they'd kill him. I ben awaiting fur it."

This is Lincoln's stepmother's cabin in Illinois, 1865. In front of it are two of Abe's cousins who grew up with him—Dennis and John Hanks. When the young Lincoln was old enough, Dennis held his hand and taught him to write with a buzzard's quill. In 1831 John helped Abe build a flatboat, and together they floated all the way down the Mississippi to New Orleans, with hogs to sell.

BLOOMINGTON, ILLINOIS

This indignation meeting on April sixteenth was typical of those held all over the North. It took place in front of the McLean County Court House where Lincoln had appeared as a lawyer in countless cases.

SAVANNAH, GEORGIA

Even the south was outraged at the assassination. This meeting of the citizens of Savannah, Georgia, was held to discuss what action the city should take in regard to Lincoln's death.

Indignation sweeps the country

All through the North citizens came together in their meeting places to discuss what they should officially do about Lincoln's death. Delegates were chosen to go to the funeral, proclamations of regret were passed, decisions on how buildings should be draped were made, and endless discussion was held over what should be done with the assassins when they were caught. Even Southern cities like Savannah, Georgia, joined in the sorrow. The city had been under the military rule of the United States for almost four months at the time of the assassination, having been occupied by General Sherman and his army on December 21, 1864. The taking of Savannah terminated Sherman's victorious march to the sea and Sherman sent Lincoln the famous telegram, "I beg you to accept as a Christmas gift the city of Savannah . . ." On the platform during the indignation meeting were the mayor and members of the city council, also the commanding Union officers of the occupation. They looked out over the largest crowd ever assembled in the history of the city. The mood was one of deep shock, many people wept, and if there were those who had something other than sorrow in their hearts, they were silent.

The stock exchange closes down

As the news of the assassination reached out across the nation, the normal Saturday morning doings of a people came to a sudden wrenching halt. But in New York City, before the official sessions of the Stock Exchange and the Gold Room were called off, a good many hungry speculators, expecting that the President's death would hurt the national credit and they would profit by it, bought gold freely. At 11:00 A.M. the stock houses closed their doors and the banks followed at noon. The brokers streamed out of the Exchange onto the sidewalk and lingered there. When a passerby called out, "It served Old Abe right!" the police barely saved him from the crowd. Another man, a block away from the Gold Exchange, was heard to say, "Did you hear Abe's last joke?" and for that he was severely beaten. During the morning a few speculators tried to make gold transactions right there on the sidewalks, but they were almost mobbed by the aroused crowd.

These photographs are believed to show downtown New York on the morning of Lincoln's death, as brokers pour out of the Stock Exchange and the Gold Room to stand irresolute and almost stupified in the streets.

AN AUTOPSY AND THEN EMBALMING

The White House room where the autopsy took place was on the second floor at the front right-hand corner of the building.

DR. CRANE, Assistant Surgeon General of the United States, attended the autopsy along with Surgeon General Barnes.

ORVILLE H. BROWNING, an old Illinois political friend of Lincoln's, watched the skull cut open.

DR. CURTIS, a pathologist at the Army Medical Museum, held Lincoln's brain in his hand and found the bullet.

DR. STONE, the Lincolns' personal physician, came straight from the death room to be an observer.

GENERAL RUCKER, of the Quartermaster Department, was there because it was his men's duty to escort the body.

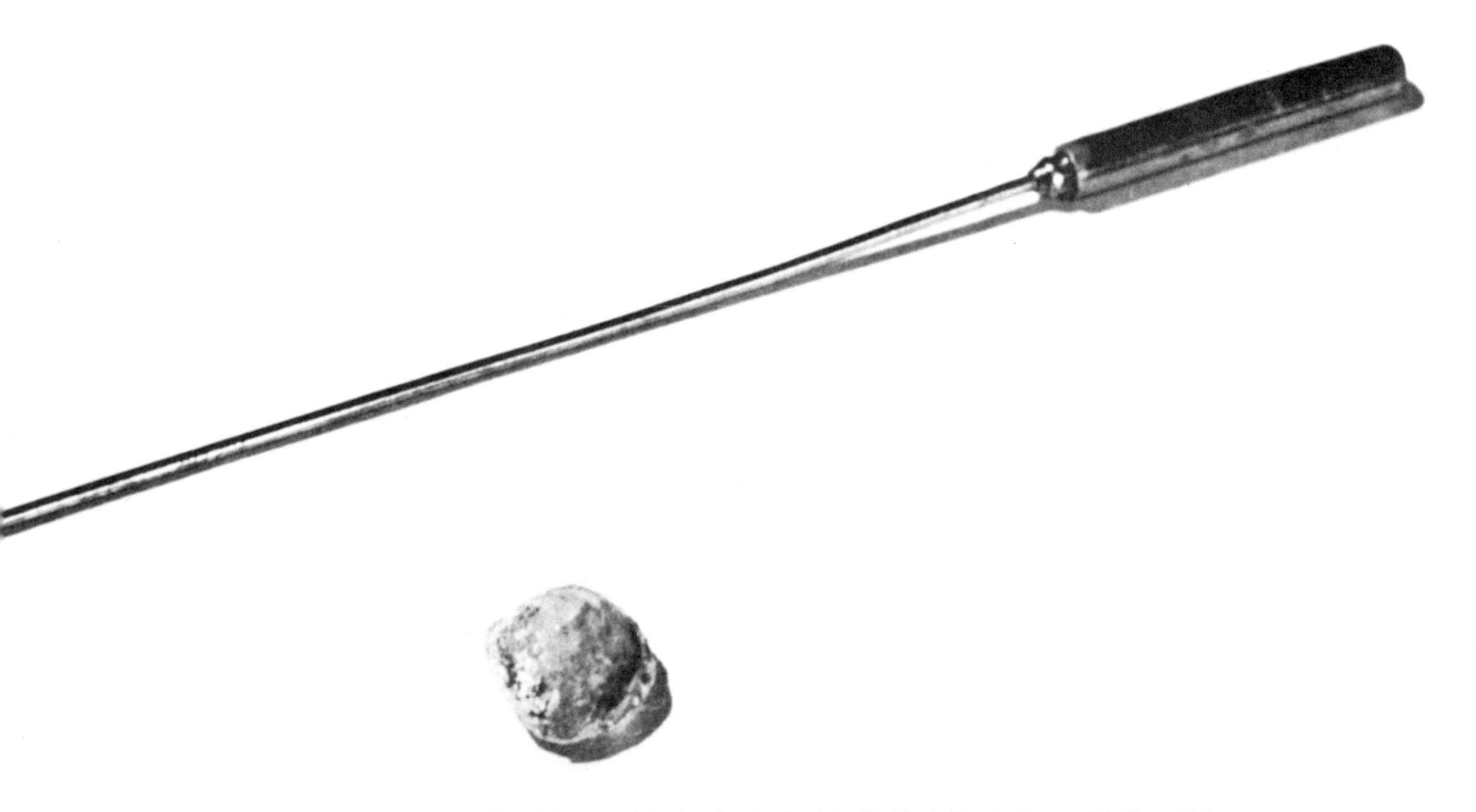

This is the silver Nelaton probe used to explore Lincoln's wound during the death night. Beside it lies the flattened bullet which fell from Lincoln's brain during the autopsy.

As Mrs. Lincoln left the Petersen House to be driven back to the Executive Mansion, she stood a minute beside her carriage and cried, "That dreadful house! That dreadful house!" A few minutes later the body of her husband was carried out and placed in a hearse, the coffin wrapped in a star-spangled flag. Then with measured tread and arms reversed, the little procession moved away—a lieutenant and ten privates. Slowly up Tenth Street to G Street the horses pulled the dead President back to the White House. Mrs. Lincoln refused to enter either her own bedroom in the southwest corner of the second floor, or Mr. Lincoln's bedroom next to it. She finally chose a room with no memories which she had fitted up for the President so that he could do some writing there. The room's shades were lowered and Mary Lincoln got into bed and began an endless tossing and sobbing. Tad had run weeping to meet her as she got out of the carriage and buried his face in the folds of her dress, and he now stood terrified at the foot of his mother's bed, watching her very near convulsions.

"Don't cry so, Mama, or you will make me cry too," said Tad. That was the only thing that stopped Mrs. Lincoln's hysterics. She could not bear to see little Tad cry.

No one could be hardhearted enough not to feel sorry for Mary Lincoln now. Her desolation was complete because she did not have the character to meet her grief with any dignity and fortitude. She hid herself away to rail against her fate, while the country buried her husband. All during the war years it had been a kind of sport to make fun of the President's wife from the West, and let her read in print that she was a dumpy woman with no taste, who wore over-gorgeous, too low-necked dresses, and that she carried whole flower gardens on her head, didn't know any better than to wear her rings on the outside of her gloves. Now, that kind of criticism was silenced, but pity could not bring liking.

In the Guest Room at the northeast corner of the second floor of the White House Lincoln's body was placed upon two boards laid across trestles. At eleven o'clock the autopsy was begun by sawing the top of the President's skull straight around on a line above his ears so that the top could be lifted off. Present were Surgeon General Barnes, Dr. Stone, the family physician, Dr. Taft, Dr. Crane, Assistant Surgeon Notson, General Rucker, who with his men had escorted the body back to the White House, and Lincoln's close friend Orville Browning. Two pathologists from the Army Medical Museum did the actual work—Assistant Surgeon J. Janvier Woodward and Assistant Surgeon Edward Curtis. Young Curtis movingly described the scene:

> *The room . . . contained but little furniture: a large, heavily curtained bed, a sofa or two, bureau, wardrobe, and chairs comprised all there was. Seated around the room were several general*

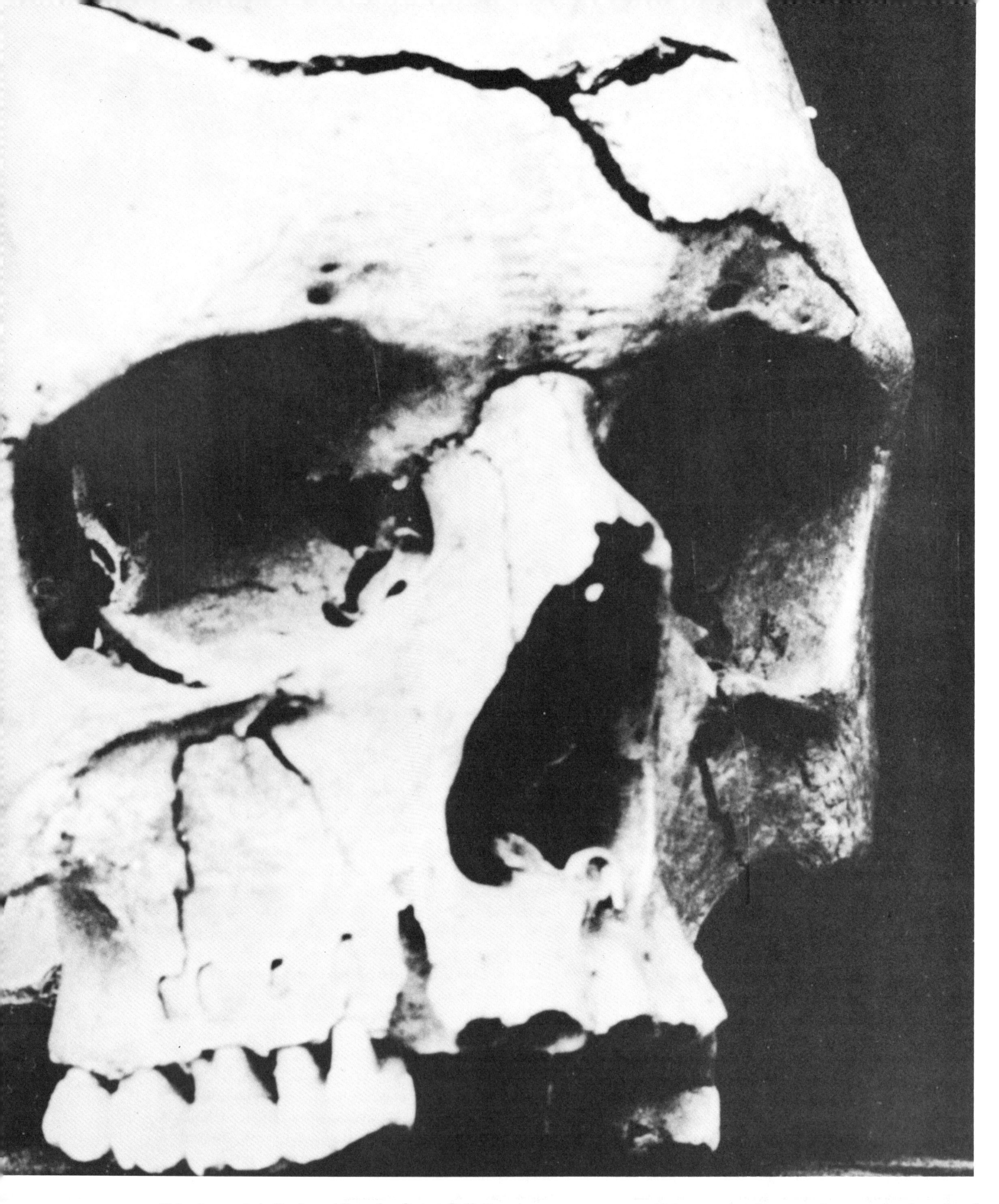

This shattered skull of a soldier who died at Bull Run shows what the autopsy found had happened to Lincoln's skull. The bullet struck this soldier in the side of his head, yet big cracks appear across the forehead. The President was struck in the back of his head, yet the orbital plates of both eye sockets had been cracked by "contre-coup," or transmitted force, the phenomenon which causes breakage at points opposite the point of impact. The description of the Bull Run soldier's skull appears just above Lincoln's case history in the official record, "The Medical and Surgical History of the War of the Rebellion," in a discussion of "cases of alleged fracture by contre-coup after gunshot injury of the skull."

officers and some civilians, silent or conversing in whispers, and to one side, stretched upon a rough framework of boards and covered only with sheets and towels, lay—cold and immovable—what but a few hours before was the soul of a great nation. The Surgeon General was walking up and down the room when I arrived and detailed me the history of the case. He said that the President showed most wonderful tenacity of life, and, had not his wound been necessarily mortal, might have survived an injury to which most men would succumb.

. . . Dr. Woodward and I proceeded to open the head and remove the brain down to the track of the ball. The latter had entered a little to the left of the median line at the back of the head, had passed almost directly forwards through the center of the brain and lodged. Not finding it readily, we proceeded to remove the entire brain, when, as I was lifting the latter from the cavity of the skull, suddenly the bullet dropped out through my fingers and fell, breaking the solemn silence of the room with its clatter, into an empty basin that was standing beneath. There it lay upon the white china, a little black mass no bigger than the end of my finger—dull, motionless and harmless, yet the cause of such mighty changes in the world's history as we may perhaps never realize.

Now the autopsy was done, undertaker Dr. Charles D. Brown, of Brown and Alexander, took over. Andrew Johnson, who had just been sworn in as the new President of the United States by Chief Justice Chase at the Kirkwood House, entered the room and watched briefly. Brown and his assistant drained Lincoln's blood through the jugular vein. Then they made a cut on the inside of the thigh and through it force-pumped a chemical preparation which soon hardened the body like marble. The face was shaved except for a short tuft left at the chin. The eyes were closed, the eyebrows arched, the mouth set in the slightest of smiles.

As the undertakers worked, Dr. Curtis suggested to the Surgeon General that Lincoln's brain be weighed. Again Dr. Curtis describes the scene:

"*. . . silently, in one corner of the room, I prepared the brain for weighing. As I looked at the mass of soft gray and white substance that I was carefully washing, it was impossible to realize that it was that mere clay upon whose workings, but the day before, rested the hopes of the nation. I felt more profoundly impressed than ever with the mystery of that unknown something which may be named "vital spark" as well as anything else, whose absence or presence makes all the immeasurable difference between an inert mass of matter owning obedience to no laws but those governing the physical and chemical forces of the universe, and on the other hand, a living brain by whose silent, subtle machinery a world may be ruled.*

The weighing of the brain . . . gave approximate results only, since there had been some loss of brain substance, in consequence of the wound, during the hours of life after the shooting. But the figures, as they were, seemed to show that the brain weight was not above the ordinary for a man of Lincoln's size.

Now Lincoln's body was covered with a white cloth and a fine cambric handkerchief was spread over his face. Upon the pillow and over the breast were scattered white flowers and green leaves. Guards were posted at the door and the doctors began to pack up and leave.

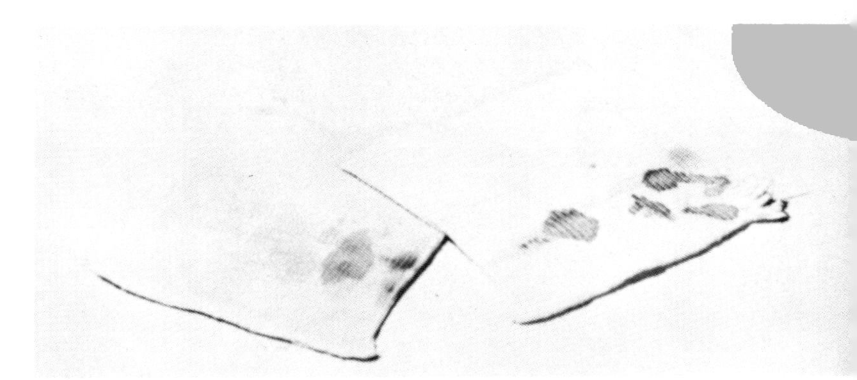

BLOODSTAINED CUFFS were cut off the shirt Dr. Curtis was wearing at autopsy and kept as a memento by his wife.

Later in the day Stanton supervised the clothing of the body—from the black suit Lincoln had worn at his second inauguration to a low collar and small black bow tie and white kid gloves. Stanton, in fact, was the busiest man in Washington that weekend. He attended President Johnson's first Cabinet meeting at noon on Saturday, and then hurried to Seward's house on Lafayette Square across from the White House to break the news to him of Lincoln's death. The Secretary, looking up from the mass of bandages that covered his slashed cheeks and the metal clamps that held his jaw together, seemed to realize what he himself had narrowly escaped, and conveyed that he would try to marshal all his forces to stay alive and get well. Back in the Guest Room, Stanton decided that the black under Lincoln's eyes that had spread down his cheeks would be left there for posterity. "Should not the undertaker use chemicals to erase this?" Stanton was asked. "No," he replied, "this is part of the history of the event."

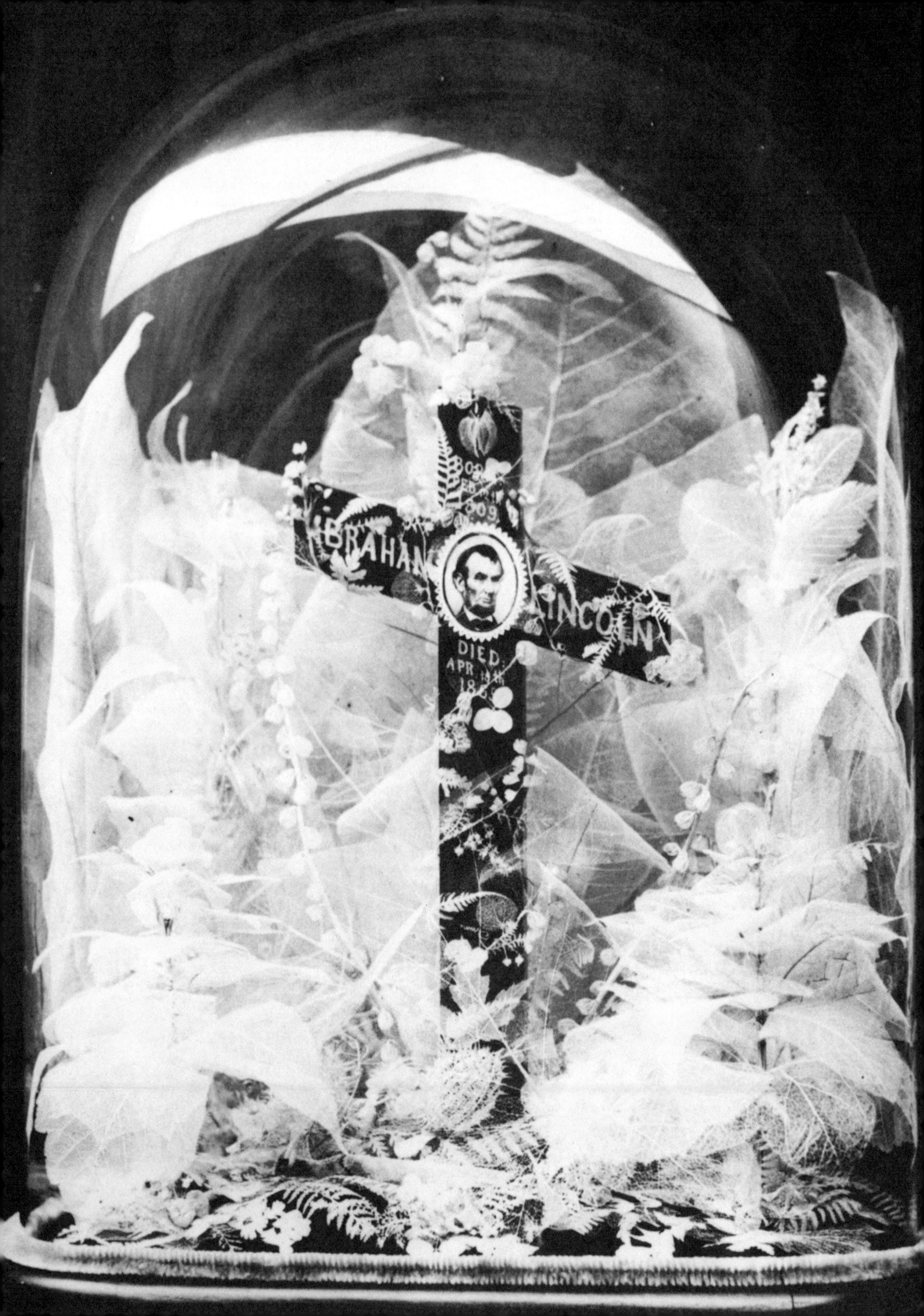
DIED
APR

OUT OF THE RAVEL OF RELICS AND RUMORS, OF REMEMBRANCES AND GUESSWORK, SOMEWHERE WAS THE TRUTH

Far from regarding it as an honor to have Abraham Lincoln die in his boarding house, William Petersen was in a black temper. The Ulke brothers had always known him to be a hard drinker and a wife driver—they were happy for Mrs. Petersen that she was at this moment visiting a daughter at school in Bethlehem, Pennsylvania. When her husband now advanced to the bed, seized one the bloodstained pillows from beneath the head of the recently expired President and hurled it angrily through the window into the yard, Henry and Julius were terrified. He soon made loud explanation—his house was a mess—all that blood and mud under foot—unwashed basins and bottles piled up and dozens of old leaking mustard plasters littering the hall. What was worse, he had read in the paper that the President died in a tenement. He would let that paper know and soon that his was one of the most respectable dwelling houses in Washington.

Shortly after nine on Saturday morning the relic hunters descended on the Petersen House. Young Fred Petersen divided up a portion of the President's shirt, tore the bloody sheets into strips, cut into small squares the towels that had been laid over the wet red pillows whenever Mrs. Lincoln had paid her visits—anything with Lincoln's blood on it would be preserved. There were locks snipped from Lincoln's head by the doctors to see the wound better, and the regular inmates of the house divided these in haste, counting them out by the single hair, as the crowds, who were beginning to knock on the front door and beg to come in, must not be allowed to see and covet these most sacred of all reminders that would soon be framed or committed to the leaves of a Bible.

HALF ORNAMENT, HALF ALTAR

This cross bearing Lincoln's name and photograph is surrounded by the skeleton leaves so popular in the 1860's, and the whole arrangement is contained in a glass dome or vitrine. Fragile tributes to the assassinated President like this one appeared suddenly on thousands of parlor tables throughout the country, taking their places alongside the family albums.

The visitors to Willie Clark's room began at several hundred a day. He was a shy young man but he soon found himself roused to lionlike fierceness to defend everything he owned from potential thieves. As they were crafty, he became crafty. He had to watch the crocheted scarf on his bureau and the pincushions, and it was a battle to keep even the most respectable-seeming people from scratching at his wallpaper with their fingernails and whipping out pocket scissors if he looked the other way—his curtains were turning out to be irresistible.

Willie had safely hidden away out of sight Mr. Lincoln's overcoat, suit, and boots and he intended to give back to Robert Lincoln the suit and coat due him. Willie found himself powerfully drawn to those huge boots and, somehow, when all the dividing was done, Willie still had the boots. He thought he had the worsted coverlet too, and the bed, and slept there as he always had the first few nights, but gradually, as the Petersen family learned how insanely anxious people were for anything that had touched Lincoln, spread and bed departed, as had even the forlorn mustard plasters. Willie's secret treasure was the candle stub which doctors had held, lighted, near the President's head to allow each newly arrived consultant to assess the brain damage.

Artists arrived to sketch the room and the deathbed, which turned out to be seventy-four and one half inches long, explaining the poor fit of Lincoln's seventy-six-inch frame—and he was wearing those stout-heeled boots when the first attempt to settle him straight down was made. Sketches were made of William Petersen, who managed not to glower in his portrait, of Henry and Julius Ulke, Thomas Proctor, the boarder upstairs who was passionate about frogs, and Henry Safford, who had waved at the door and invited the bearers in. Willie Clark refused to be sketched, refused to lend a photograph of himself from which a sketch could be made, shrank back into the safety of his own privacy and would not speak a word concerning his three women relatives framed on his bureau—not even to tell that they were Ida, Clara, and Nannie. But he

graphically described the President's long pointed toes sticking out from under the coverlet and he placed and named for the artist everyone present at the moment of death.

Outside in the city people were saying a good many things about that death room. The rumor was that three unannounced acts had taken place in that room before the body left. That a sort of preliminary embalming had taken place by a hurriedly chosen but famous embalmer—a Dr. Holmes, who had succeeded in the impossible job of filling with embalming fluid the bullet-riddled body of Lincoln's close friend, Edward D. Baker, who had been killed at Ball's Bluff. But, the story went on, when word came to those in the death room that the family had chosen Dr. Charles D. Brown, who had embalmed Willie Lincoln, Dr. Holmes hastily repacked his injecting syringes and chemicals and departed.

Also, it was positively stated, a death mask was made in the Petersen House, and the owner of the death room was awarded the knife that spread the plaster.

And, it was just as positively stated, a photograph had been taken of the bed the President died in, and it showed blood on the pillow.

All three rumors were denied by the residents of the house. Had they been true, and admitted, Secretary Stanton's wrath would have been terrible and his punishment swift.

Over at Ford's Theatre, the police had found and taken to police headquarters, as being allied to the assassination, Booth's black slouch hat, the President's tall beaver hat, Booth's derringer pistol, Dr. Taft's cape, one spur, one empty opera-glass case, one brass button, and one India-rubber button.

Lieutenant Newton Feree from Ohio, who had wandered into the Lincoln box just after he had been carried away, found it "one pool of blood"; he picked up and took away half of the President's collar. A policeman named Clarvoe was carrying around in his pocket one half of the President's cravat. One of the actors had found Lincoln's ebony cane leaning against a chair in the box and had managed to get it to his lodgings unreported. Several bloodstained programs were found on the box floor and one made its way to Kansas. The bar which Booth used to barricade the entrance door to the little hallway was found by Isaac Jacquette, who had been attending the play. He took it home to his boarding house, where he sawed off a piece of it for an officer who thought he wanted a relic, then decided he didn't! While this was theft of government property, Jacquette went unpunished, but a soldier named Bedee, who picked up some papers that fell out of Lincoln's pocket as he was carried across Tenth Street, immediately turned them in to Stanton in the Petersen House and was locked up in prison for a week, protesting every minute that he had not kept the papers. The confusion was so great it was simpler to arrest him than investigate. On the other hand, Stanton himself generously gave away an assassination item that belonged with Booth's pistol, as evidence—he presented the dagger which Paine had used to slash Secretary Seward to the invalid soldier nurse, George Robinson, who had defended him. Robinson took his relic home and astonished the natives of

MEMENTO OF ASSASSINATION

This paper cross was sent to a friend by Francis Lieber, professor of Political Science at Columbia, who was in charge of moving the Rebel Archives into Ford's Theatre when the government refused John Ford's plea to let him open up again as a theatre. Lieber wrote to a friend, "I found a small portion of the paper hanging still covering the wall of the box in which our President, Lincoln the Forgiving, was assassinated. . . . I send you a part of this melancholy and yet sadly endearing memento."

the tiny island, Isle-au-Haut, off the coast of Maine, with his great knife and its bloody history. A New Hampshire man, Private William H. Keyes, found Lincoln's gold-rimmed glasses in the gutter of Tenth Street and got them back home to New Hampshire without being caught.

When the theatre box had been stripped of everything that was not undeniably theatre furnishings, like the rocking chair the President had sat in, so that not even an India-rubber button remained, then the surreptitious scraping off of wallpaper began. Each shred was given some special significance—"where our beloved President's head must have rested when he leaned his head back"; or "a place he must have put his hand on entering the box." The curtains of the box had gone too—snip, snip, snip—"the very part of the lace he pulled back to look down at the audience."

During the first shocked, hectic days after the assassination, Secretary Stanton devoted a large part of his attention to the situation in Ford's Theatre, which he had already decided should never again be used for its present purpose, even if he had to tear it down, stone from stone. On Sunday Stanton dispatched Judge of the Supreme Court of the District of Columbia Abram Olin to the the theatre, along with Clara Harris, Senator Ira Harris, and James Ferguson, keeper of the restaurant north of Ford's. They had a hard time getting in because Maddox, the property man, and Griffith, head carpenter and builder of the theatre, had locked the doors and refused to come and open them. Finally they broke a window. The party of four went up to box Number Seven, the murder box, and with a lighted candle examined the hole Booth had bored in the door. One of the party sat in Lincoln's rocking chair while another put his eye to the hole and tested whether it had offered the desired view—the back of a head. It did. They then took special note of the fact that the bits of wood displaced by the boring and the pieces of plaster gouged out of the wall in the hallway to make a mortise for Booth's wooden bar had vanished. Someone had cleaned up.

In the days to follow Stanton himself visited the building and went over Booth's path inch by inch, stationed soldiers every few yards upstairs and down, and had the actors give an entire performance of *Our American Cousin* so it could be studied for possible clues to the assassination. The only thing that evolved clearly was that Booth had chosen the moment of shooting to match the lone appearance on the stage of only one performer.

For reasons he did not explain, Stanton locked up scores of people he suspected, including the Ford brothers from the theatre. Yet he allowed the policeman, John Parker, who had gone with Lincoln as his only protection to the play and had become so interested in the sound of the actors' voices that he moved from outside the President's entry door to a seat where he could see as well as hear, to go back to the White House and continue service with his guard's job there. The only punishment Parker suffered was a tongue lashing from Mrs. Lincoln, who called him into her bedroom and

A RELIC OF THE MOURNING
Mourning ribbons like this one, with its picture, its dates (in this case the birth date wrong by a year), and its simple, sad sentiment, were worn by millions all over the country.

Anything to do with that night of dying became a cherished relic.

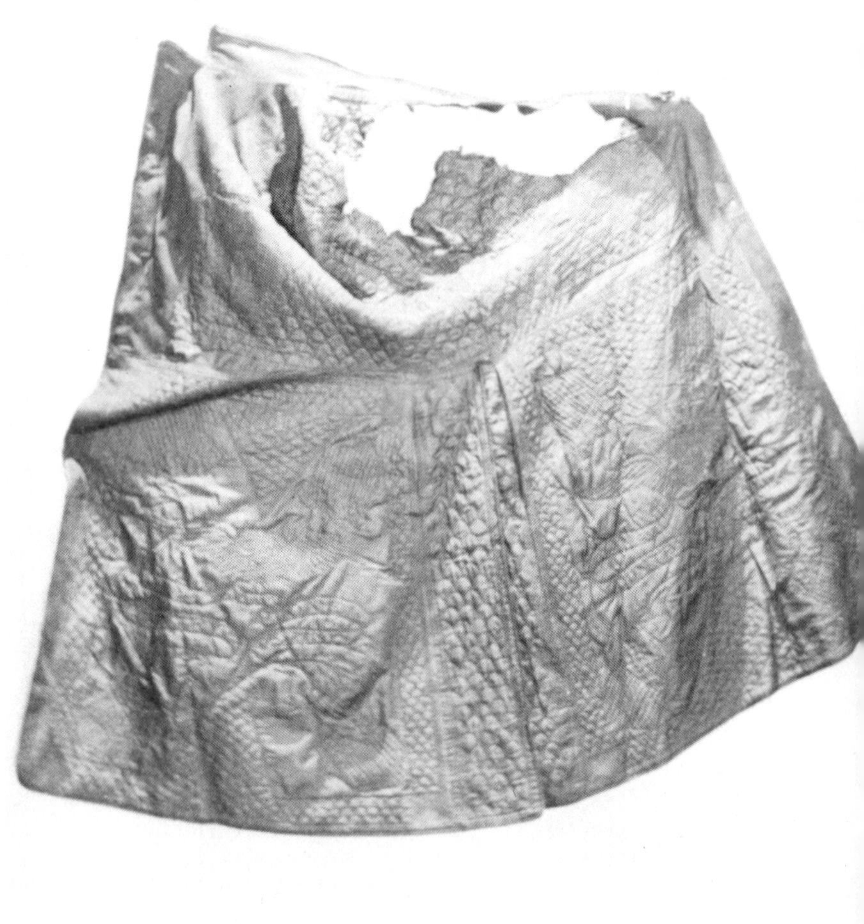

told him she knew he was a conspirator and had murdered her husband. Then she waved him back into the hall and he continued life, a free man. Stanton was not interested in little fish now. He had made a bold decision, and he was not bothering to wait for evidence—he knew. He simply announced that John Wilkes Booth had been the tool of the Confederate leaders, offered one hundred thousand dollars for the capture of Jefferson Davis and began to vilify the South just as Lincoln's dream of an era of peace and trust and devotion to a common country again was dawning. This was all Stanton's idea, and so vindictive and bitter was his attack on the government at Richmond, proclaiming that traitors had now turned murderers and promising vengeance, that he turned the whole recent climate of mercy and forgiveness into the tragedy of hate again.

Stanton ran the country singlehanded for the first days after the assassination, and no one looked to newly sworn-in President Johnson to make decisions. Johnson merely received delegations in his office in the Treasury Building, seemed to mention the name Lincoln very seldom, and assured people he would punish treason. The country was uncertain about him. Some said he was a lowborn Southerner who would take out his bitterness on the upper classes he had envied, and some countered that as a tailor born in poverty, who could not read until he was grown but who still had struggled and risen through elective office to the Presidency, he must be strong. Still, during those first days of relic hunting and exchanging theories and memories and planning for Lincoln's trip West, a certain fear was widespread: was the new President of the United States a chronic drunkard? Was Johnson a slave to liquor, or simply a man who had been ill on March fourth at Lincoln's second inauguration and misjudged the amount of brandy needed to carry him through a public ceremony?

Everyone knew the astounding fact that Andrew Johnson had disgraced himself by delivering an incoherent,

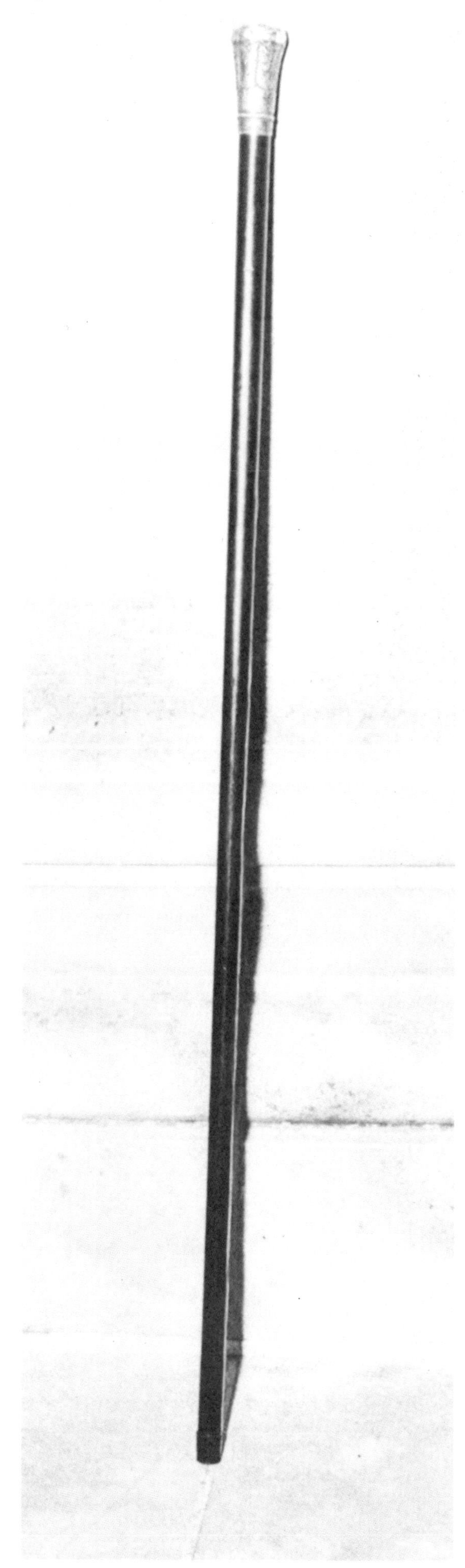

The frock coat, overcoat, and pants Lincoln was wearing when he was shot were left in Willie Clark's room. They were returned to Mrs. Lincoln, who gave them to the White House doorman, Alphonso Donn. Lincoln's hat was found in the box, was taken to police headquarters and exhibited at the trial of the conspirators. Lincoln's ebony cane, which had a silver head with "A. Lincoln" engraved on it, was found in the theatre box leaning against a chair by an actor from *Our American Cousin.*

idiotically senseless stump speech in the Senate chamber, and that Lincoln had later defended him, saying: "I have known Andy Johnson for many years; he made a bad slip the other day; but you need not be scared. Andy ain't a drunkard."

For the nation it could only be a humiliation and a worry that on the very day of Lincoln's assassination, twenty-four hours before Johnson was to become President, there had appeared in the *New York World* a long and frank appraisal of his alcoholism, likening him to a common gutter derelict. It was the *London Times'* correspondent's report to Britain on Johnson's behavior at his swearing-in as Vice-President, just three weeks earlier.

The column was peppered with "All eyes were turned to Mr. Johnson as he started, rather than rose from his chair, and with wild gesticulations and shrieks began . . . his behavior was that of an illiterate, drunken rowdy . . . 'He is drunk,' said one, 'He is crazy—this

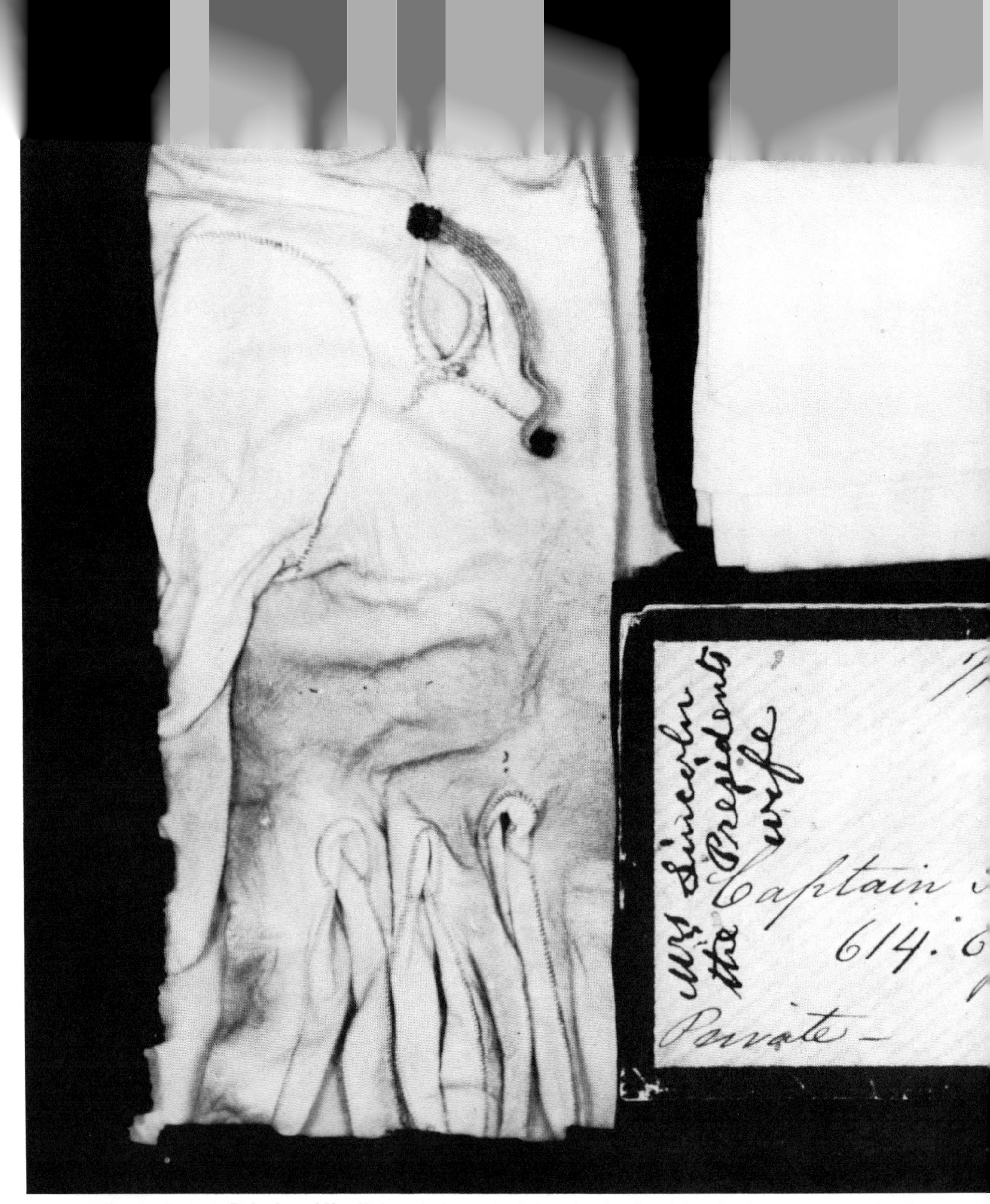

Millionaire Benjamin Richardson of New York received one pair of gloves found in Lincoln's pocket the night of his death and

is disgraceful.'" The British journalist wrote of how he met, after the ceremony, with a Democratic Senator who said, "The country is disgraced, and I pray God for the health and long life of Abraham Lincoln. I never prayed for him before, nor knew how valuable his life was to the country. Should he die in the four years, which calamity may Heaven in its mercy avert, we should have Andrew Johnson as President, and sink to a lower depth of degradation than was ever reached by any nation since the Roman emperor made his horse a consul." A member of Congress came up and asked the Britisher to be sure to tell the people of England that

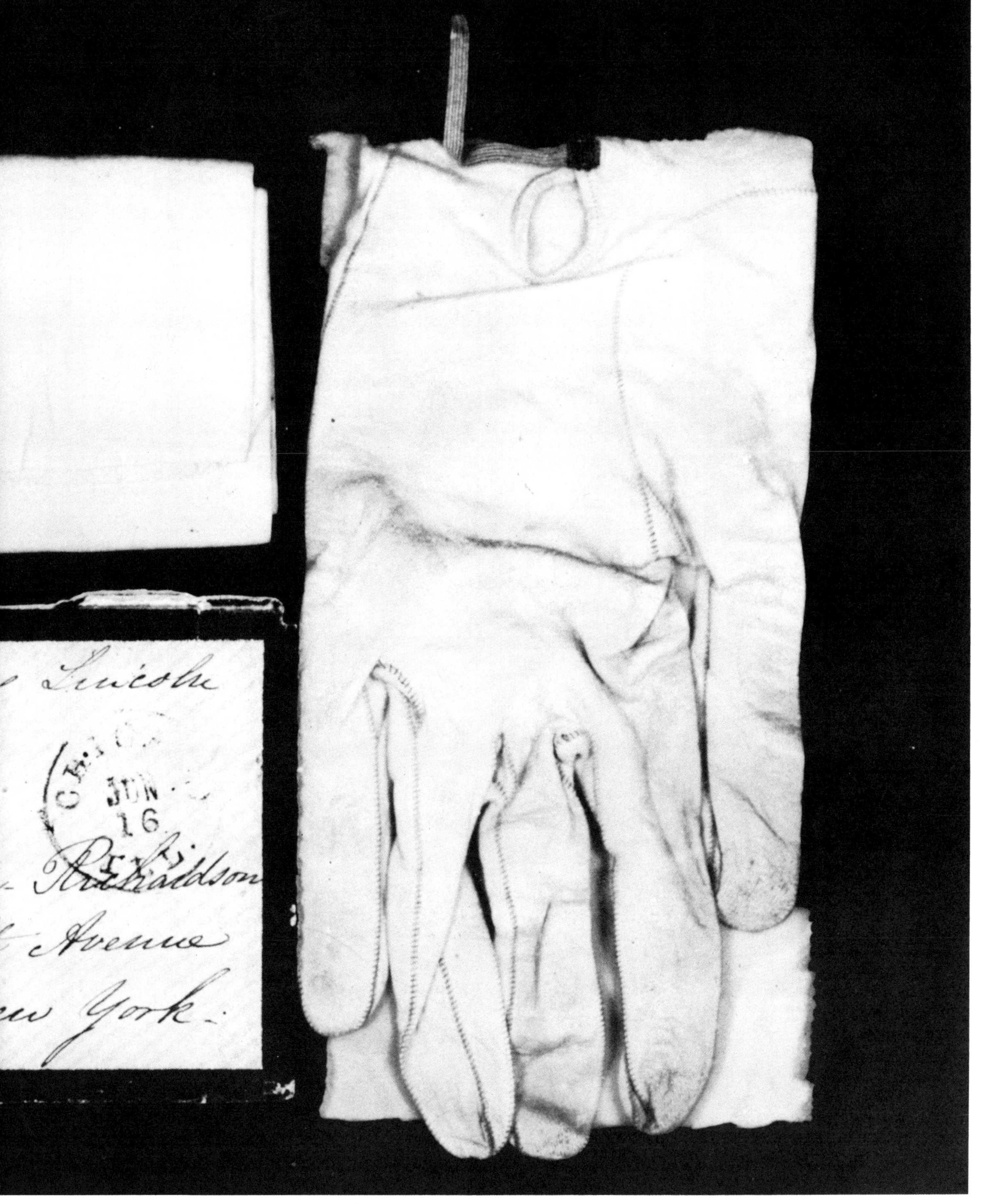

the handkerchief he carried to the theatre—framed them to hang on his dining-room wall.

"Mr. Johnson will never recover from his scandalous conduct—he is ruined as a public man forever."

The morning after the newspaper article appeared the "ruined" Vice-President succeeded Lincoln. Rumors flew that he had been in a drunken stupor the night of the assassination, that he had been almost impossible to arouse in the morning and appeared at his hotel room door, ignorant of any bad news, with puffy eyes and hair matted with actual mud—he looked as though he had been on at least a month's spree. Along with this story was the one that it took both a doctor and a barber working at top speed, and with desperate measures, to

Willie Clark kept Lincoln's black leather boots with their gay maroon goatskin tops, which were left behind in Clark's room on the death night.

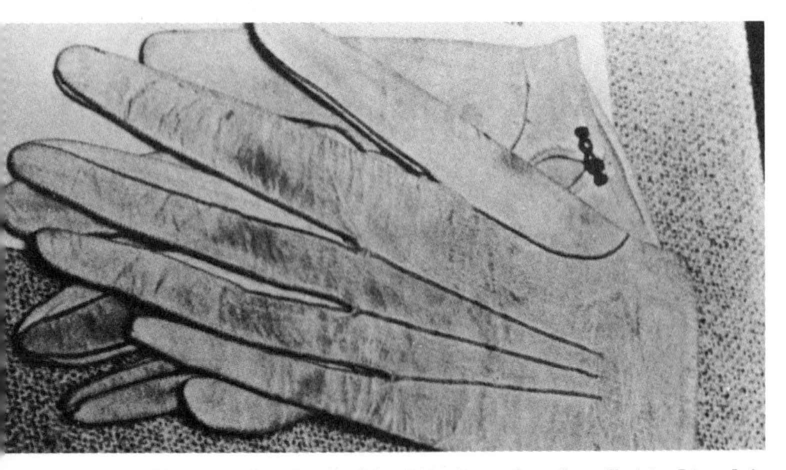

The second pair of white kid gloves found stuffed in Lincoln's overcoat pocket was given by Mrs. Lincoln to her sister's son-in-law, Edward L. Baker, editor of the *Illinois State Journal*.

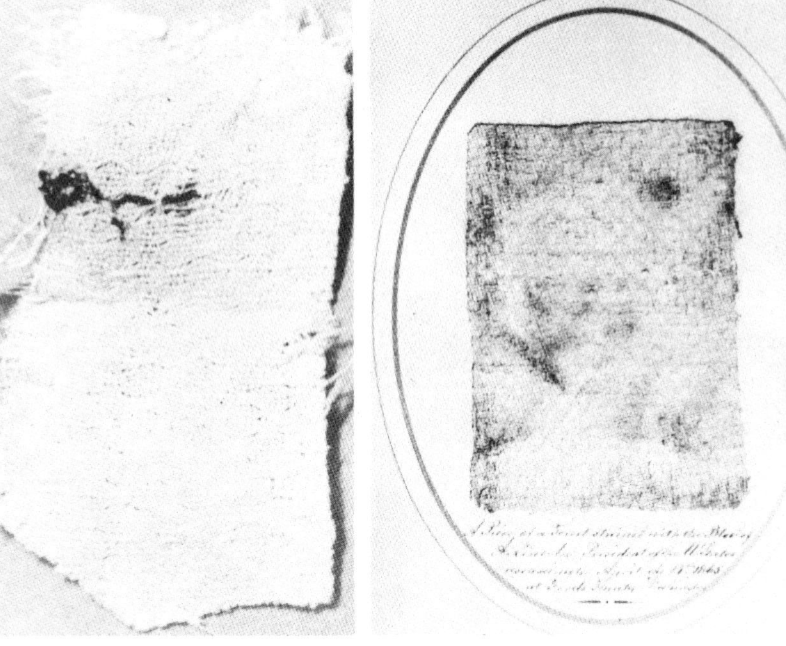

These are swatches of the towels that were laid over the bloodsoaked pillows every time Mrs. Lincoln visited the death room in the Petersen House.

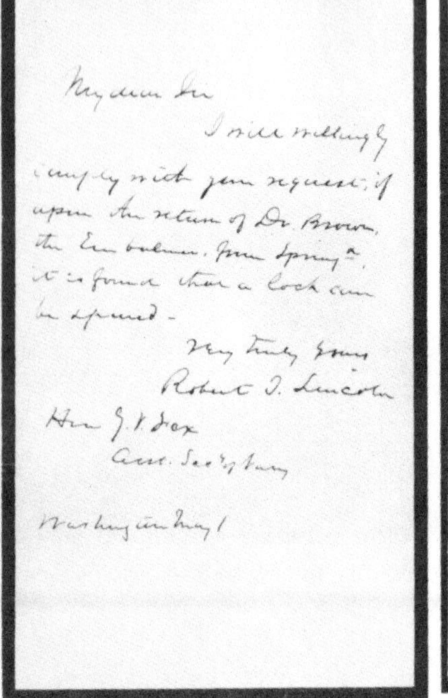

My dear Sir

I will willingly comply with your request, if upon the return of Dr. Brown, the Embalmer, from Springfd. it is found that a lock can be spared -

Very truly Yours
Robert T. Lincoln

Hon G. V. Fox
Asst. Sec'y Navy

Washington May 1

From
Robert T. Lincoln

Hon G V Fox
Asst. Sec'y Navy

One of the most treasured relics was a lock of Lincoln's hair. This one was sent to a friend by Robert Lincoln.

The red, white, and blue Irish worsted coverlet under which Lincoln died was last exhibited in Springfield on the fiftieth anniversary of the assassination. Then it vanished.

SURRAT. BOOTH. HAROLD.

War Department, Washington, April 20, 1865,

$100,000 REWARD!

THE MURDERER

Of our late beloved President, Abraham Lincoln,

IS STILL AT LARGE.

$50,000 REWARD

Will be paid by this Department for his apprehension, in addition to any reward offered by Municipal Authorities or State Executives.

$25,000 REWARD

Will be paid for the apprehension of JOHN H. SURRATT, one of Booth's Accomplices.

$25,000 REWARD

Will be paid for the apprehension of David C. Harold, another of Booth's accomplices.

LIBERAL REWARDS will be paid for any information that shall conduce to the arrest of either of the above-named criminals, or their accomplices.

All persons harboring or secreting the said persons, or either of them, or aiding or assisting their concealment or escape, will be treated as accomplices in the murder of the President and the attempted assassination of the Secretary of State, and shall be subject to trial before a Military Commission and the punishment of DEATH.

Let the stain of innocent blood be removed from the land by the arrest and punishment of the murderers.

All good citizens are exhorted to aid public justice on this occasion. Every man should consider his own conscience charged with this solemn duty, and rest neither night nor day until it be accomplished.

EDWIN M. STANTON, Secretary of War.

DESCRIPTIONS.—BOOTH is Five Feet 7 or 8 inches high, slender build, high forehead, black hair, black eyes, and wears a heavy black moustache.

JOHN H. SURRAT is about 5 feet, 9 inches. Hair rather thin and dark; eyes rather light; no beard. Would weigh 145 or 150 pounds. Complexion rather pale and clear, with color in his cheeks. Wore light clothes of fine quality. Shoulders square; cheek bones rather prominent; chin narrow; ears projecting at the top; forehead rather low and square, but broad. Parts his hair on the right side; neck rather long. His lips are firmly set. A slim man.

DAVID C. HAROLD is five feet six inches high, hair dark, eyes dark, eyebrows rather heavy, full face, nose short, hand short and fleshy, feet small, instep high, round bodied, naturally quick and active, slightly closes his eyes when looking at a person.

NOTICE.—In addition to the above, State and other authorities have offered rewards amounting to almost one hundred thousand dollars, making an aggregate of about **TWO HUNDRED THOUSAND DOLLARS.**

"Do recognize him some where and kill him . . ."

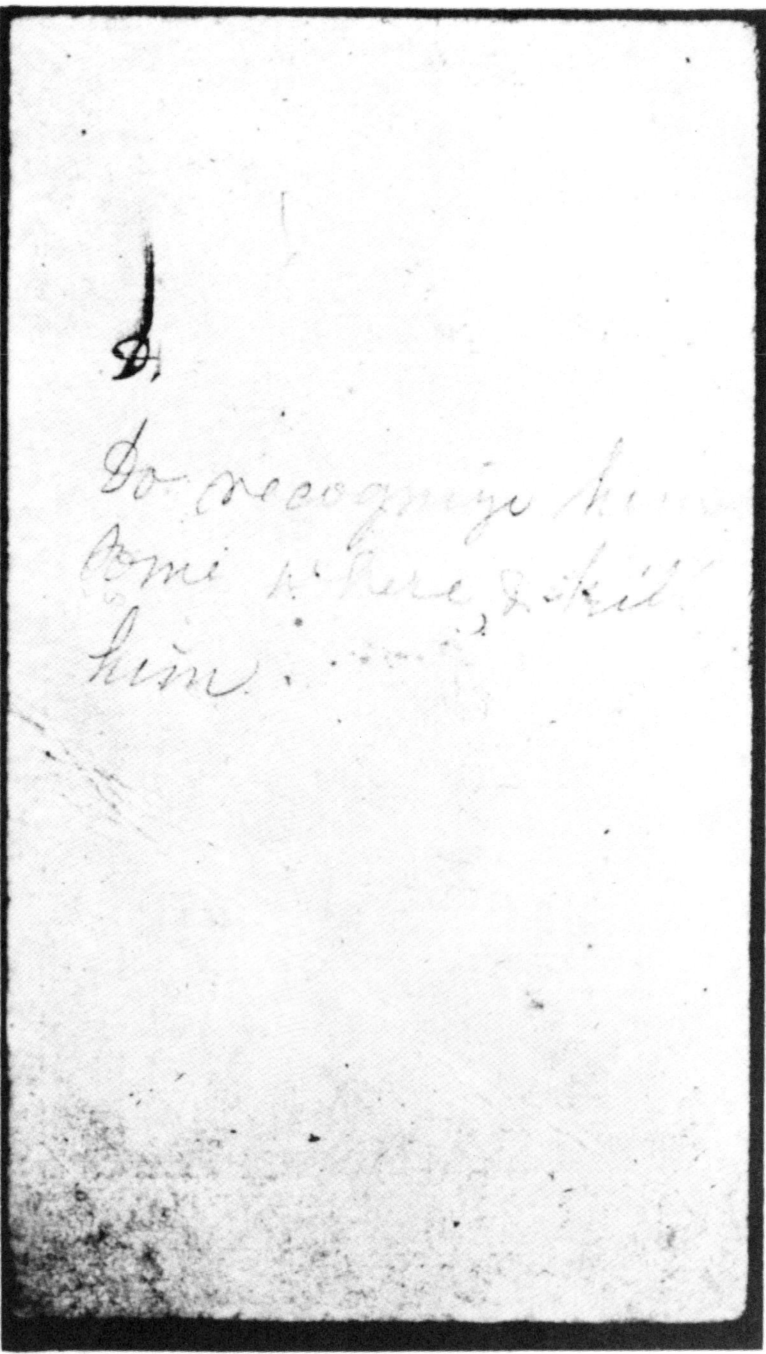

The rewards spurred a search for the assassins by several thousand soldiers and detectives, and many months after Booth's death, even far into 1866, wrangling went on among committees and Congress itself as to how the reward money should be divided. Finally, each of the twenty-six soldiers who had surrounded the barn in which Booth had been trapped and shot received $1,653.85, their commanding officer Edward P. Doherty got $5,250, and the chief of detectives La Fayette C. Baker received $15,000 as having supplied the brains for the capture. Almost every family who kept a photograph album on the parlor table owned a likeness of John Wilkes Booth of the famous Booth family of actors. After the assassination Northerners slid the Booth card out of their albums; some threw it away, some burned it, some crumpled it angrily but hung on to it as a memento of the nation's betrayal, and some wrote their hearts' prayers on the backs of the pictures. In the case of this portrait of Booth the writer began in ink, changed to pencil, scrawling, "Do recognize him some where, and kill him . . ."

get him in condition for the 10:00 A.M. swearing-in on Saturday morning.

On the other hand Secretary McCulloch, who attended the ceremony in the Kirkland House conducted by Chief Justice Chase in the presence of the Cabinet, thought the new President handled himself very creditably, seemed properly grief-stricken at Lincoln's sudden death, and was quiet and dignified . . . Johnson begged the Cabinet with great earnestness to remain as now composed, and to support him in his arduous and heavy burdens.

Later, as Johnson began to make his bitter spur-of-the-moment denunciations of the South, McCulloch remarked it would have been better if Johnson had been stricken dumb on assuming the Presidency—his written speeches were fine but whenever he spoke without preparation he became so wild he could easily be mistaken for a drunkard.

For a few days after the murder people talked a lot about what they had seen, and "blew up" scraps of information and guesswork for the thrill of dabbling in a real-life mystery. There had been nearly two thousand people in the theatre and eighty-four over in the death room and twenty-five bearers of Lincoln's body, and their stories were emerging crazily.

Eight of the bearers insisted that theirs had been the honor of carrying the head. One, a New York grocer who had been on a sight-seeing trip in Washington, announced he had run up and supported an elbow, had moved along with his other hand on Lincoln's pulse, and recalled giving the weeping crowd the news that the injury would be fatal. One remembered that the President's body had sagged in the middle until two men were assigned to reach in and push upward—he had been a pusher. As another told it, the victim made the trip extended perfectly flat on a shutter wrenched from a theatre window. One of the clearest recollections had him transported sitting upright in the rocking chair in which he had failed to rock out of range of John Wilkes Booth's huge bullet.

The picture of Booth's escape from Ford's Theatre was given earnestly, and with bewildering variations.

Booth put one hand on the box rail, vaulted over it, and sailed through the air the twelve feet to the stage. In jumping, his right spur turned the framed engraving of Washington completely over, snagged the blue Treasury guard's flag festooned around the front of the box, and a shred of the blue material fluttered behind his heel all the way. Booth rose, flourished his dagger, shouted "Sic Semper Tyrannis," and strode out of sight.

Some said that the blue flag was not draped around the box, but up on a staff that stood straight up against the box's central pillar, but Booth managed to flip his spurred heel up there and make the tear, then he grasped the flagpole, slid his hands down its length and dropped the eight feet to the stage. Booth rode the rail first as though it were a saddle and his gait crossing the stage was a slow limp. He also coasted down the front of the box as though he were sledding, ran at top speed to the exit opposite and didn't say a word. He landed on his hands first; he was hurt dreadfully; he went by, moaning with pain. He soared fifteen feet from a crouched position, sauntered slowly to the footlights as though he were part of the troupe, flashed his knife blade in the gaslight, hissed "Sic Semper Tyrannis," with deathly pale face and eyes glittering, almost emitting fire, turned and with defiantly unhurried stage gait stalked off the stage.

In two curious variations, Booth hopped across the stage like a toad and the blue cloth hopped along just out of time behind him. And he was so completely paralyzed from the fall that his helpers had to throw a rope to him and he was pulled off behind scenes.

A young girl eyewitness contributed the fact that Booth had asked her just the day before whether "tyrannis" was spelled with two r's or two n's. She agreed with the versions of Booth's swift escape, but added an extra morsel—the maddened crowd had heaved her up on the stage and in a half-faint she realized the actor who played Lord Dundreary was fanning her with his wig. He volunteered that he had been standing alone in center stage when Booth fell heavily exactly beside him. But the actor Harry Hawk was also volunteering that he had been alone on the stage when Booth fell heavily.

The story of the President's last moments in the death room over at the Petersen House were just as baffling and fuzzy. To some in the room Lincoln's breathing was a frightening thing—a deep snoring, a wild gurgling. To others, it had a musical quality, and Stanton likened it to an Aeolian harp.

There were watchers by the bedside who heard not a sound of any kind; the President left the world after agonizing long minutes of utter silence. The only way of knowing it was all over was to watch the doctors with their fingers over the heart, the big artery in the neck and the two wrist pulses. When they darted looks at each other of question and then agreement, Dr. Barnes made the announcement.

Some said that Stanton rose from his knees, smoothed Lincoln's eyelids, and pulled down the shades. Maunsell B. Field, Assistant Secretary of the Treasury, says convincingly that right at that time he noticed that Mr. Lincoln's eyes were not quite closed, so he smoothed and closed them.

But now comes the real and fascinating conflict. Dr. Leale recounts, "Then I gently smoothed the President's contracted facial muscles, took two coins from my pocket, placed them over his eyelids, and drew a white cloth over the martyr's face."

Thomas McCurdy Vincent of the War Department says it was he who smoothed the eyelids and placed the coins. It was Vincent who had at 1:30 A.M. written down at Stanton's dictation an announcement of the President's death to be sent when the words became fact—a dictation which Mrs. Lincoln in the front room overheard and which caused her acute premature agony, caused her to cry wildly, "Is he dead? Oh, is he dead?"

Vincent writes, "Soon after eight the devoted War Minister had ordered all to be arranged for the removal of the body to the Executive Mansion and left me as his representative until the transfer should take place. It

THOMAS M. VINCENT

MAUNSELL B. FIELD

CHARLES A. LEALE

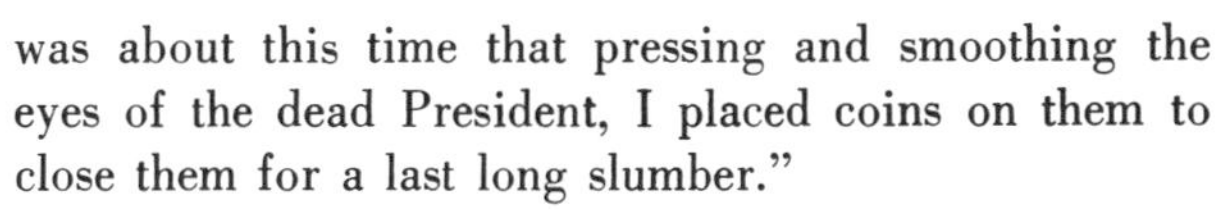

GEORGE V. RUTHERFORD

was about this time that pressing and smoothing the eyes of the dead President, I placed coins on them to close them for a last long slumber."

These two statements made Colonel George V. Rutherford angrily indignant because it was he and he alone who had smoothed and placed coins on Lincoln's eyes. He resolved to produce something a little more convincing than the mere words of honorable men. He would get up an exhibit of the very coins themselves that he had placed—silver half dollars—and he would use black sealing wax and impressive black ribbon and secure the signed certification of three men no one could question. He got Montgomery Meigs to testify that, after Lincoln died, Stanton told Rutherford to place pennies on Lincoln's eyes, which he did, "but immediately substituted two silver half dollars." Rutherford got General Christopher C. Augur, Commanding Department of Washington, to make a sworn statement for the exhibit that he had removed those same coins from the eyes, on taking the body from the box that same morning at the White House. Lastly he got General Daniel H. Rucker of the Quartermaster's Department, whose men had escorted Lincoln in his temporary coffin from the Petersen House home to the White House, to swear that he had received from General Augur these same coins and deposited them in his safe.

IT WAS GOOD-BY TO WASHINGTON

Here and on the following six pages is the Washington that Lincoln knew, a city now preparing to pay its last respects to the fallen President with a great state funeral. This photograph, never before published, was taken from the roof of the Smithsonian in 1863 by Mathew B. Brady. The structure in the foreground is the highest tip of the most easterly of the Institution's fantastic red sandstone towers. The empty fields leading toward the Capitol were the grounds of the Mall, for which was planned landscaping and extension west to the Potomac. (Today the Washington Monument and the Jefferson and Lincoln memorials stand, along with the Smithsonian, on this same great sweep of land.) The prominent building at the right was erected a few years before the war to house the National Guard Battalion. During the war it became Armory Square Hospital, and it was from this building that Dr. Charles Leale, after operating all day, came to Ford's Theatre on the assassination night.

In 1857 the work of taking down the old low dome of the Capitol had begun and the new dome was not finished until December 1863, shortly after the picture was taken. Montgomery Meigs, who was in charge of the project, devised a huge scaffold, which rested on the floor of the rotunda of the Capitol and rose through the dome hole; a derrick on top lifted the nine million pounds of iron plates that made up the new dome and set them in place on a series of ribs.

At the time of Lincoln's funeral Washington was a sprawling, simple city of about seventy-five thousand people. It was a city of little frame houses and raggedy, unpaved streets, in the midst of which, and looking very much out of place, were set half a dozen great marble buildings—the Patent Building, the Post Office, the Treasury Building, the White House, the Capitol. Through this city ran the canal at the upper left of the picture. It had formerly been used for small boats to take people from the Potomac to the Eastern Branch. But now all the sewers of Washington emptied into it and the bodies of all the animals that died were flung into it. People held their noses as they hurried across the high bridges that spanned it. No one seemed to mind the existence of this pestilence-breeding, sluggish water way which reeked, as John Hay once put it, of "the ghosts of 20,000 drowned cats." When the wind was right, the smell wafted into Lincoln's bedroom and office windows.

THIS DREARY TRACT of land comprises the boggy Potomac flats through which the Old City Canal moves stagnantly, south of the Executive Mansion in the left background and the Treasury Building at the right—almost at the end of its sickeningly slow journey to empty into the river. The mud flats bordering the canal were used during the war to quarter beef cattle for the army which were slaughtered as need arose. Considering the presence of these

cattle and the vile old canal which poisoned the fair Potomac, no wonder that every member of the President's family was sick one week after eating locally caught shad. Lincoln's office looked out on this scene, but he could also look above and far beyond it at the lovely countryside that stretched to Mt. Vernon and Alexandria. Just out of this photograph's range, to the left, rose the stump of the unfinished Washington Monument.

The most familiar landmarks

This is the Lee Mansion across the Potomac, which Lincoln could see from any of the west windows of the White House.

This side view of the Lee Mansion shows where Lincoln discovered unburied soldiers in their coffins, which prompted the beginning of Arlington Cemetery.

Never again would Lincoln gaze out on Lafayette Square, the little park surrounded by an iron fence, across Pennsylvania Avenue from the White House. Once Tad had locked his father in it and refused to give him the key, an imprisonment which delighted the President, though it badly wasted his time. Looking out every day on the little square, the President could always see the bronze statue of General Andrew Jackson that the government had paid Clark Mills, the sculptor, fifty thousand dollars to model. Charles Sumner said the work was so dreadful he was ashamed to have to walk by it with visitors from Europe, and it was generally made great fun of.

From any of the west windows of the White House—Mrs. Lincoln's bedroom or the Prince of Wales Guest Room, where the autopsy and embalming took place—the President could look across the river at the old Lee

Once Tad locked his father in this little fenced-in park across Pennsylvania Avenue from the White House.

Mansion with its eight huge Doric columns, copied from an old temple near Naples. Arlington House was the home of Martha Washington's grandson, George Washington Parke Curtis, who left it to his daughter, the wife of Robert E. Lee. The Lees abandoned their country seat with its spectacular view of Washington, two hundred feet above the Potomac, when Lee decided to fight for the South. The North used the Mansion as a hospital during the war, and on the afternoon of May 13, 1864, President Lincoln and Quartermaster General Montgomery Meigs rode across the Long Bridge to pay a visit to the wounded soldiers in Arlington House. Out by the side garden gate were piled twelve wooden coffins awaiting burial, but nothing could be done because the report had just come that the soldiers' cemetery in Washington was full. Both Lincoln and Meigs agreed that the twelve soldiers should be buried immediately, here beside Arlington House. Meigs issued the order, graves were dug, services read, and the first body lowered into the earth there was that of a Rebel soldier. This was the beginning of the setting aside of about two hundred acres for a National Cemetery and it began to fill quickly. Three days before Lincoln's assassination, on the evening of his last speech, when all the windows of the White House were lighted with candles, and the President stood reading in the center window of the second floor, the windows of the Arlington Mansion were also illuminated. And looking across the river, the people of Washington watched rockets being fired from the Arlington lawn where thousands of ex-slaves sang "The Year of Jubilee."

Farewell to the memory of the nation's Father

During both his inaugural addresses Lincoln faced this much ridiculed, half-naked statue of George Washington.

From in front of the east steps of the Capitol this Jupiter-like statue of Washington faced Lincoln as he read both of his inaugural addresses. Here, in this unpublished photograph by Mathew B. Brady, Brady's nephew and assistant, Levin C. Handy, stands in front of the little iron fence that surrounds the statue. In 1832 the government had given the commission to make this statue out of Italian marble to young Massachusetts sculptor, Horatio Greenough, and he worked on it for eight years without a day off. It almost sank the ship that brought it to the United States in 1841. When it was transferred to the rotunda of the Capitol, for which it had been planned all along, its twelve tons almost crashed through the rotunda floor and a solid column of masonry had to be put below the statue to support it. But it was not long before all agreed that because the light was so dim and poor inside the rotunda it should be moved outdoors and sit facing the East Capitol steps. The whole story broke young Greenough's heart, for he knew it was not the light in the rotunda, but that public opinion was that his statue was not worthy to be there in that hallowed spot. His statue had become a laughingstock, for he had portrayed Washington not in his everyday clothes but naked to the waist, with a sort of Roman toga draped over one shoulder and his right hand pointing to the sky like some ancient god. People in the 1800's did care what Washington had worn. They could go into the Patent Office and see his uniform on exhibit and it annoyed them to see the father of his country in the East Capitol Park half-naked in a toga.

Lincoln looked out of his office window every day of his Presidency and was reminded by the stump of the Washington Monument how short is a country's memory of her great men. Contributions for its erection had simply stopped at one hundred and fifty-three feet and the plans called for a height of six hundred feet. In 1848 Lincoln, as a young Congressman from Illinois, had stood on the Fourth of July with the rest of Washington's population and watched Grand Mason Benjamin B. French lay the cornerstone of this tribute to the first President, pouring wine and oil on it, placing in the hollow inside of the stone over one hundred objects representative of American life in the mid-nineteenth century, including coins, newspapers, daguerreotypes of portraits of George and Martha Washington, to be sealed up and preserved for some far future generation. French trusted, in his speech, that no one would refuse the honor of contributing his mite to this National Monument and then made a remark that would be disputed less than twenty years later:

"No more Washingtons shall come in our time . . . that human form has not yet been shaped to receive the eternal fire to make it another Washington."

In April 1865 people were saying that human form had indeed been shaped, but it had been taken from them, and the nation was again mourning, again wondering what monument it could raise to a great memory. It would be eleven years more before Americans would begin putting the remaining marble blocks on the Washington shaft.

Funds for the Washington Monument, begun in 1848, had run out, and at the time of Lincoln's funeral it still stood unfinished.

WASHINGTON BIDS A MAJESTIC FAREWELL

The business of saying good-by to the President was to take the city of Washington almost a full week. The plan was for Lincoln to be carried downstairs to the East Room in his huge coffin on Monday night, and starting Tuesday morning he would be on view there to the public. Wednesday was to be the day of the official funeral, followed by a procession from the White House to the Capitol, where he would lie in state in the Rotunda until Friday morning. Finally a special train would take him slowly north, then toward Springfield through a country of sorrow on almost the same route he had taken east four years before.

George A. Harrington, Assistant Secretary of the Treasury, was put in charge of the funeral preparations, and now he issued orders for the building of a catafalque in the East Room of the White House where the ceremony would take place. Upstairs in her room Mrs. Lincoln was wracked day and night by the sound of nails being hammered as carpenters worked on the huge structure. She cowered and put her fingers to her ears, saying every blow sounded like a pistol shot. She sent a request to Secretary Harrington, begging him not to dismantle the catafalque until she had moved out of the White House, which meant it would stand there—the "Temple

Early comers to Washington's great funeral procession took places on the portico of the Treasury Building and held them through the day, the papers said, "as though by squatters' rights."

of Death" it came to be called—for five whole weeks, while visiting citizens snipped away at it and tore off sizable strips of the black cloth, even the expensive black satin rosettes, as mementos.

Every care was taken not to disturb Mary Lincoln. Visitors to the Guest Room where Lincoln lay on the undertaker's cooling board tiptoed past her room. Only close friends of the family were admitted here, along with Members of the Cabinet and both Houses of Congress and their wives. On Monday evening the men who carried the dead President past Mrs. Lincoln's door and downstairs to the East Room took off their shoes, so that she would not hear the shuffle of feet and know what was going by.

On Tuesday Lincoln belonged to the people. Early that morning the line began forming outside the White House and was soon a mile long, six and seven abreast. Promptly at nine-thirty the west driveway gate was opened, and the crowds silently filed in through the heavily draped South Portico. The entire huge front of the White House was dripping and festooned with mourning.

It was a cloudy day, but the outdoors seemed brilliant compared to the sepulchral gloom and darkness people stepped into when they crossed the threshold. They moved through the dim great hall into an almost wholly dark Green Room and turned left into the East Room. The East Room ran along the entire east side of the White House and measured forty by eighty feet with a ceiling twenty-two feet high. It occupied an exact quarter of the entire house. Just enough light sifted through its venetian blinds to keep the crowd from stumbling—it was as though they peered at things through a late twilight. In the center of the room stood the "Temple of Death"—the catafalque. Since it reached up as high as eleven feet from the floor, the middle one of the three enormous, low-hanging crystal chandeliers had had to be removed and its gas pipe capped, but at each end of the room, north and south, the other two were there, completely shrouded, like giant bunches of grapes in black bags. The eight tall mirrors over the eight marble mantelpieces were swathed from top to bottom with black cloth over their frames and white cloth stretched the length of their glass. From all the room's cornices hung black streamers, but it had been impossible to cover the blood-red and gold velvet wallpaper, which Mrs. Lincoln had so extravagantly sent for from France—she actually dispatched a decorator on an ocean steamer to bring it home. Nor had the undertaking director attempted to shroud the windows' blood-red draperies of rich watered silk and lace, but he had had them drawn almost the whole distance across, each to the other, to effect a more awesome atmosphere. There was nothing whatever that he could do about Mrs. Lincoln's twenty-five hundred-dollar wall-to-wall Brussels carpet with its background of pale sea-green and its gay repetitive weaving of fruits and flowers. The structure in the center of the room which drew everyone's eye, irresistibly, offset a thousand times the abandoned character of the carpet.

The catafalque which bore Abraham Lincoln's coffin had been built at top speed and with no regard for economy. It had been designed by Benjamin B. French, Commissioner of Public Buildings, who was in charge of everything about the funeral that had directly to do with Lincoln's body. He was a 33rd degree Mason and a Past Grand Master of Freemasons of the District of Columbia, and he designed a catafalque for Lincoln that closely resembled the elegant Lodges of Sorrow which were the central feature of Masonic funerals. Four seven-foot-high posts were set ten feet apart at the head and foot of the catafalque and sixteen feet apart along the sides. From the tops of these posts rose an arched canopy to the height of eleven feet from the floor. The upper side of the canopy was made of black alpaca, and the finest black velvet decorated its sides, with sweeping festoons of black crape. Sixteen enormous black satin rosettes were set at the highest point of each festoon. The underside of the canopy was white fluted satin, which caught and reflected a little of what light there was on the face below.

The dais under the canopy on which the coffin lay was eleven feet long and three feet high and was covered with rich black cloth. But the coffin was actually more than four feet off the ground because there was a long ledge around the base of the dais which people were supposed to mount and walk along as they viewed Lincoln. Thus all were forced to make a near and extremely intimate inspection.

The fifteen-hundred-dollar coffin, which had been ready since late Sunday afternoon after marathon work by the undertaker for more than twenty-four hours, was the last glorious word in funeral trappings. The wood of the shoulder-flare style coffin was walnut but not an inch of it showed, for it was entirely covered with the finest black broadcloth. It was six feet six inches long on the outside and must have been a tight fit on the inside for its six-foot-four-inch tenant, the white satin lining being quilted and lavishly stuffed to make the resting place a soft one.

Inside the walnut case was an extra heavy lining of lead. On each side were four massive silver handles and on the center of the lid there was a shield outlined in silver tacks, in the center of which was a silver plate bearing the inscription:

ABRAHAM LINCOLN
16TH PRESIDENT OF THE UNITED STATES
BORN FEBRUARY 12, 1809
DIED APRIL 15, 1865

There was one unique, unexpected feature of this coffin that had not been ordered by the family or Commissioner French. On either side there were four shamrocks, formed by silver tacks, their three leaves showing clearly the outlines of the Irish national emblem. The embellishment was never explained—it was probably dreamed up by an Irish undertaker's artist who had been told to design something beautiful and meaningful. In the center of the largest leaf of each trefoil was a silver star, and there was a star upon each end of the coffin. The

GENERAL ULYSSES S. GRANT,
mourning crape hanging from his arm sat all alone at the head of the coffin at the White House funeral and wept.

lid was hinged to fold back a third of the way down, so as to expose the face and shoulders.

In the gloom of the great East Room the people who came to pay their last respects to Lincoln were directed by officers to the foot of the catafalque, where they divided into a single line on each side, mounted the step and walked along beside the coffin, pausing to look down at the face on an average of one second each. The greater part of the body seemed to be sunk snugly deep down in the coffin, but the head rose up high on a dainty white silk pillow. The crowd was a mixture of men and women and children. In accordance with the custom of the times which accepted the fact that grief, to be deep, must be heard there was a great deal of sobbing aloud. At about 1:00 P.M. a large number of invalid soldiers arrived, some limping, some with canes or sticks or crutches, some with bandaged heads or arms in slings. Without a single sound, they took a last look at the face of their honored Commander-in-Chief.

At 5:30 P.M. the public was shut out and for the next two hours special groups were admitted to the East Room. Principal among them were about four hundred men and women from Illinois, who had been arguing and pleading since the assassination to have Lincoln interred in their State. They had finally won out and were jubilant. They were composing all kinds of statements saying that Lincoln belonged to the state which had first recognized his greatness, and they had resolved that citizens of Illinois would not only wear crape on their left arms for six weeks, they would also wear crape on their hats.

The minute the special off-hours viewers had left,

Drawing of the East Room funeral service failed to show the raised platform

carpenters were admitted to the East Room in force. They had a big job to do before the official funeral the next morning. They began to build a series of steps arranged as in an amphitheatre, beginning low, about five feet away from the catafalque, and growing higher back to the East Room walls, so that everyone invited could have a clear view of the dead President and the clergymen conducting the funeral. Secretary Harrington had the steps separated into sections by the laying down of thin white ribbons in an effort to solve the unrewarding and impossible task of assigning places to the people who really deserved to be present. Small cards were placed in each section, with the name in handwriting of the delegation assigned to that space. The hammering went on through the night and into Wednesday morning, right up to the time the first invited guests arrived.

and wrongly included Mrs. Lincoln who never made an appearance.

Special trains had been running, jam-packed, into the city of Washington for the last two days and people had been driving in from towns and villages in carriages or buggies or even hay-wagons—the authorities figured that six thousand people slept Tuesday night on floors of houses or hotels (Willard's Hotel. turned away four hundred applicants), or in their vehicles or on blankets spread on whatever grass plots they could find. Washington was bursting—there were one hundred thousand human beings in the city and sixty thousand of them were prepared to watch a procession of forty thousand on Wednesday, following Lincoln's official funeral at the White House. The people had arrived with wisps of black crape already encircling their left arms and, those who could get them, with small tintypes of the President dangling on black ribbons pinned above their hearts. The gas streetlights burned all night and crowds moved slowly through the avenues in a dazed way, as though it were high noon. There was a feeling that each person was mourning a member of his family.

At sunrise the people who had been sleeping were waked by the booming of cannon in all the forts encircling the city, with the counterpoint of tolling bells in church towers and firehouses. It was a radiantly beautiful day—warm, cloudless, with a bright sun, and as early as eight o'clock there were throngs on Pennsylvania Avenue outside the White House and under the trees of Lafayette Square Park across the way. The heavy black draping all across the great front of the Mansion contrasted with the spring gaiety of the bright-green lawn surrounding it and of all the trees in blossom. The magnolias fortunately were blooming early, and some of their flowers had been picked and strewn on the lid of the coffin.

Every house and store in Washington was shut tight for the day. The rich had sent messengers to other cities to buy mourning decorations when the supply in the capital gave out, but even the poorest shanties had their bits of black cloth tacked up, snippets and ends cut off and thrown away as elaborate festoons were measured for the houses of the well-to-do. Actually, it was these humble fluttering shreds that made people choke up. The big displays only filled them with awe.

By eleven o'clock tickets were being presented and the majority of those invited entered the funeral chamber through the Green Room. In the Blue Room, the adjoining oval parlor, appeared the great names. It was filled almost full with the late President's personal cavalry guard from Ohio, who had ridden their matched black horses wherever Mr. Lincoln went. A path two and a half feet wide was opened in their midst, and along this path and through the Green Room passed General Grant, Admiral Farragut, members of the Supreme Court and the Diplomatic Corps on their way to their allotted spaces in the gloom of the East Room. At two minutes to twelve President Johnson and his friend Preston King entered, followed by ex-Vice-President Hamlin and the Cabinet, and for everyone there was the shock of Seward's absence and the thought of how near they had come to standing beside two coffins today.

Lincoln's complexion had always been dark, but now, instead of being even darker, it was unpleasingly lighter, a grayish putty color. Around his mouth he still had the faintly happy expression that those who watched him die saw come over his face a few minutes after he stopped breathing. The trouble was that the smile was frozen on a face that was unfamiliar in its unresponsive

GENERAL WILLIAM TECUMSEH SHERMAN, shown here with mourning crape on his arm, missed the funeral because he was in North Carolina trying to negotiate a peace treaty with General Johnston.

Washington's funeral car, drawn by six white horses, carried the coffin on a platform eleven feet high.

stoniness. Gone was the mobility which so entranced anyone who watched him in life, the magic lighting-up of the features that made a plain man handsome when his mind struck sparks.

At the head of the coffin was a fresh, fragrant cross of lilies, sent by Mrs. Lincoln's intimate friend, Mrs. Orne, of Philadelphia, a well-known writer for women's magazines. At the foot was the oversized anchor of white rosebuds which had stood there all during yesterday's viewing and was wilting badly. A small amount of light was shed on the coffin by a pair of tall wax candles in silver candlesticks on a mantel.

At the four corners of the catafalque were four officers of a special guard of honor, three of them standing like statues, but the fourth, Brevet Major-General David Hunter, was restless, pacing back and forth and leaning with a gauntleted hand on the pole of the catafalque. The two silver stars on his shoulder shone in the candlelight, and the mourners could see his paper collar standing up stiffly.

At the foot of the coffin sat Robert Lincoln along with the husbands of his mother's two sisters who had come on from Springfield, Ninian Edwards and Clark M. Smith, and two of his mother's first cousins, Dr. Lyman Beecher Todd and General John B. S. Todd. Lincoln's two young secretaries, John Nicolay and John Hay, stood beside Robert. Mrs. Lincoln would have been at the foot of the coffin, too, had she been there at all. Instead, she remained upstairs in bed the entire day.

General Grant, with tears in his eyes, sat alone at the President's head, facing the perfect cross of lilies. He would always say that the day of Lincoln's death was the saddest day of his life. Just a little over a year before, on March 8, 1864, he had paid his first visit to the White House after being made Lieutenant General. It was the evening of a weekly reception and Mr. Lincoln, surrounded by citizens in the oval Blue Room, spied him, knew him immediately from his photographs. He stepped up the line to greet his new head of the armies, took hold of him, and moved him along to Mrs. Lincoln, saying "Here is General Grant. What a surprise! What a delight!" And afterward the shy soldier had been swept into the East Room by a throng of admirers, had been swung up on a red brocaded sofa and been forced to stand there while the almost hysterical guests—twice the number now here for the funeral in the same space—struggled to get near him and have a good look. Ladies' clothes were torn in a sort of genteel riot before he escaped.

President Johnson stood at the east side of the coffin and behind him was the Cabinet. Standing neatly in their appointed squares were the clergy, members of the Supreme Court, governors of states, officers of the Army and Navy, a tremendous New York delegation, members of the Senate and House, members of the boards of the Christian and Sanitary Commissions, forty mourners from Kentucky and Illinois, the pall-bearers, heads of bureaus, the assistant secretaries, the

Diplomatic Corps, and many others, such as the nurse who had taken care of Willie Lincoln in his last illness. At the time of the assassination she herself was ill in a hospital, of typhoid fever. But she was determined to look for the last time on Mr. Lincoln's face and she was carried down the hospital stairs and brought to the White House. There were only six other women present—Secretary Chase's two daughters, Kate Chase Sprague and Miss Nettie Chase, Mrs. Stanton, Mrs. Usher, Mrs. Welles and Mrs. Dennison.

To the Diplomatic Corps, gorgeous in their golden coats and shining medals, what was taking place was more than a funeral. The foreign ambassadors looked at President Johnson standing there with his arms crossed, Mr. Lincoln's same Cabinet ranging behind him, and they marveled at the smooth transfer of power which the Constitution of a republic had devised.

Just before the first of the four ministers who were to conduct the service began speaking, Johnson and Preston King stepped up to the coffin, mounted the foot-high ledge at its side and looked down concentratedly at the face for a moment, then retired to their places a few feet back. Johnson had been visited by many delegations in his office in the Treasury Building since Lincoln's death and he was trying to show everyone that he was going to be a strong president. In the last few days he had taken to beginning all his interviews by praising Lincoln, lamenting his loss, and saying all his—Johnson's—efforts would go to carrying on the great work he had begun—Lincoln's policies would be his policies. This he invariably followed up by a statement that treason was the most vicious of all crimes, and those guilty of it must be punished. "Very vigorous" said some, "Vindictive" said others, and "We will have no trouble now" said all those who had opposed Mr. Lincoln's gentle and forgiving attitude toward those who had rebelled.

At exactly ten minutes past twelve Dr. Hall began the Episcopal burial service: "I am the Resurrection and the Life saith the Lord; he that believeth in me, though he were dead, yet shall he live, and whosoever liveth and believeth in me shall never die."

Bishop Simpson of the Methodist Episcopal Church delivered a prayer in which he likened Lincoln to Moses, and when he was done, all six hundred listeners were in tears.

FORD'S THEATRE on the day of the Washington funeral. After the assassination the theatre was never again opened for performances. In time it was bought by the government from owner John Ford. At first it was used for storing Confederate records, then as the Army Medical Museum in which the most popular exhibit was several vertebrae of John Wilkes Booth --those pierced by the bullet that killed him and cut from the base of Booth's neck in the autopsy.

Lincoln's pastor, Dr. Gurley, gave the funeral sermon.

It was a cruel, cruel hand, that dark hand of the assassin, which smote our honored, wise, and noble President, and filled the land with sorrow. But above and beyond that hand is another which we must see and acknowledge. It is the chastening hand of a wise and faithful Father. He gives us this bitter cup. And the cup that our Father has given us, shall we not drink it?

He went on:

Oh, it is a mysterious and most afflicting visitation! . . . In the midst of our rejoicings we needed this stroke, this dealing, this discipline; and therefore He has sent it.

Dr. Gray, Chaplain of the Senate and a Baptist, closed the services with a prayer asking God's blessing on practically everyone—on Lincoln's family, on Johnson, on Seward, on the Cabinet, on the commanders of the Army and Navy, on all the soldiers and sailors, on the ambassadors from foreign courts. "God of Justice," he ended, "and Avenger of the Nation's wrong, let the work

The mighty funeral procession turns down Pennsylvania Avenue and sweeps dramatically toward the Capitol.

of treason cease, and let the guilty perpetrators of this horrible crime be arrested and brought to justice. . . . Send speedy peace unto all our borders. Through Jesus Christ our Lord. Amen."

While the funeral was going on, simultaneously all across the nation and even in Canada twenty-five million people were hearing similar sermons and prayers in their churches, hearing that Lincoln's work on earth was finished and that God had removed him purposefully; hearing how regretful it was that Lincoln had died in such low surroundings; hearing him likened to Washington, the saviour of his country; to Moses, leading his people to the edge of the Promised Land but not allowed to enter—even to Christ—for Lincoln had been murdered on the anniversary of the Crucifixion.

After the White House services the six hundred people went outside, blinking in the sudden strong sunlight. The twelve veteran reserve corps sergeants who were to be the only ones to lift the coffin until it reached the Springfield tomb, now carried it—lid closed—outdoors and placed it on the funeral car, which was waiting with

This view of the funeral procession, taken during a pause in the marching, shows the approach to Capitol Hill up Pennsylvania Avenue. This full scene, with the hill and Capitol in the distance, is published here for the first time.

its six white horses at the Mansion's front door. The platform on which the coffin rested was eleven feet off the ground, high enough so that everyone in the crowd along the streets would see the object of greatest interest. Much of the height was accounted for by the wheels of the car, which were enormous, though seemingly frail, with spokes that looked too spindly for the important journey they were about to make.

As the procession began to move, the minute guns took up their regular booming, and again the church and firehouse bells began to toll. Lincoln's old friend and self-appointed bodyguard Ward Hill Lamon had arranged the great procession and he had done it well. Some of the units had been waiting hours on side streets and they joined the marching lines just as had been planned. Leading the procession and preceding the coffin on its high black car along Pennsylvania Avenue—full of ruts and potholes made from dragging heavy war supplies over it for four years—was a detachment of colored soldiers, the second troop to enter Richmond at its surrender. Officers of the Army, Navy and Marine Corps followed. Then marshals, the clergymen who had conducted the funeral, the doctors who had attended the President on his deathbed, the twenty-two pallbearers, General Grant, and Admiral Farragut and civilian mourners.

Just behind the hearse came Mr. Lincoln's favorite horse, branded *U.S.*, bearing his master's boots reversed in the stirrups. Many people who had seen the President riding this horse now remembered the tall figure with the plug hat slipped back on his head, the long stirrups. Behind the hearse Robert Lincoln and Tad rode in a carriage together. Tom Pendel, the doorkeeper of the White House, rode up in front with the coachman. The two brothers rode close enough to their father's body to see the men's hats in the crowds along the sidewalks being removed by the hundreds as the colossal coffin passed by with all its silver ornaments shining in the bright sunlight.

Seward was watching, propped against his pillows at the window of his house, but it was all a vague dream to him and he afterward remembered he saw black plumes nodding on the top of the funeral car. There were no plumes. There was at the top of the funeral car a gilt eagle, covered with crape.

Many convalescent soldiers had left their beds in the Washington hospitals to march, out of respect to their late Commander-in-Chief, and though some were too weak to go far, there were those who were actually on crutches who hobbled all the way to the Capitol.

The Negro citizens made one of the most impressive sights of all. They walked in lines of forty, straight across the avenue from curb to curb, four thousand of them. They wore high silk hats and white gloves and marched holding hands.

The scene was solemn, impressive, and unforgettable as the procession swept around into Pennsylvania Avenue from Fifteenth Street—and suddenly, movingly, the whole mile-and-a-half distance leading to the Capitol

A colorful marcher in the procession was California hunter Seth Kinman, who had recently presented Lincoln with an elk-horn chair of his own construction. Lincoln, he said, was the first to occupy it—he had fought off hundreds of eager sitters.

Another mourner, Frederick Douglass, the six-foot tall, fiery civil rights leader, was one of the first Negroes ever to be entertained socially at the White House. He was received by Mr. Lincoln in the East Room on March 5, 1865, and told the President his inaugural address the day before had been a "sacred effort." Said Lincoln, "There is no man's opinion that I value more than yours."

came into view. Every window, housetop, and tree was weighted down with silent watchers, the sidewalks were crowded, and there were many Negro couples with very young children. The grandeur and sadness were indescribable. Every face in line was solemn—the majority tear-streaked. The measured maddeningly slow-motion tread of the marchers, the halting roll of the wheels of gun carriages over cobblestones, the mingling into one unearthly wail of dirges from the thirty interspersed bands—and on, on, without let up, the beat, beat, beat of the muffled drums was almost unbearable. Eyes watching the heroic dark pageant often had to turn away as people forced themselves to think momentarily of some everyday matter and let the blinding film curtaining their eyes clear.

Most of all, it was those heart-stopping sounds, intensifying and exalting the sights, that made the day unforgettable.

And legends were born that day. Hundreds said that in the blue sky above the procession shone an entirely new and exceedingly bright star that had never been seen before. It was like the story that was to grow up about the wood thrushes of the country. It would be said that no wood thrush sang a note for a whole year after Lincoln's death.

When the funeral car reached the East Front of the Capitol at three-thirty, it stopped in front of the great East Portico and the east front steps. At that moment the tail of the procession was just rounding the corner of the Treasury Building and starting up Pennsylvania Avenue. The high platform of the hearse car made it difficult for the Veteran Corps sergeants to grasp the coffin and so it first had to be worked onto a stand that was placed beside the hearse. At last it was swung up on the eight pairs of shoulders and the men strained to move their heavy burden at just the right slow climbing pace up the long, long flight of steps.

Only a select few were invited to enter the rotunda and see Mr. Lincoln installed on his second catafalque, to lie in state. Benjamin B. French entered first, close behind the sergeants who were slowly proceeding to the rotunda's center. The rotunda was dark, and French had covered all the sculpture and the massive paintings with black crape. He had also designed the catafalque here as he had created the one at the White House. This one was much simpler and neater than his first effort.

Now members of the family drew near—also Nicolay and Hay, the four clergymen of the funeral, the deathbed physicians, President Johnson, Generals Grant, Halleck, Hunter, Meigs, the honorary pallbearers, the Illinois and Kentucky delegations. Dr. Gurley began reciting, "It is appointed unto men once to die—the dust returns to the earth as it was and the Spirit unto God Who gave it. All flesh is as grass, and all the glory of man as the flower of grass. The grass withereth and the flower thereof falleth away. We know that we must die and go to the house appointed for all living. . . ."

A few minutes later all had departed except the Guard of Honor.

At eight o'clock Thursday morning the doors were opened to the public. All day long people entered in a double line from the west side of the Capitol, parted to form single lines as they walked the length of the catafalque, joined again to go out by the great eastern door and down the long stone stairway—the spot where many present now had seen Lincoln twice sworn in as President.

During the day Noah Brooks got permission to climb alone up the winding stairs that led to the dome and from far above he looked down. He described it:

> *From that lofty point, the sight was weird and memorable. Directly beneath me lay the casket in which the dead President lay at full length, far, far below; and like black atoms moving over a sheet of gray paper, the slow-moving mourners, seen from a perpendicular above them, crept silently in two dark lines across the pavement of the rotunda, forming an ellipse around the coffin and joining as they advanced toward the eastern portal and disappeared.*

And so it was over. On Friday morning Lincoln would begin his slow, mercilessly public, and daily interrupted seventeen-hundred-mile journey.

STANDING BEYOND WORKMEN'S SHACKS and an idle derrick is the newly completed Senate building. The thousands who sorrowed and who thrilled at the sight of columns draped in black like these, flags at half-mast and, at the sound of drums and the dirges, would have winced if they had examined the cost in dollars of saying a poetic farewell to Lincoln. Nothing was poetic about the lists of expenses. The total undertaker's charge came to $7,459. The platform in the East Room that the delegations stood on cost $358.14, the six white horses $75. The government was billed for mourning clothes for the White House servants—"one full black suit clothes for Peter the footman: $125"—was a typical charge. All the Senate and House and members of departments charged their armbands and badges to the government. The men who draped the Capitol rotunda made sure they charged for overtime when they had to work late Tuesday and Wednesday nights. And even the public gardeners working in the White House conservatory and the government botanical garden put in their bills for flowers supplied to decorate the East Room and the catafalque, padding their requisitions heavily. Such was the confusion that even claims like these were approved. Everyone who had a claim was urged to make it immediately and everybody did. There were hundreds of hack-owners putting in their bills for eight dollars, the standard price for use of a hack on the funeral day. Chief Justice Chase put in a special bill for eight dollars for his carriage in the procession, but the members of the Cabinet paid their own way.

The total Washington funeral bill came to thirty thousand dollars, right to the penny.

Lincoln's third son, Willie, is shown at six in Springfield, then five years later just after the family's arrival in Washington.

THE LOST SON WHO MADE THE JOURNEY HOME WITH HIS FATHER

Lincoln was not to travel home to Illinois alone. Along with him on the special train, Mary Lincoln decided, would go their little twelve-year-old son, Willie, who had died three years before and whose remains were in a crypt in Georgetown's Oak Hill Cemetery.

William Wallace Lincoln's story reaches back nine months and three weeks before his birth and concerns the reason why Mary and Abraham Lincoln so desperately wanted a new baby just then. Their three-year-old second son Eddie had died on February 1, 1850, leaving the parents anguished. Very little is known of small Eddie except that he loved kittens, that his eyes always brightened when someone said the word "Father," that his hair fell over his brow in silken waves, and that once Lincoln went shopping in the capital to find some plaid stockings for his "dear little feet." He slipped away from this world in an early dawn, after a gradual weakening through fifty-two days. The death record gave the cause as consumption.

Eddie's funeral service was held at eleven the next morning in the Lincolns' brown cottage on Eighth Street in Springfield and Lincoln asked Dr. James Smith to include in the service the hymn "My faith looks up to Thee. . . ." Mrs. Lincoln had not eaten and would not, but her husband seated himself at the table and swallowed his breakfast, saying, "Mary, we must live." He had been to Hutchinson's Cemetery and for fifteen dollars bought a family burial plot, and now tiny Eddie was to be the first committed to this earth. He ordered a marble slab with the name and date—a dove with outstretched wings to be carved at the top and lower down the words "Of such is the Kingdom of Heaven." A week later an unsigned twenty-four-line poem called "Little Eddie" appeared in a Springfield newspaper. The central theme was "Pure little bud in kindness given—In mercy taken to bloom in Heaven," and many readers believed the contribution had been written by Abraham Lincoln himself, with whom religion, according to his wife, was "a sort of poetry in his soul." The father bore his grief silently, only writing one letter to his stepbrother to say, "We miss him very much." In odd moments he wondered about the strange dream he had had the night before the baby's death, in which he seemed to be sailing swiftly on an unknown ship, toward an unknown shore.

Then, on December 21, 1850, appeared Willie, a perfect, beautiful boy, to be rocked in Eddie's cradle and dressed in Eddie's first clothes. Always, through Willie's twelve years of life, he was to be bound up in his parents' thoughts and love with the child they had lost. In a queer way Eddie was a part of Willie and when Willie had to die in Washington, Willie was Eddie too. It was a dreadful double death—they were losing Eddie all over again.

Of course Lincoln knew in his reasoning mind that when he left to assume the Presidency in Washington he was leaving Eddie behind, and he put it in words to his friends gathered at the station on the rainy morning of February 11, 1861. No one could know his sadness at saying good-by. "Here my children were born," he said, "and here one of them lies buried."

Still, when Willie walked into the door of the White House at his father's side, little Eddie was far from being left behind.

Willie was a quiet, thoughtful boy who wanted to be good as much as Tad wanted to be naughty. Tad would not pay attention to his lessons and at twelve could neither read nor write, whereas Willie studied faithfully, and at eight, on a trip to Chicago with his father, was able to write very creditably to his best friend in Springfield, Henry Remann. "Dear Henry," he began, "This town is a very beautiful place. Me and father went to two theaters the other night. Me and father have a nice little room to ourselves. We have two little pitchers on a washstand. The smallest one for me the largest one for father. We have two little towels on top of both pitchers. The smallest one for me, the largest one for father. We have two little beds in the room. The smallest one for me the largest one for father." And so on. Other than being a student of "The Three Bears" Willie had a good memory, memorized long portions of the Bible for Sunday School, and told his mother and father he was going to be a preacher when he grew up.

But William Wallace Lincoln, named for the family doctor back in Springfield, caught cold and developed a fever after riding his pony in a slushy half-snow during the last days of January 1862. At first his mother merely kept him indoors and near a fire, but as the first week in February began and the boy seemed worse she put him to bed and called the doctor. She was planning a large reception in the White House for the night of February fifth and the question was whether she ought to recall the invitations. The doctor reassured her—he thought Willie would be better by then. But Willie was burning with fever on the night of the fifth, as his mother dressed for the party. He drew every breath with difficulty. She could see that his lungs were congested and she was frightened. Nevertheless she put on the daringly low-necked dress with the black lace trimming in which she had planned to be such a sensation. She was standing, black flounces gathered up by loops of ribbon on the side and artificial flowers bound into her own hair, with her unusually long train spread out behind her, when Mr. Lincoln came into the room. She never knew what he was going to say and in this case it was, "Whew! Our cat has a long tail tonight." Her exquisite bosom and lovely arms were her best features and the First Lady

Willie was born nine months after the Lincolns lost their second son, Eddie, whose tombstone this is.

never lost an opportunity to have them admired. "Mother," said the President, "it is my opinion, if some of that tail was nearer the head it would be in better style." Mary Lincoln was not pleased. She turned away coldly but the Marine Band was already playing downstairs so within the moment she took her husband's arm and composed herself to make an entrance.

Eight hundred invitations had been mailed and the red, green, and blue parlors were crowded with guests—members of the Senate, the Diplomatic Corps, the House, the Cabinet, governors of the states, officers of the Army and Navy. It was a crush, definitely the brilliant affair she had wanted so badly. Exotic flowers from the presidential greenhouse were in vases every few yards, and the day before she had personally told the leader of the band, Francis Scala, just what to play. The guests were invited for eight, but it was nine-thirty before the great majority of the company began to stream in and surge around the Lincolns, who were receiving in the center of the East Room.

In the dining room which was thrown open at midnight was a long table with a gigantic looking-glass upon it bearing massive confections of sugar. Most recognizable were Fort Sumter, a warship, a temple of liberty, a Chinese pagoda, a Swiss cottage, and a fountain with glasses around it filled with what looked like beer. The actual supper had been supplied by Maillard and whispers were going around that it had cost thousands of dollars.

Yet there was no joy in the evening for the mechanically smiling hostess and her husband. They kept climbing the stairs to see how Willie was, and he was not doing well at all. With fear clutching at their hearts, they went downstairs once more to hear the singers of the evening, the Hutchinson family, give a frighteningly real rendition of the song "Ship on Fire," which required simulation of a violent thunderstorm at sea, the frightened screams of the trapped passengers, a mother pressing her babe to her bosom of snow, "a tramp, a rout, an uproar of voices—'Fire! Fire!' "

The cheeks of the sailors grew pale
at the sight—and their eyes glistened wild in the gleam
of the light—and the smoke in thick wreaths mounted
higher and higher—Oh God it is fearful to perish by fire!

By the next morning the household knew that Willie was seriously ill. Not only Dr. Stone but consulting doctors were called in. The newspapers decided that the boy's affliction was bilious fever, but those who saw the sick boy knew the trouble concerned his breathing apparatus. Now one of the parents was always with Willie and a nurse was ordered to be sent from one of the hospitals where she had been caring for wounded soldiers. After a week Mrs. Lincoln found herself worn out and too weak to get up from bed any longer. For her son the doctors held out no hope. The patient was wandering of mind and did not recognize the distracted loving face of the tall man who bent over him.

Death came in the afternoon of February 20, 1862.

High above Rock Creek in Georgetown's Oak Hill Cemetery is the Carroll tomb where Lincoln buried Willie.

The father covered his face with his hands and wept uncontrollably, convulsively, chokingly. At last he could speak and looked at Willie long, very long, as if he could not turn away. "My poor boy," he said, "He was too good for this earth. God has called him home. I know that he is much better off in heaven, but then we loved him so. It is hard, hard to have him die!"

The funeral was held in the East Room. Willie had been embalmed and lay seeming only asleep in his imitation rosewood coffin, first placed in the Green Room where his friends might pass by and see him.

The service began with the East Room packed with very much the same people who had been present at the party that was such a brilliant success two weeks before, but now there was not a smile, only tears on every cheek, and the faces of the children from Willie's Sabbath School class looked stricken. Dr. Gurley read from the

Scriptures—by his own choice and no prearrangement with the parents, happening to stress the words on Eddie's marble slab out in Springfield—"For of such is the kingdom of Heaven." Privately, after the service, Dr. Gurley told people that shortly before death Willie had asked him to take the six dollars that were his savings out of the bank on his bureau and give them to the missionary society.

The carriages of the funeral procession stretched for so many blocks that they took a long time to wind their way up to the heights of Georgetown and to the beautiful Oak Hill Cemetery with its crown of oak trees. There had been a terrible storm in the city that day—steeples of churches had fallen, roofs had been torn off houses, people who tried to walk on the streets were blown along and had to grasp at railings and lamp posts to stop themselves. Now all was still and the hundreds of people climbed out of their carriages and walked through the gates of the cemetery to the beautiful little red stone Gothic chapel with its blue stained-glass windows. Here, over the coffin, more prayers were said by Dr. Gurley and at last everyone filed slowly away and Willie was left alone beside the altar. It was generally supposed that his embalmment was for the purpose of sending the boy back to Springfield and that the journey would be made soon. Actually, Mr. Lincoln had accepted the offer of his friend, the clerk of the Supreme Court, William Thomas Carroll, to have Willie placed in one of the crypts of the Carroll tomb, and the next day the President returned without publicity to see Willie taken from the chapel to the tomb. Nothing could have been more peaceful or more beautiful than the situation of this tomb and it was completely undiscoverable to the casual cemetery visitor, being the very last tomb on the left at the extreme far reaches of the grounds, at the top of an almost perpendicular hillside that descended to Rock Creek below. The rapid water made a pleasant rushing sound and the forest trees stood up bare and strong against the sky.

Beside himself with grief, Lincoln visited the tomb, and, newspapers claimed, he twice had the crypt opened to look upon his son.

Word soon got about that Mr. Lincoln had been back to the tomb twice to have Willie's coffin opened so that he could look at him again. Dr. Charles Brown had embalmed Willie so perfectly that he did really seem to be only sleeping, and Lincoln could not bear to leave him alone in the cold tomb. Long ago, when he had lost his first love, Anne Rutledge, he had been distracted by the thought of the rain falling on her grave.

Back in the White House the President tried to go back to his work for the country but his spirits were so low and his heart so crushed he could not keep his mind on anything. When Thursday came around and Willie had been dead one week, he shut himself up in his room and no one knows how he gave way to his sorrow. The next Thursday he was even more depressed, and disappeared again. This continued until he received a call from Dr. Francis Vinton, of Trinity Church, New York, who explained that Mr. Lincoln was behaving like a heathen. To give way to his feelings was sinful and furthermore he was responsible as a leader to the country which had elected him, and he was utterly failing the people of this country.

"Your son is alive in Paradise," said Dr. Vinton.

The President had hardly listened to the minister's talk. He had turned deaf ears to him and dull uncomprehending eyes until somehow the four words "Your son is alive" reached him. He jumped up from the sofa saying, "Alive! Alive! Surely you mock me."

"No, Sir, believe me," said Dr. Vinton, "it is a most comforting doctrine of the church, founded upon the words of Christ himself."

For some minutes Mr. Lincoln sobbed and repeated the words "Alive? Alive?" After the interview there was no more shutting himself up on Thursdays and the President, with a mighty effort, went back to the routine of his office work.

He fullfilled his oath to the people, but after work hours his heartbreak sometimes proved too great to hide.

Now, three years later, the undertakers removed Willie from his vault, enclosed his little metallic coffin in a new black walnut one more suited for the occasion, and took him to the depot where the funeral train stood ready for departure. The actual funeral car, heavily draped in black, was divided into three sections. In the center section the guard of honor would live. In the rear compartment was a bier waiting to receive Lincoln. It was in the front compartment on a second bier that Willie's double coffin was placed. His father would join him soon for the long trip West and home.

PART III

THE LONG JOURNEY HOME BEGINS

Abraham Lincoln's funeral procession back across his land to Illinois was the mightiest outpouring of national grief the world had yet seen. Although at the time the camera was a crude, unwieldy machine requiring long exposures and laborious processing, still that new invention was there all along the way to record the great spectacle of tribute. Here are the pictures it made, along with a detailed account of that memorable journey one hundred years ago.

HOMEWARD BOUND... FIRST STOP BALTIMORE

This engine, decked in black and wearing a picture of Lincoln over

At 6:00 A.M. on the morning of Friday, the twenty-first of April, a small group met once more in the rotunda of the Capitol, and Dr. Gurley said another prayer, beseeching God to "watch over this sleeping dust of our fallen Chief Magistrate," and praying that the Lord "watch over it as it passes from our view and is borne to its final resting place in the soil of that state which was his abiding and chosen home." All present then followed the coffin through a light drizzle to the depot, where the new President was waiting to say his last farewell. The funeral train consisted of nine cars and the engine—plus a pilot engine that would run ahead to make sure there would be no accident—and the actual funeral car that was to hold Lincoln and his son was second from the rear. The engine was heavily draped in black. All brass fittings were highly polished and then craped. There were little flags here and there, covered with black cloth, and a large photograph of Lincoln over the cowcatcher was framed with a wide black border. Three hundred people riding in eight railroad cars—a ninth for their baggage—were to accompany Lincoln on the seventeen hundred-mile trip which had been carefully planned by a committee of Illinois citizens. It was to include every city at which Lincoln as President-elect had stopped on his trip eastward to Washington in February 1861—with the exception of Cincinnati. The officials of Cincinnati expressed themselves as deeply offended by the decision, even though it was explained to them that the diversionary loop south would make the trip too lengthy. In the end the route included Baltimore, Harrisburg, Philadelphia, New York, Albany, Buffalo, Columbus, Indianapolis, Chicago, and Springfield, and a delegation from Cincinnati came to the Columbus funeral.

In addition to the numerous Senate and House members, some of the more noteworthy among the men selected to make the journey with the President's body as guests of the government were the two Springfield brothers-in-law, Edwards and Smith, the two Todd first cousins of Mrs. Lincoln, Brigadier-General Edward D. Townsend representing Secretary of War Stanton, Rear Admiral Charles H. Davis representing Secretary of the Navy Welles, Major-General David Hunter, who had been chief of the guard of honor at the funeral, Ward Hill Lamon, Judge David Davis, Dr. Gurley, Dr. Charles Brown, the embalmer, and Thomas Pendel, the tall doorkeeper of the White House, who had put Tad to bed on the death night and who, in his build, resembled the President so greatly that when he returned from the funeral Mrs. Lincoln would send him to pose in Lincoln's clothes for a portrait of her husband.

At one minute before eight o'clock Dr. Gurley said the last Washington prayer. All heads were uncovered as bells tolled and the Baltimore & Ohio engine, puffing smoke from its wide-mouthed stack and with its logs of wood for refueling piled up just behind the engineer's cab, moved at a snail's pace out of the depot. A Negro regiment was lined at the track's side, and through the windows, as the train increased its speed, the funeral party saw the motionless repetitive figures at wooden attention, topped by incongruously nonwooden, grief-convulsed features. Good-by, Father Abraham! And for Father Abraham, it was good-by forever to Washington.

First stop Baltimore.

The city fathers of Baltimore had studied the fabulous details of the gigantic procession in the Capital and

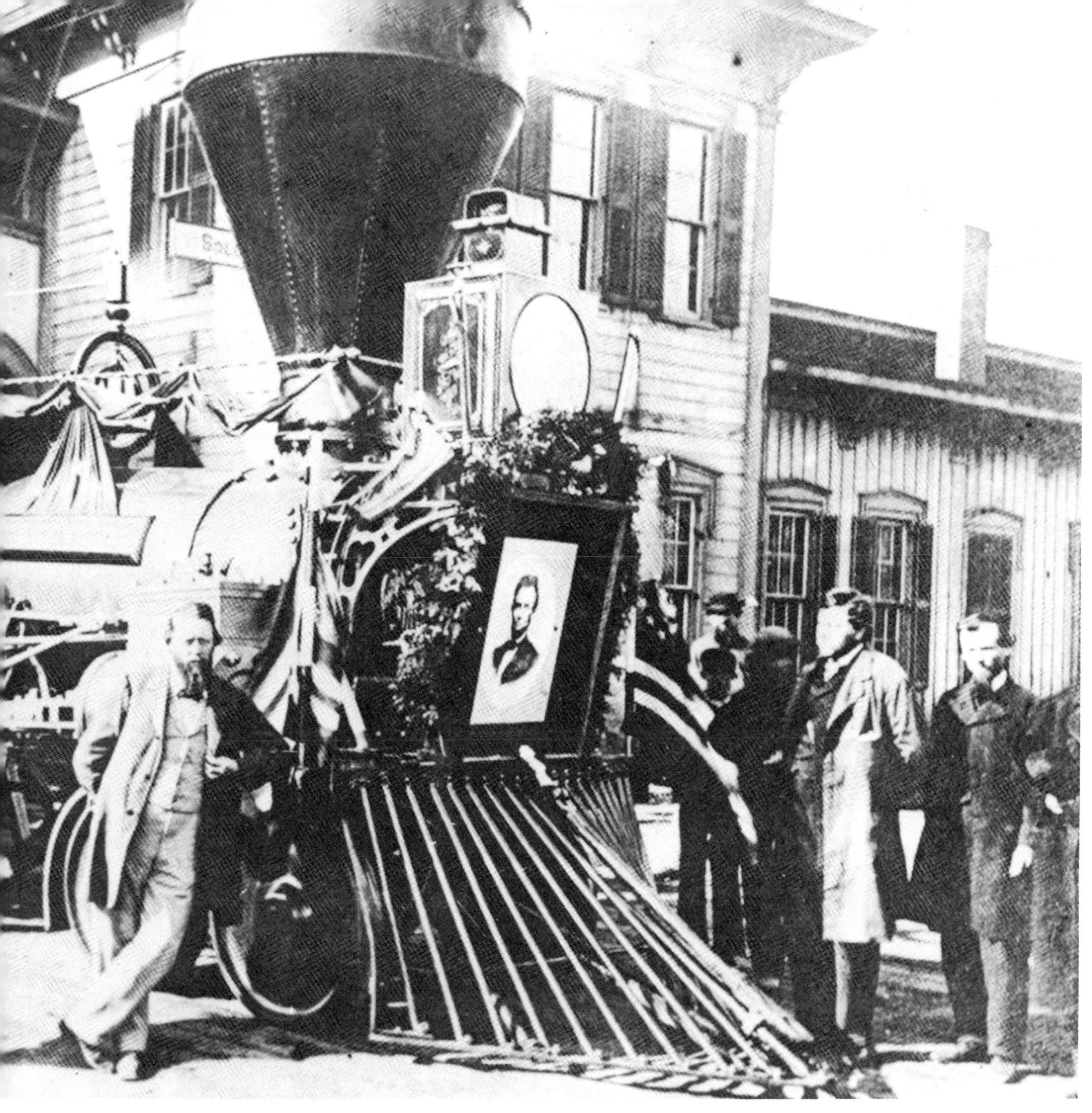

its cowcatcher, is one of many that took part in the long funeral trip back to Illinois.

they in turn organized a tremendous undertaking of their own. But, alas, Friday dawned cold and rainy. Whereas it had only been sprinkling in Washington, it was pouring in Baltimore. Still the people gathered in closely packed masses along the procession route during the two hours that the funeral train was traveling toward them at twenty miles an hour. Just before ten o'clock the train arrived. As in Washington, minute guns boomed, church and fire-house bells tolled. The schedule gave Baltimore a scant four hours. The coffin was removed by its Veteran Corps sergeants and brought out into the streets jammed with people, among whom small boys were elbowing their way, doing a brisk business in selling crape and photographs of Lincoln. People seemed to have small change available even though they had been warned to leave their watches and money at home—there would be an army of pickpockets. Now the coffin was placed in what Baltimore newspapers described as the most beautiful hearse ever constructed. The frame was of genuine rosewood, gilded, and the back and two sides were of French plate glass three quarters of an inch thick. The thing that Baltimore was most proud of was a new invention. The coffin did not just rest on a hard, unresponsive black platform, it rested on patented elliptic springs, allowing the body to ride with astounding smoothness—not one annoying jolt. The procession of military and civic representations was so enormous that it took three hours to get to the Merchants' Exchange where the coffin was opened for viewing. Ten thousand people looked on Lincoln's face but many thousands more were disappointed, for at two o'clock sharp—there was no arguing—Lincoln had to go.

It was as if the funeral committee had sworn an oath to heaven never to fall a minute behind in their iron-bound cross-country schedule. There was no one to intercede for the long lines of schoolchildren standing patiently in the rain—all the schools had been closed—and they had to be content with a glimpse of the four sleek black horses and, behind glass, the smooth-riding coffin.

THUNDER AND LIGHTNING IN HARRISBURG

At every town along the way from Baltimore to Harrisburg that afternoon entire populations were waiting alongside the tracks of the Northern Central Railway, the second of twelve lines to be used. Babies were held up to see the black "choo-choo" train, old and sick people were carried to the stations and sat in chairs. Governor Andrew Curtin of Pennsylvania and his staff had boarded the train at the state line, and this became the custom of governors—to ride with the train through their states. Only at the station at York the engine made a stop. General Townsend had had an urgent request from the ladies of that town and he graciously allowed six of them to enter the funeral car and place a three-foot-wide cartwheel of red, white, and blue flowers on Lincoln's coffin. On the train the superintendent of the Railway Telegraph had in his pocket something unheard of—a "pocket" telegraph. He could be in touch with the authorities in Washington, in case Stanton had any new orders about the trip, or with the poor frustrated city fathers in Harrisburg who were beginning to realize that the big mourning pageant they were preparing so frantically was going to be ruined by rain. For now the heavens really opened and there was a deluge. By the time Harrisburg was reached, a little after 8:00 P.M., violent thunderstorms had developed and the big procession had to be given up. Despite the rain, the crowd at the station was packed so tight that people thought they would suffocate. The Veteran Corps sergeants removed the body to the hearse, which had been constructed by the city at frenzied speed. It was drawn by four white horses, already something less than white. Jagged streaks of lightning flashing across the dark sky and claps of thunder heightened the effect of the church and fire-house bells tolling and the boom of the cannons, as the crowds and the military accompanied the hearse to the House of Representatives in the State Capitol. There was a new invention in Harrisburg too—the streets were lighted by special "chemical" lights, and their yellow glow punctuated every so often by the white flashes of lightning allowed the people really to see the gorgeous hearse, with its white satin streamers and rosettes and silver stars, as it passed by.

In the House of Representatives a catafalque was waiting. The upholsterer who had erected it had had quite a challenge disguising certain pieces of furniture in the room. He had taken yards of black cloth and draped it in tasteful folds from the head of the catafalque's dais over the clerk's desk so that the desk

Here, flanking the funeral train which stands in the Harrisburg station, are Admiral Charles Davis who represented the Navy on the trip West and General Edward D. Townsend who represented the Army.

Harrisburg's House of Representatives (fluted black cloth disguising the clerk's desk and the speaker's stand) awaits the arrival of the coffin.

At Lancaster, Pennsylvania, ex-President James Buchanan was there at the depot to watch the funeral train pass.

was invisible. Then a second mound of black swept up behind the first one and concealed the speaker's stand. In the tapestry behind the two mounds was a splendid portrait of Lincoln.

Harrisburg was not going to be caught the way Baltimore was, with its citizens miserable because such a small percentage had been able to view. Now, with the permission of General Townsend and Admiral Davis, the coffin was opened at 9:30 P.M. and thousands passed it in a double line that separated, then joined again and exited, until midnight. Promptly at eight o'clock the next morning the long waiting lines were admitted again, for the funeral train had to leave the city at eleven. Before the doors were opened the undertaker had re-chalked Lincoln's face to try to hide the growing discoloration. Also, the body literally had to be dusted—the coffin being opened and exposed so often that the face and hair and close-cut beard seemed to attract particles out of the air, particles that must have been breathed down upon the dead President in the many sighs of the mourners.

In the morning—Saturday, April twenty-second—it was still raining, but Harrisburg was going to have its procession, rain or no. By 8:30 A.M. the church and firebells were tolling and minute guns were being fired. At ten o'clock forty thousand people were on the streets to watch the four horses, washed white as snow during the night, pull the hearse from the Capitol to the depot. To see Lincoln off were volunteers with arms reversed, drummers beating out the dead march on their muffled drums, cavalry with horses reined in so they would not prance too much, clergy on foot, the Governor and other authorities, fire companies, Knights Templar, and, as in every funeral procession, completely separated from each other as the orders of the day called for—"White citizens on foot—Colored citizens on foot."

At quarter past eleven the funeral train pulled out of the Pennsylvania Railroad depot on its way to Philadelphia. Over the countryside, through towns, past cities, it headed east. Not a third of the way to Philadelphia, the train moved slowly through Lancaster where there was an enormous crowd at the depot and a huge sign: ABRAHAM LINCOLN, THE ILLUSTRIOUS MARTYR OF LIBERTY, THE NATION MOURNS HIS LOSS. THOUGH DEAD, HE STILL LIVES. Ex-President Buchanan was in his buggy at the depot—Buchanan, who in the months before Lincoln's inauguration had allowed the Southern states to steal government arms from its forts and to prepare for war while the President-elect sat helplessly from November to March in his Western hometown.

Just before the train pulled into Lancaster it had to pass through a tunnel and just inside the tunnel stood old Thaddeus Stevens, the stormy, relentless, clubfooted congressman who had been such a harsh irritant—pushing Lincoln, pushing him to emancipate the slaves before the President felt the time was right for it, and after the Emancipation Proclamation pushing him to give the freed men suffrage, and then at the war's end, to be sterner with the South. On the afternoon of April 14, just before Lincoln left for Ford's Theatre, Thaddeus Stevens and Ben Wade, the Ohio abolitionist, had come to the White House and threatened Lincoln that if he didn't go along with their ideas on reconstruction, there might be such a thing as impeachment for him.

Now, as the car bearing the coffin passed Stevens, he took off his hat for a second and then replaced it.

Stevens would spend every ounce of energy left in his body fighting President Johnson who, on thinking it over, would not begin by punishing treason but would try to carry out Lincoln's merciful plans to heal the wounds of the war and reunite the country. And when Johnson thwarted his plans to subjugate the South, Stevens would lead the fight to impeach Johnson. And when Stevens lost that fight he would also lose his life. Drained of his fierce energy, he died on August 11, 1868, and lay in state in the rotunda of the Capitol just where Lincoln had lain. He was buried in a small Lancaster graveyard with these words, which he had written himself, on his stone:

> *I repose in this quiet and secluded spot, not for any preference for solitude, but finding other cemeteries limited by charter rules as to race, I have chosen this, that I might illustrate in my death the principles which I advocated through a long life—"Equality of man before his creator."*

At the entrance of the Lancaster tunnel old Thaddeus Stevens, who had been a continual thorn in Lincoln's side, took off his hat for a second as the car bearing the coffin passed.

Three years later Thaddeus Stevens lay in state in the Capitol's rotunda just where Lincoln had lain, beneath a statue of his old adversary which was temporarily on exhibit there.

BEDLAM AND VIOLENCE IN PHILADELPHIA

Philadelphia's elaborate hearse (below) sits in front of shop of the undertaker who designed it before being taken to meet the funeral train at the station (above).

Something new was added to the viewing of Lincoln in Philadelphia. For the first time there was real violence and people actually got hurt in the frantic crush to push inside Independence Hall where the lying-in-state took place. The trip into Philadelphia had been orderly. The population of every town along the way was out beside the tracks to stand in silence, or kneel, as many did, as the train passed. All the shops were closed and the plows stood deserted in their furrows or, if a mile away, a solitary farmer was at work behind his plow, horse and plow were now halted, and the tiny distant figure knelt. For miles before the Philadelphia station was reached there were no gaps in the crowd—just solid lines. The train arrived at Broad Street Station a little after four-thirty in the afternoon—a good two hours ahead of time by the official schedule—but then the careful organization of Philadelphia's town fathers began to go to pieces and it was almost six-thirty before the coffin was put on the hearse and the immense procession that had been planned got under way. The hearse, a marvel of black cloth and silver fringes and tassels, was the first of the funeral cars to have white plumes as well as black. Three big white feathers nodded at the top center of the canopy as eight black horses—the largest number of horses yet—hauled Lincoln toward Independence Square. Afterward Philadelphians claimed that theirs was the most gigantic, the most impressive procession of any in all the cities. Eleven divisions marched to the inevitable booming of cannons, tolling of bells, firing of minute guns, roll of muffled drums and slow dirges. At the square, when the Old State House was passed, a

At left the 9th Union League Regiment lines up waiting for the hearse which is shown above being drawn up jam-packed Broad Street.

large transparency was uncovered—a picture of Lincoln with a background of a huge coffin, spectacularly lighted by gas jets which formed letters that spelled out HE STILL LIVES. A band high up in the steeple of the State House played dirges, and Independence Square was lighted by sixty red, white, and blue calcium lights which turned people's faces the color they were closest to. The coffin was placed in the East Wing of Independence Hall where the Declaration of Independence had been signed, not many yards from the old Liberty Bell against which had been propped a big anchor of flowers. The viewing that night was by invitation only, handpicked people admitted by cards from the Mayor. These special guests were stopped at 1:00 A.M. and as they departed they passed the long lines of the general public which were already forming to be admitted at 5:00 A.M. Sunday morning. By daylight the lines reached west as far as the Schuylkill River and east as far as the Delaware, and the Camden ferry boats were landing huge loads of would-be viewers from New Jersey. Most people arrived in the line exhausted because the city interpreted literally that man and beast should rest on the Sabbath and therefore no horsecars were running. Understandably, on Sunday morning Philadelphia was keyed up, on edge, at fever pitch. When pickpockets began to terrorize a portion of the line, it suddenly surged into a mob, far out beyond its guiding ropes. Then the ropes were cut—by "villains," the newspapers explained—and bedlam broke out. People who had been almost up to the entrance windows were sent back by the police to the end of the three-mile-long double lines, to begin all over again the wait of five, six or seven hours. Now the crowd was completely out of control as the police fought to keep order. Bonnets were pulled off women's heads, hairpins scattered in every direction, women's hair fell down to their waists, whole dresses were ripped off, there were screams and shrieks and every few minutes a female fainted and had to be extricated from the spot and passed along over people's heads. Crushed hoops and crinolines littered the Square. One young lady had her arm broken, and word got out that two little boys were dead, but they were finally revived. The police must have known what the emotions of the Philadelphia viewers would be because, unlike the arrangements in other cities where viewers could get right up next to the coffin and stop a second for a really close look at Lincoln's face, here a strong balustrade had been built on each side of the coffin to prevent the crowds from obtaining too close a view—the closer people got to Lincoln's face, the more inflamed their passions became. In line with this the police would not let the viewers stop for even a second at the coffin. Even so, people had to be prevented from trying to touch Lincoln's face and in many instances actually trying with a sort of insane desperation to kiss the forehead and the gaunt cheeks. When it was all over at 1:00 A.M. Monday morning, Philadelphia claimed that three hundred thousand people had looked on Lincoln, many of whom must have remembered his words at Independence Hall on Washington's Birthday, 1861, on his trip east to be inaugurated. Explaining how his political feelings all sprang from the Declaration of Independence and that he felt that the promise of equal chance for all men that the Declaration put forth was the binding principle behind the Confederacy, he had then said ". . . But if this country cannot be saved without giving up that principle . . . I would rather be assassinated on the spot than surrender it."

The people of Philadelphia remembered Lincoln best from Washington's Birthday, 1861, when, on his trip east to be inaugurated, he had spoken to them at Independence Hall. In the large picture at the right Lincoln is shown just before that speech in the left-hand corner of the flag-draped platform. The enlargement of a portion of this same picture (above) shows the President-elect just coming onto the speaker's stand, taking off his hat to the crowd.

NEW YORK GETS TWO DAYS TO EXHIBIT ITS GRIEF

Lincoln's coffin was removed from the railroad car at Jersey City and taken across the Hudson to New York City by ferry. Here in this woodcut a second ferry follows with Willie and the funeral car.

In the mammoth procession that New York City put on for Abraham Lincoln, Brooklyn, which had a rivalry going with her neighbor, was given the tail position to walk in. Then on top of that Brooklyn was told that there would be an extension of the tail, for Negroes were going to be allowed to march too. Five thousand had planned to walk, but a command had come from the Tammany-controlled City Council, "No Negroes marching!"—and "Positively no black people in our procession." The Negroes were indignant. They felt if a horse of the President's could follow immediately behind the hearse in Washington, the race he had freed could march and honor him in New York. They felt particularly ashamed and deserted, with their best friend gone.

Finally a telegram arrived from Washington "It is the desire of the Secretary of War," it said, "that no discrimination respecting color should be exercised in admitting persons to the funeral procession tomorrow. In this city a black regiment formed part of the escort." The City Council gave in, but now it was too late to get the five thousand. Too many of them had been intimidated. But Police Superintendent John Kennedy, who had been fighting for colored people to be allowed on the New York horse coaches, was determined the Negroes should march and be protected. About three hundred of them finally did, with two platoons of police preceding them and two more following, but whenever the Negro marchers, carrying their big motto TWO MILLION OF BONDSMEN HE LIBERTY GAVE, came in sight the only applause of the day broke forth—the crowds cheered and waved handkerchiefs. Grief equalizes all, their presence seemed to cry. But the Negro marchers' dream of following their Emancipator's funeral car was only a dream, for by the time they started to walk at the tail end of the huge procession, the coffin at the head of the line had not only left New York but was a good way up the Hudson. In fact West Point cadets were saluting the funeral train by that time.

For New York City the ceremonies had begun the day before. Covering itself in black so that it became a city transformed, hardly recognizable, New York waited as the funeral train slowly made its way from Philadelphia through the early morning darkness of Monday, April the twenty-fourth. At dawn the train stopped in the Trenton station for about half an hour. Trenton as a city was very hurt because it was the only state capital on the entire funeral route where Lincoln was not lifted off the train and a funeral service held in an imposing building. However, it was observed by a guest on the train, looking out of his window at the Trenton citizens, that "it did not occur to the male part of the throng that a general lifting of the hat would have been a silent but becoming mark of respect to the dead." Far different, he observed, at Newark, a city of eighty thousand inhabitants, where every man removed his hat and the feeling was so deep that women, too, took off their bonnets out of respect.

The train arrived in Jersey City at 10:00 A.M. Since

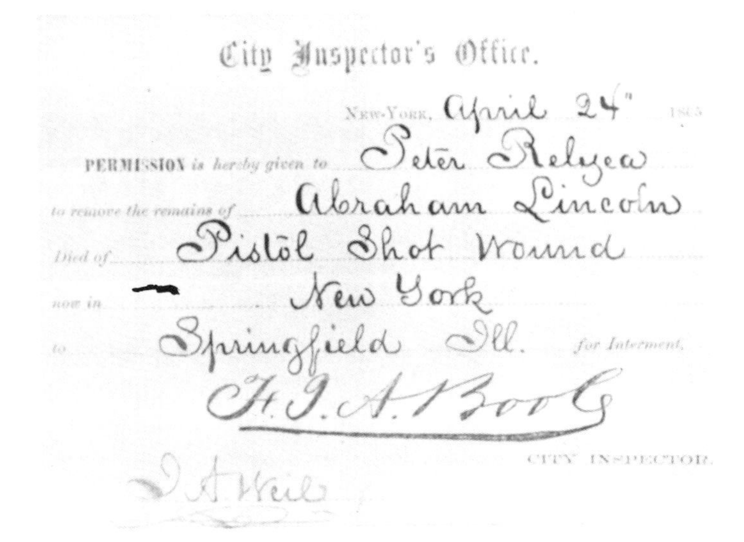

City Inspector's Office.

New-York, April 24" 1865

PERMISSION is hereby given to Peter Relyea

to remove the remains of Abraham Lincoln

Died of Pistol Shot Wound

now in New York

to Springfield Ill. for Interment.

F. I. A. Boole

CITY INSPECTOR.

I. A. Weil

The drawing at left shows the start of the procession from the Desbrosses Street ferry landing to City Hall. The Seventh Regiment forms a hollow square around the small hearse that bears the coffin. Above is the New York permit which was necessary to remove the remains of Abraham Lincoln, dead of "pistol shot wound." Below is the glorious hearse to be used in the grand funeral procession the following day. It had been designed and constructed by Peter Relyea, the official undertaker of the city of New York, who had labored day and night over his work of art. Here Relyea in high hat stands at the right of his creation.

Down Broadway toward City Hall where
the viewing will take place,
the small first-day hearse is hauled past silent crowds.

Along the route of the funeral

early morning there had been crowds outside the depot, but only special ladies and their escorts were admitted to take their places in a gallery which ran around the inside of the depot. Very much in view was the depot's large clock, its hands not at 10:00 A.M. but fixed instead at 7:22—the moment of Lincoln's death.

Suddenly there was a clanging bell and the pilot train arrived, then the nine cars of the funeral train slid in silently and everyone for a mile around jumped as a German singing group—the Liederkrantz Society of seventy-five voices from Hoboken—thundered forth with an appropriate dirge—"Integer Vitae." New York had been building a magnificently glorious hearse for the procession the next day but it would have been risky to bring it with its easily wind-borne plumes and its fragile Temple of Liberty pinnacle across the Hudson. Very sensibly the coffin was transferred to a small, rather subdued hearse and carried across the river by ferry. A second ferry took the train's funeral car, with Willie in it, and a third took the big car that carried the official

procession New Yorkers darken rooftops and invade trees. Good window positions sold for up to one hundred dollars a person.

escort which journeyed straight through to Springfield. Here in New York a new engine, a new pilot engine and seven new cars, as was customary, would be supplied by the new line officiating, the Hudson River Railroad.

New York's shoreline forest of masts was thin today—there had been a favorable wind the day before and many ships had gone to sea or headed up the coast—but what ships were out in the river as the ferries passed lined up their crews and tolled their bells. Many sailors watched from high up in the rigging, indistinct dark specks against the brilliantly sunny April sky. As the first ferry drew in to the wharf at the foot of Desbrosses Street, a big crowd was waiting with the most prominent feature, New York's crack Seventh Regiment, wearing the same gray uniforms in which they had answered Lincoln's first call to protect the Capitol in '61, to escort him now to New York's City Hall. Along the way the chimes of Trinity Church rang out over and over "Praise God from Whom all blessings flow," and mingled with the chimes were the powerful voices of the bearded

THE NATION MOURNS.

Germans, now rendering the Pilgrims' Chorus from *Tannhaüser*. The Seventh marched with such curious exactness that they seemed like mechanical toy soldiers. Their rhythm almost hypnotized the crowds so that after the hearse had passed they kept on standing in their positions, motionless. The park outside City Hall was bursting its iron fence, its trees bent down like bushes with enormous berries on them—the adventurous small sons of the poor. The sons of the rich stood patiently in line, holding their mamas' hands. The lines stretched more than a mile uptown beyond the Bowery and way down Pearl Street. In all, more than twenty thousand people were in view.

The coffin was now carried into the building and up the twenty-two right-hand steps of a circular staircase under the rotunda. Here it was set down on a black velvet-covered dais which was tipped up at the head so that those coming up the twenty-two steps could see Lincoln's face all the way. The dais was in the doorway leading to the Governor's Room. Cutting off the bright light from the top of the rotunda was a specially constructed black-cloth ceiling which made the whole scene exceedingly dim. So dim that four chandeliers above the dais had had to have their gas jets turned on, throwing a ghastly green light over the room.

Lincoln had been shaken up during this last trip and the embalmer and undertaker needed half an hour for

Lincoln's coffin has just been carried up the steps of City Hall between throngs of waiting viewers to the dais which stands ready inside.

THE ONLY PHOTOGRAPH OF LINCOLN IN DEATH

This is the only known photograph of Lincoln in death. It was taken by New York photographer Jeremiah Gurney, Jr., as the body lay in state at the top of a circular staircase under the rotunda. To capture the funeral scene with Admiral Davis and General Townsend at either end of the coffin, Gurney focused down from a high alcove on the other side of the rotunda. The picture at the right is a detail of the over-all scene. Gurney planned to have his historic photograph on sale within a few days, but, on hearing a picture had been taken, outraged Secretary Stanton issued orders to break all the plates. Telegrams went repeatedly from New York to Washington pleading that the picture be allowed to be preserved, but Stanton remained adamant. Finally the plates were broken, but General Dix, in charge of the military in New York, had already sent Stanton a single print to show him how unobjectionable it was. Twenty-two years later Stanton's son, Lewis, found it among his father's papers and sent it to Nicolay with the suggestion that he and Hay might want to use it in their ten-volume life of Lincoln. Instead, it was laid away in the Nicolay papers, which eventually went to the Illinois State Historical Library. The picture did not come to light until 1952 when a fifteen-year-old boy, who was such an avid student of Lincoln that he had been granted the use of the Hay and Nicolay papers, stumbled upon it.

Spurious photographs of Lincoln in death

Each one of the photographs shown here has been claimed in recent years to be Lincoln in death. It was the custom of the times to take such pictures—many photographers advertised that recording the dead was their specialty. Each of these pictures, handed down in families from generation to generation, have histories behind them which at the very least convinced their owners that they were the real thing.

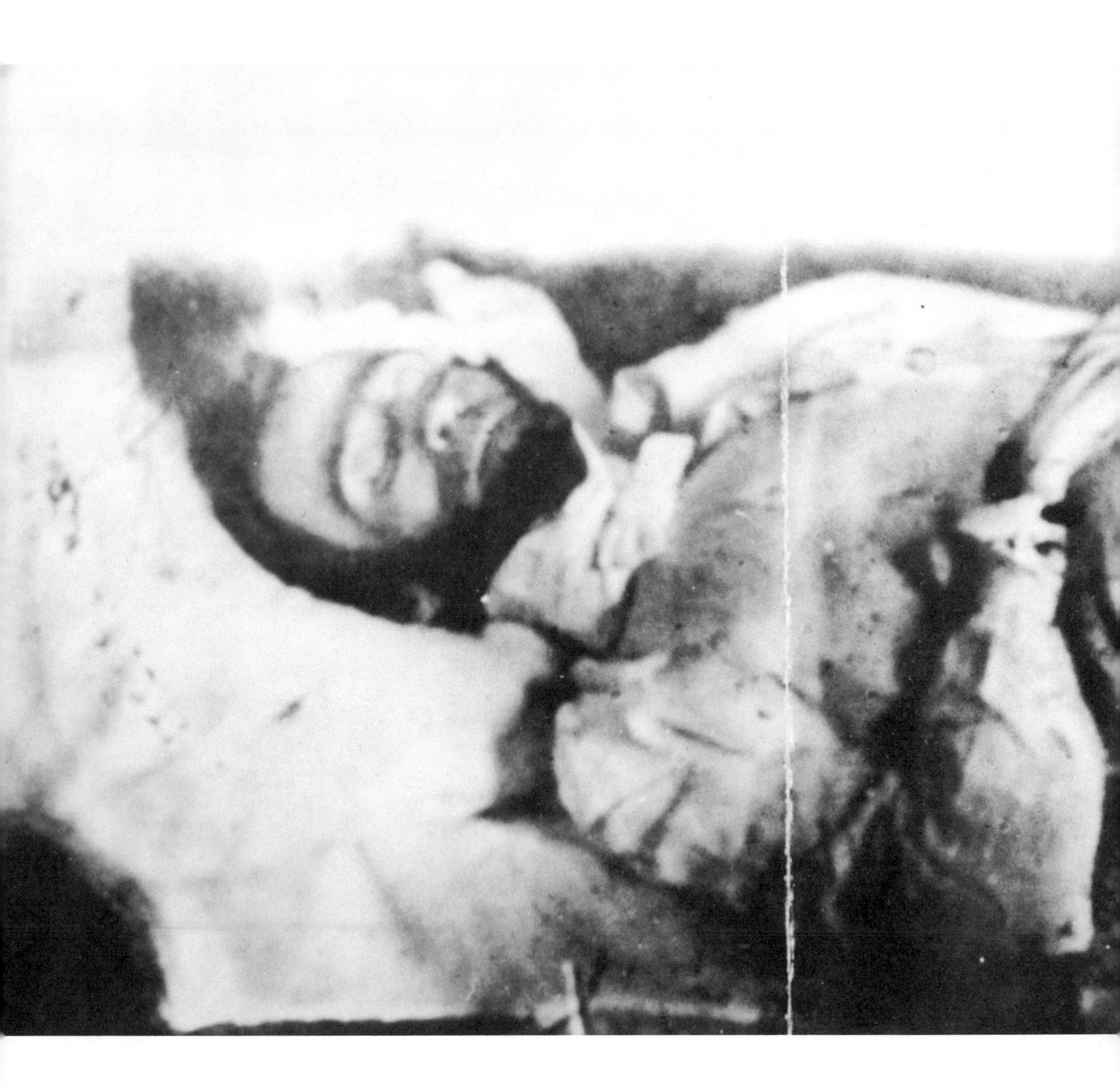

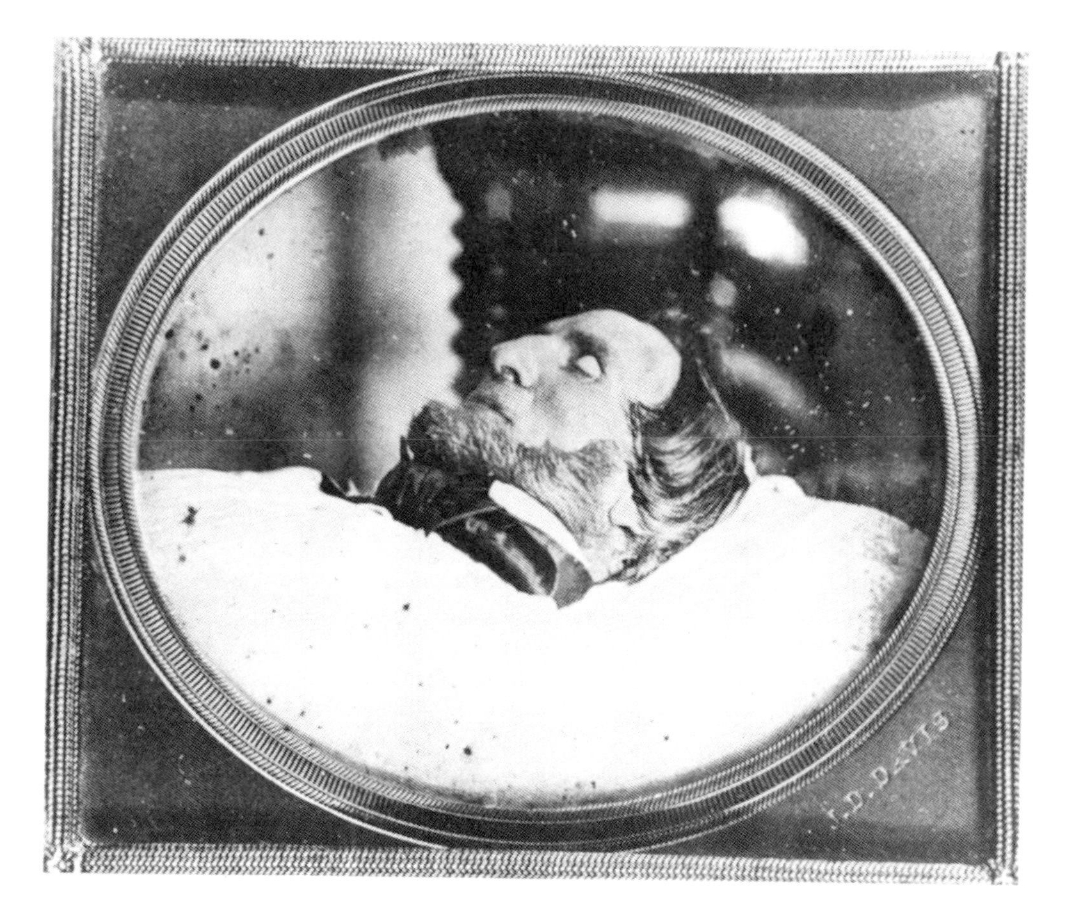

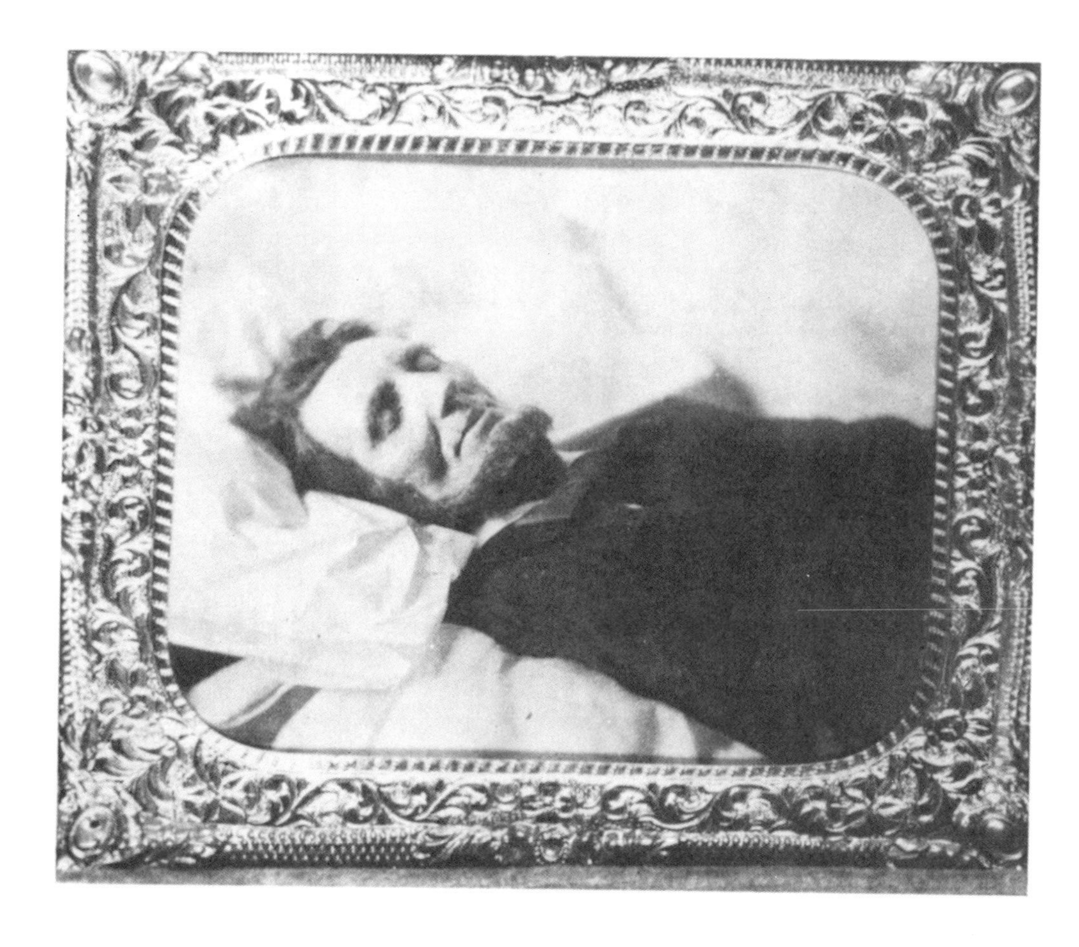

dusting, adjusting, and re-dressing him in a clean collar and shirt. Then a privileged few were allowed to place flowers on the coffin. Among them was a mother with her eight-year-old son who laid two initials, A.L., made of white flowers, up near the opening where Lincoln's breast showed. The mother then handed out slips of paper to the reporters present, saying that her son's name was Master George Washington Irving Wellington Bishop and would they please print his full name in the papers. So, by a quirk of fate, this freakish family offering appears before our very eyes today, for now, before the public was admitted, Jeremiah Gurney Jr., photographer, was granted exclusive rights to take pictures of the noble dead. Of the many long exposures made in the frustratingly inadequate light only one exists today—the only known photographic record of Lincoln in death. And there, as plain today as they were then, are little Master Bishop's flower letters—A.L. (*see* page 162).

Sometime after 1 P.M. the public was admitted. Immediately it became obvious how poor the viewing arrangements here really were. The people had to come in through the basement, walk like moles through dark halls, feel their way up narrow stairs, and then two by two approach and mount the right-hand circular twenty-two stairs. On and on the crowds came to see that unbearably sad sight. There were more than half a million people out there in the streets and the lines were only passing the coffin at eighty persons a minute. Outside there was some muttering that Mayor C. Godfrey Gunther had made this foolish plan on purpose. Boys in the trees in the park began whistling and yelling back and forth. Irresponsible groups charged the legitimate lines and police scattered a couple of thousand people, hitting them freeely, and as everyone thought, unnecessarily cruelly on their heads with their clubs. But there was no dangerous or vicious rioting as there had been in Philadelphia. The throngs that waited through the night, surging toward the tiny, inadequate opening that had been provided for the viewing, were irritable and pathetically disappointed but they still let themselves be directed like sheep by the police. Many of the women who did get in tried, as in Philadelphia, to kiss Lincoln's face and were immediately jerked back. Some just kept their hands covered with their shawls and at the right moment their fingers stole out and gave a quick touch. Police Superintendent John Kennedy was there with his official cane, pointing out viewers who were getting away with anything. One policeman especially had an exhausting time—as each woman walked along beside the coffin with her eyes drawn backward irresistibly to Lincoln's face, she did not see the first isolated step down on the right-hand side and invariably stumbled into the officer's arms.

On the morning of Tuesday, April twenty-fifth, the

In New York's gigantic funeral procession Lincoln's coffin was borne uptown by Peter Relyea's huge and elaborately decorated hearse, which was drawn by sixteen horses.

lines of now almost hopeless people were longer, if anything, than the day before. One thing only occurred to break the boredom of the wait—someone threw a lighted cigar at the black festoon just under the huge banner proclaiming "THE NATION MOURNS," flames rose high for a moment, but a brave officer climbed up and tore down the mass of burning material and others stamped out the fire on the stone steps.

Inside, in the Mayor's Room, a Captain Parker Snow had arrived and was talking earnestly with General Dix. Snow was an explorer with both arctic and antarctic experience and he had two relics he would like to have placed in the coffin, to be buried with Lincoln. The first was a fragment of a page from a prayer book on which the only word that could be read was "Martyr." It had been found, he said, under the skeleton of one of Sir John Franklin's men, lost in that explorer's unsuccessful expedition. The second was a minute scrap of material that could have come from a uniform, presumably worn by the skeleton. General Dix humored Snow by dropping his offerings in beside the body, undoubtedly knowing very well that they would soon be swept out in one of the undertaker's frequent and thorough coffin cleanings.

Now it was Peter Relyea's moment of glory. Peter Relyea was the official undertaker of the city of New York. He had been issued a permit to transport Abraham Lincoln—dead of "pistol shot wound"—through New York on his way to Springfield, Illinois. For three days, right out on the streets at the junction of East Broadway and Grand Street, Relyea had been building the elaborate New York funeral car before marveling crowds. He had been living with it, sleeping there with it, and up to the last available second adding one more flag or plume or silver star. Now a little before one o'clock in the afternoon Relyea led his glorious catafalque into the park enclosure in front of City Hall, and walking in front of the sixteen gray horses, he turned the hearse car entirely around so that it would face west and be ready to set forth for the procession up Broadway. The Relyea work of art just about paralyzed all beholders with its magnificence. Its platform was huge—fourteen feet long and almost seven feet wide. Up on the roof of the canopy was a gold and white temple of Liberty with a half-masted small flag fluttering from its dome, a fitting crown to the twelve big craped national flags that rose in clumps of three from each column. Up inside the canopy was white fluted satin that matched the inside trimmings of the coffin, and hanging down from the satin, so that it would dangle straight over the coffin, was a glittering gilt eagle, wings spread, craped, of course, so it could not glitter too brightly and by

The procession approaches Union Square, where the ceremonies took place. At the left of the picture, in the second-story window of their grandfather's house, are six-and-a-half-year-old Theodore Roosevelt and his brother, Elliott.

any possibility strike a cheerful note. Absolutely nothing could be seen of the sixteen horses except the very lower portion of their legs, the tips of their noses, and their long gray tails. Each was wearing a combination blanket-dress with a sort of black snood that rose up over its head. Each pair was led by a Negro groom in high silk hat.

At two o'clock, with Lincoln aboard the Relyea creation, the procession began to move. And what a triumphal procession it was! Led by a squad of mounted police who made sure the street was clear ahead, it started off with a hundred dragoons with black and white plumes and red, yellow, and blue facings on their uniforms. Then generals and their staffs, and following them the rich coffin on its rich catafalque. There were eleven thousand of the military marching. There were Irishmen, and small Irish children, marching in bright green, but with black rosettes in their left lapels, and Zouaves with baggy red trousers, but with black ribbons on their chests. The resplendent, parrot-colored representatives of foreign nations rode along in their carriages, each with an armband or a craped sword. There were eight divisions of civilians. One was made up of trades—cigar makers, caulkers, waiters, drygoods clerks, sheet-iron workers, plumbers, painters, tailors, carpenters. There was the division containing medical men, lawyers, members of the press, the Century Club, the Union League Club. The fourth division was made up almost entirely of Masons and other lodges and the eighth division was civic societies from Brooklyn. Then finally, at the end, the three hundred well-guarded Negroes.

The procession took three hours and forty-eight minutes to pass each point on its route. It went up Broadway to Fourteenth Street, over to Fifth Avenue, up Fifth to Thirty-fourth Street, and across Thirty-fourth to Ninth Avenue to the Hudson River Railroad Depot. Single positions in windows along Broadway rented from fifty dollars to one hundred dollars for the afternoon. At Chambers Street a shaggy St. Bernard dog loped out from the crowd and walked along with the hearse car, immediately under the canopy. A whisper spread about, started by his master, that dog and master had recently paid a visit to Lincoln in the White House and the President had patted the dog kindly on its head. Could the dog have known whom he trotted along beside in the shadow of the great catafalque?

So it was with New York. All through the afternoon church and firebells tolled, one hundred bands wailed, minute guns boomed, muffled drums beat out their monotonous, spine-chilling message, and there was no other sound in the great city except the crunch and rattle of the gun carriages and the shuffle of human feet and the clippity-clop of horses' meticulously blacked hoofs.

In New York's farewell eleven thousand of the military marched along with seventy-five thousand just plain people.

ALBANY POSTPONES ITS TRAVELING MENAGERIE

It was a little after 4 P.M. on the afternoon of Tuesday, April twenty-fifth, when the "Union," the same engine that had brought Lincoln over these tracks four years ago on the run from Albany to New York, now tolled its bell as it started on the reverse trip. In a few moments the only unpleasant sights of the trip were passed—the abattoirs and pigsties and garbage dumps that infested the dockside area of New York. But a mile or two out of the shabby old Hudson River Railroad Depot the train broke into open country and from there until Albany was reached at eleven o'clock that night the scenery along the great Hudson River was majestically beautiful.

The route of the train passed through a succession of small towns and now the twenty-mile-an-hour rate of speed seemed too fast, for each town had gone to enormous trouble to work up a tableau and inscribe a motto or build an arch, or do all three. Where there was no station but just a road crossing, there was often a minister with his parishioners, all kneeling, singing a hymn. At Yonkers the people were lined up and the men raised their hats. At Tarrytown there was a tableau—young girls in white with wide black sashes—the effect was chaste and mournful. At Sing Sing guns were fired and an arch of black velvet and evergreens reached across the tracks. At Peekskill the train stopped and a band played a dirge while guns fired. At Garrison, across from West Point, all the uniformed cadets had come across the river with their band and now silently they walked through the funeral car, past the coffin. At the Academy guns were fired and

With black dripping from its building fronts Albany awaits the arrival of the funeral train.

all eyes looked across the water at the sunset—a red fireball sinking, leaving a sky so brilliant with color that eyes used to acres of funeral black were stabbed by the glory. Now they were passing through the little towns where Willie Lincoln had so delighted his father on the trip east by knowing the exact scheduled moment of every stop and departure. It was during the Empire State run in 1861 that, in a small village, Lincoln had called for the little girl who had written to suggest that he grow whiskers. "I have a little correspondent in this town," he had said, and small Grace Bedell came out of the crowd and along the platform of the train. "See, I grew these whiskers for you, Grace," Mr. Lincoln said. Now in 1865 Grace was keeping his letter that began "My dear little Miss . . ." and though some snowflakes had gotten on it the day she opened it outside the post office and though a candy in her pocket melted next to it, this was her treasure—especially now, because of what had happened. At Poughkeepsie the train made quite a stop—the whole hilltop was black with people, guns were fired and church and firebells tolled. Old Matthew Vassar had cut blossoms from his magnolia tree as an offering, and they were placed in the compartment where the coffin was. Four years earlier, at sixty-nine, Mr. Vassar had given his life savings, four hundred thousand dollars, to found in Poughkeepsie a college for females that would give them as good an education as was offered to males at Harvard or Yale.

It was eight-ten when the train left, and the stars were suddenly visible, pricking through all over the darkening sky. The rest of the way it was torches and bonfires at every town. Then, at eleven, the train arrived in East Albany. The coffin was moved to the State House, and all through the night the citizens of Albany and the neighboring countryside passed by it.

The next day there was another procession but this time the three hundred people accompanying the train, except for a portion of the military, went straight to the two hotels in which the City of Albany had agreed to put them up for the night. They were worn out emotionally from such a concentrated, never-ending mourning ceremony, and there were six more funerals ahead of them. That night State Senator Andrew Dickson White, the future president of Cornell, walked by Lincoln's coffin and thought again what he had first thought when he met the President at the White House—that this was the saddest face he had ever seen. But that first time the sadness had vanished magically when someone in the East Room, where he was receiving, had said something to Lincoln that struck a spark and then his whole countenance had lighted from within. There was something thrilling about the change, and the way the eyes that had been dull as he shook hands had suddenly shone with a curious compelling radiance. But now, thought White, there was only that same first look of "quiet melancholy."

At noon on Wednesday, the twenty-sixth, Albany's grand parade got under way with a specially built catafalque, the marchers, the bands, the tolling bells. Today Lincoln was drawn by six white horses. Another very different kind of procession had been advertised for the twenty-sixth. Van Amburgh's great traveling menagerie was in town and everyone knew there was a "splendid giraffe, two sloth bears from Hindustan, an enormous grisly bear, a fine royal Bengal tiger, lions, leopards, a spotted axis deer, and a large black ostrich." Van Amburgh quickly proclaimed, "There will be no exhibition given until the President's remains have left the city, and the grand parade announced for this morning will be postponed until tomorrow." Then lest anyone be offended at the rapid following of the first procession by the second, "There is no circus attached to this menagerie which is purely a geological (sic!) exhibition." Then to make sure, "This is a great moral exhibition . . ."

Albany was probably the only one of the funeral cities that had the chance to pick up its spirits so rapidly after being drenched in woe. And Albany would not only have the animals but also a piece of news everyone had been waiting for. The morning papers on the twenty-seventh carried a statement by Secretary Stanton that John Wilkes Booth had been tracked down and killed.

PART IV

NO FUNERALS FOR THE ASSASSINS

On the twelfth day after the assassination Booth was finally cornered and killed. Eight conspirators in the crime were tried by a military commission who ruled that three be sentenced to life imprisonment at hard labor, one, to six years, also at hard labor, and the other four to be hanged by the neck until they be dead.

THE ASSASSIN IS TRAPPED IN A BURNING BARN

On the morning after the assassination a posse of two thousand soldiers galloped out of Washington in pursuit of Booth, who had been joined by the conspirator Herold at the Navy Yard Bridge on his wild escape into the Maryland night. On April the twenty-sixth, a detachment of twenty-five soldiers, in the charge of a lieutenant and accompanied by two detectives, finally tracked Booth and Herold down in a tobacco barn at the Garrett farm near Port Royal, Virginia, less than sixty miles from the Capitol. With the barn surrounded, Herold decided he wanted to surrender. He reached his hands out of a crack in the barn door, was manacled, led out and tied to a tree. He began shouting his innocence in a stream of talk and when ten minutes later he was still babbling he was told to shut up or they would gag him. Booth had made up his mind to die before being taken. In the darkness outside, Lieutenant Doherty had made a decision too, to smoke his quarry out by fire, and on his order a soldier made a rope of straw, lit it, and threw it onto a hay pile just inside the building. In a few moments sheets of flame lighted the barn. Silhouetted by the roaring fire Booth stepped closer to the door, peering at the slats as if to find a target outside. Sergeant Boston Corbett, stationed at one of the corners, saw Booth through the slats, a crutch under one arm, trying to hold and aim his carbine with the other. Breaking Stanton's order to bring the assassin back alive, Corbett suddenly, compulsively, fired and the bullet struck Booth in the back of the head, in almost exactly the same place Lincoln had been hit. Booth sagged limply onto the barn floor, soldiers rushed in and he was dragged outside onto the grass, then as the heat from the fire began to roast everyone he was carried further off to the porch of the Garrett house. At first he seemed dead but water was dashed on his face and his lips began to move. "Tell my mother . . ." an officer bending close to Booth's face heard him say, ". . . tell my mother I died for my country, and . . ." now the voice was only a whisper, ". . . I did what I thought was best." He asked that his paralyzed arms be lifted so that he could see his hands, and looking at them he said his last words, "Useless. Useless." Two and a half hours after Corbett's shot was fired, just as the brilliant morning sun was rising, Booth died.

After being shot in the back of the head, the dying Booth is dragged out of the flaming tobacco barn.

A search of his pockets turned up a few sad mementos of the life that had just ended—a compass, an almost burned up candle, a diary, pictures of five women —four actresses and Booth's fiancée Lucy Hale, the daughter of the Senator from New Hampshire. The diary was impounded by Stanton for two years and when it was finally released there were eighteen pages cut out of it. What remained told the story of the dread decision to murder Lincoln, the entry shown on this page. For the first time the world learned of Booth's statement that he had only switched from kidnaping to murder on the very day of his crime.

April 14, Friday, the Ides.—Until today nothing was ever thought of sacrificing to our country's wrongs. For six months we had worked to capture, but our cause being almost lost, something decisive and great must be done. But its failure was owing to others, who did not strike for their country with a heart. I struck boldly, and not as the papers say. I walked with a firm step through a thousand of his friends, was stopped, but pushed on. A colonel was at his side. I shouted Sic semper before I fired. In jumping broke my leg. I passed all his pickets, rode sixty miles that night with the bone of my leg tearing the flesh at every jump. I can never repent it, though we hated to kill. Our country owed all her troubles to him, and God simply made me the instrument of his punishment.

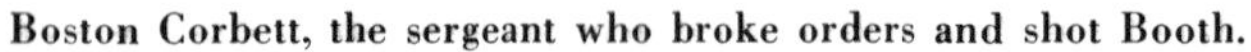
Boston Corbett, the sergeant who broke orders and shot Booth.

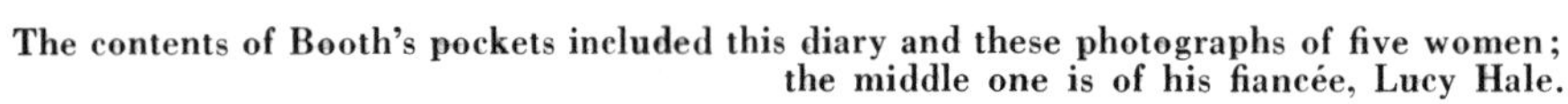
The contents of Booth's pockets included this diary and these photographs of five women; the middle one is of his fiancée, Lucy Hale.

Later entries in the diary told the bitter, desperate story of Booth's last days.

> *After being hunted like a dog through the swamps and woods, and last night being chased by gunboats till I was forced to return, wet, cold and starving, with every man's hand against me, I am here in despair. . . . I have too great a soul to die like a criminal. Oh! May He spare me that and let me die bravely. I bless the entire world. I have never hated or wronged anyone. . . .*

When Booth died on the porch of the Garrett Farm, it was just beginning to be light and in that moment the cocks began to crow. Immediately the dead man

Booth died on the porch of this farmhouse near Port Royal, Virginia.

was sewn up in a saddle blanket with a needle and thread borrowed from the Garrett household. An old Negro with a starved-looking horse and a rickety wagon was told he had to drive the body to Belle Plain on the Virginia shore where a boat was waiting. The trip was slow and the Negro terrified. At one point his hand was covered by the blood which constantly trickled through the blanket, and he wailed that it would never come off, that it was murderer's blood. Herold rode alongside the wagon between two soldiers, his legs tied to his stirrups. Over and over he tried to explain how he had met Booth only by chance and knew nothing of Lincoln's murder.

The dead man and the living conspirator were brought to Alexandria on the steamer, the *John S. Ide,* and then taken by tug to the Washington Navy Yard by its commanding officer, Admiral J. B. Montgomery. When the tug arrived at the Navy Yard, it was 2 A.M. on the morning of April twenty-seventh, and the body and the prisoner were immediately transferred to the ironclad *Montauk.* Booth's body was laid on a carpenter's bench

Below decks on this ironclad warship, the *Saugus*,
half of Booth's accomplices
were held in chains.
Another ship, the *Montauk*, was the temporary prison
for the other conspirators.

Here in this makeshift dungeon in the bowels of the *Montauk* several conspirators were held chained and hooded before being removed to the Old Penitentiary.

The identification of Booth's body and the autopsy is held on the deck of the *Montauk*.

on the deck while, below, Herold joined four other suspected conspirators in rigid manacles and ankle chains with heavy balls attached. During the next day more than ten people who knew Booth well identified him, even though his appearance was greatly changed, his face shriveled and yellow from exposure and starvation, contorted from the suffering he had gone through with his broken leg and disguised by the fact that his mustache had been shaven off and his whole face was now covered with an eleven-day-old beard. On the back of his right hand were the crude initials J.W.B. which as a boy he had put there with india ink—anyone who knew him knew those initials. The dentist who had filled Booth's teeth just a few weeks previously forced open his mouth and identified the fillings. Dr. Barnes, Surgeon General of the United States, who had been in charge of Lincoln's autopsy, now performed an autopsy on Booth, taking from the body some vertebrae to show where the bullet had passed. Dr. John Frederick May, who had also been one of the surgeons at Lincoln's death bed, made one of the conclusive identifications. At first Dr. May said the corpse bore no resemblance to the handsome actor. Then he asked that the dead man be placed in a sitting position to see if, upright, the body reminded him of Booth. It did, but only faintly. May asked that the body be turned over. A few months before, the doctor had operated on the back of Booth's neck to remove a large fibroid tumor. Before the incision had healed, Booth had engaged in a strenuous love scene with the actress Charlotte Cushman, breaking it open and eventually causing an ugly and unmistakable scar. There it was, May pointed out, exactly as he had described it to Barnes. The identification was certain.

After the autopsy the body was left unguarded for a few moments, and the officer in charge returned to find a group of prominent people with Southern sympathies who had managed to get on board, among them a young lady who had just snipped off one of Booth's black locks. As Secretary Stanton had given orders that no relic from Booth's person should be obtained by anyone, the lock of hair was taken by force from the young lady and the Rebel visitors put off the boat.

A big crowd had gathered at the Navy Yard on shore and was straining its eyes to see what was done to dispose of the body. They saw Chief Detective La Fayette C. Baker and his cousin Luther B. Baker lowering the body into a small boat with the help of two sailors who rowed first down the Anacostia River toward the Potomac, turning to the left hand jut of land—Giesboro Point where all the battle-worn, skin and bone old horses were taken to be shot. While the Bakers were still in sight of the people they played with and rattled a big chain and ball they had in the boat with them, pretending they were going to weight the body down and throw it into the river. When their ruse was complete and the people on shore could no longer make out the boat, they had it rowed across the mouth of the Anacostia to the point of land on the other side—Greenleaf Point—on which stood the Old Penitentiary on the Washington side of the Arsenal grounds. In the darkness of the night of the twenty-seventh of April Booth's body, sewn in a tarpaulin, was carried ashore and into the building, and a room was unlocked. The room had been the big dining area when the Old Penitentiary was new in the early days of the century, but now it was used to store ammunition. With a guncase for a coffin, the canvas-shrouded body was buried under the floor, the bricks all replaced and the door re-locked. Booth would stay there in this grave for four years, until, after continued pleas by Edwin Booth and "Johnny's" mother, President Johnson allowed them to have the body and bury it in an unmarked grave in the family plot in Baltimore.

To confound the crowd straining its eyes on shore, the chief of the United States Detective Bureau and his cousin pretend to throw Booth's shrouded body into the Potomac.

Later that night, Booth's body is secretly buried beneath the floor of the ammunition room of the Old Penitentiary

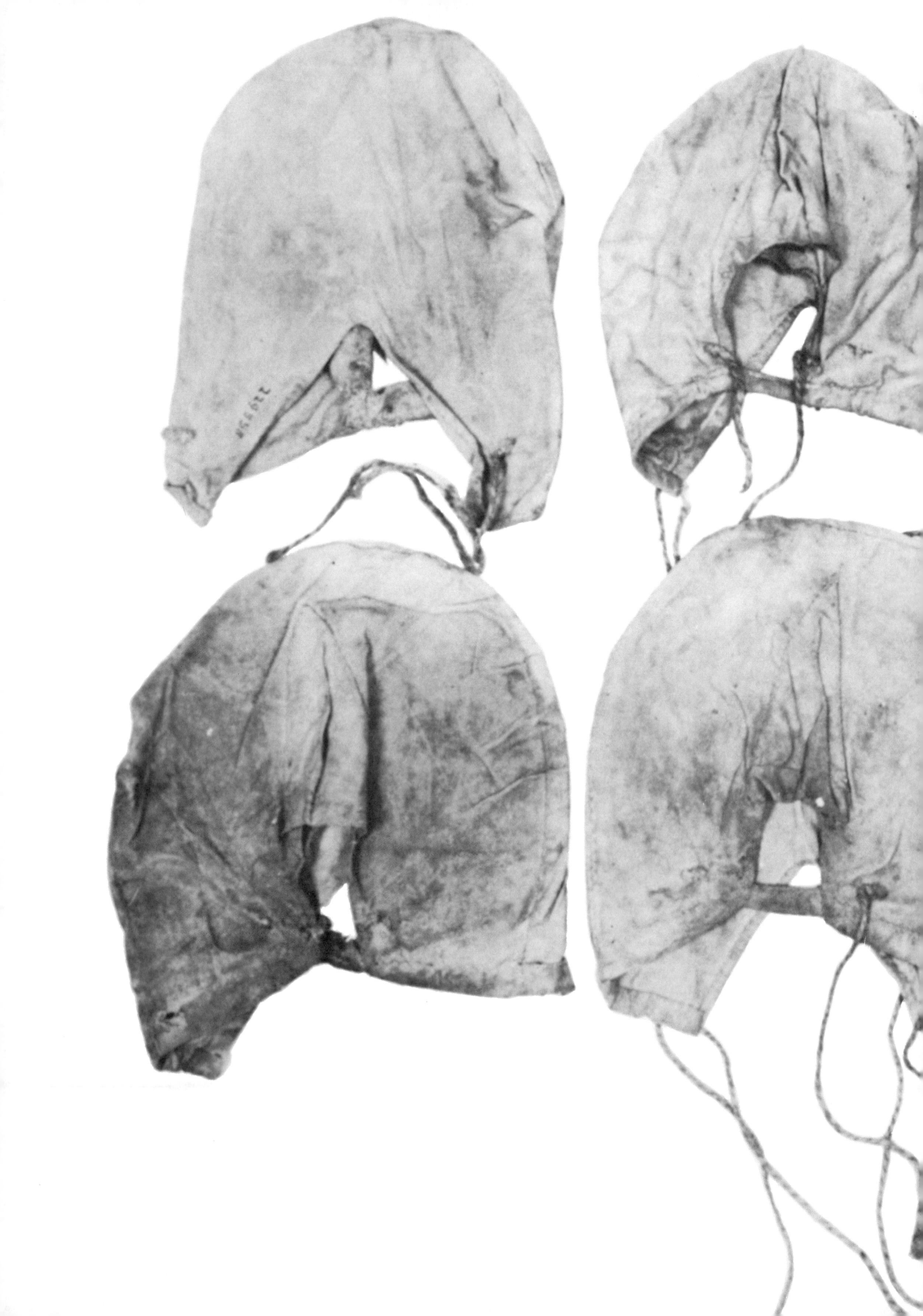

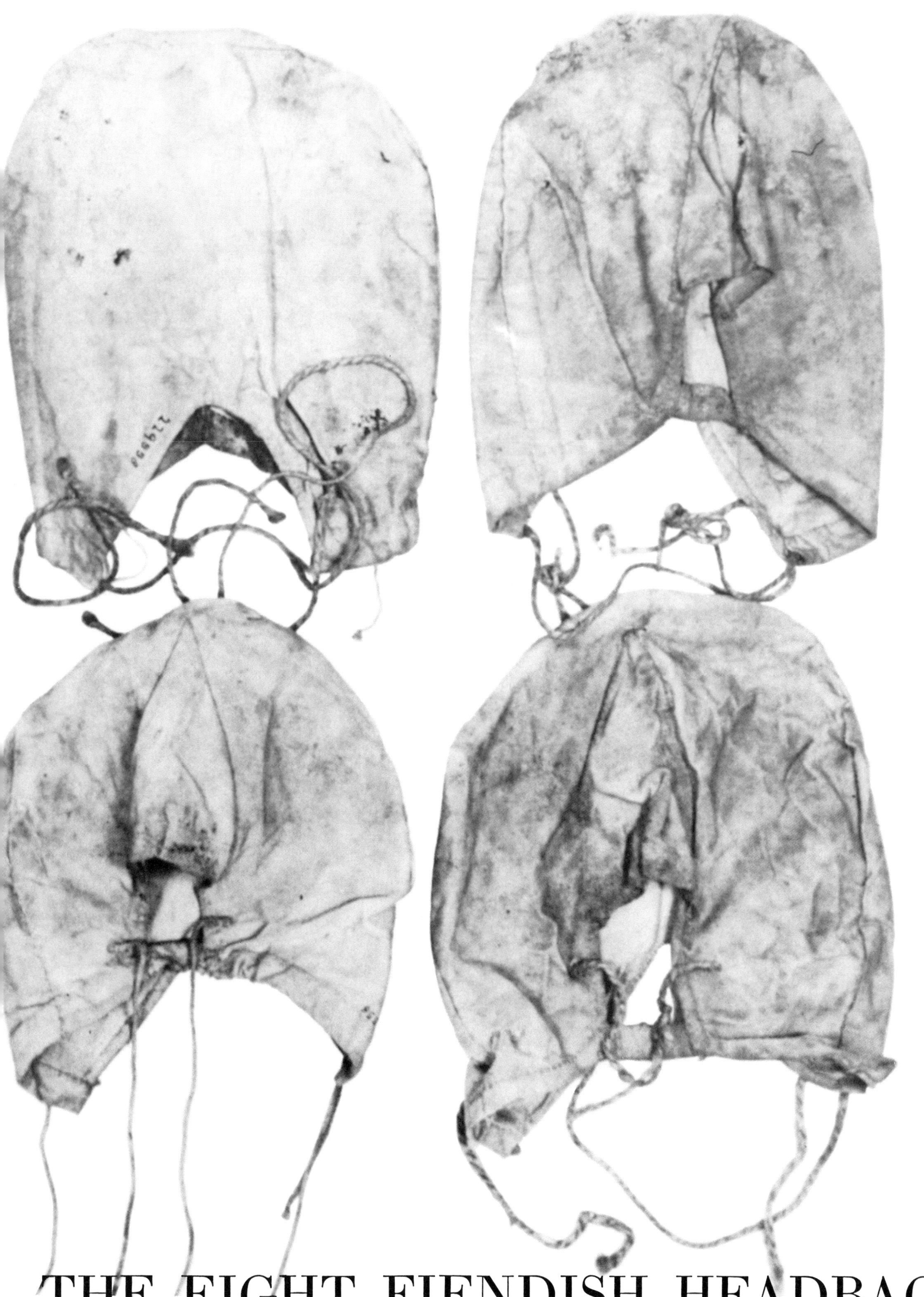

THE EIGHT FIENDISH HEADBAGS
FOR THE WRETCHED ACCUSED

Although from the start Booth was known for certain to be the murderer, in the wild turmoil of the crime's aftermath scores of suspected accomplices were arrested and thrown into prison. When these were finally winnowed to the eight prisoners—seven men and a woman—considered guilty enough to try in court, Stanton invented an unusual and spectacular torture for them. He ordered eight heavy canvas hoods made, padded one-inch thick with cotton, with one small hole for eating, no openings for the eyes or ears. Stanton ordered that the headbags be worn by the seven men day and night as a preventive to conversation. Hood number eight was never used on Mrs. Surratt, the owner of the boarding house where the conspirators had laid their plans, Stanton knew the furor of indignation that would cause. A ball of extra cotton padding covered the eyes so that there was painful pressure on the closed lids. No baths or washing of any kind were allowed, and during the hot breathless weeks of the trial the prisoners' faces became more swollen and bloated by the day, and even the prison doctor began to fear for the conspirators' sanity inside those heavy hoods laced so tightly around their necks. But Stanton would not let them be removed, nor the rigid wrist irons (above), nor the anklets

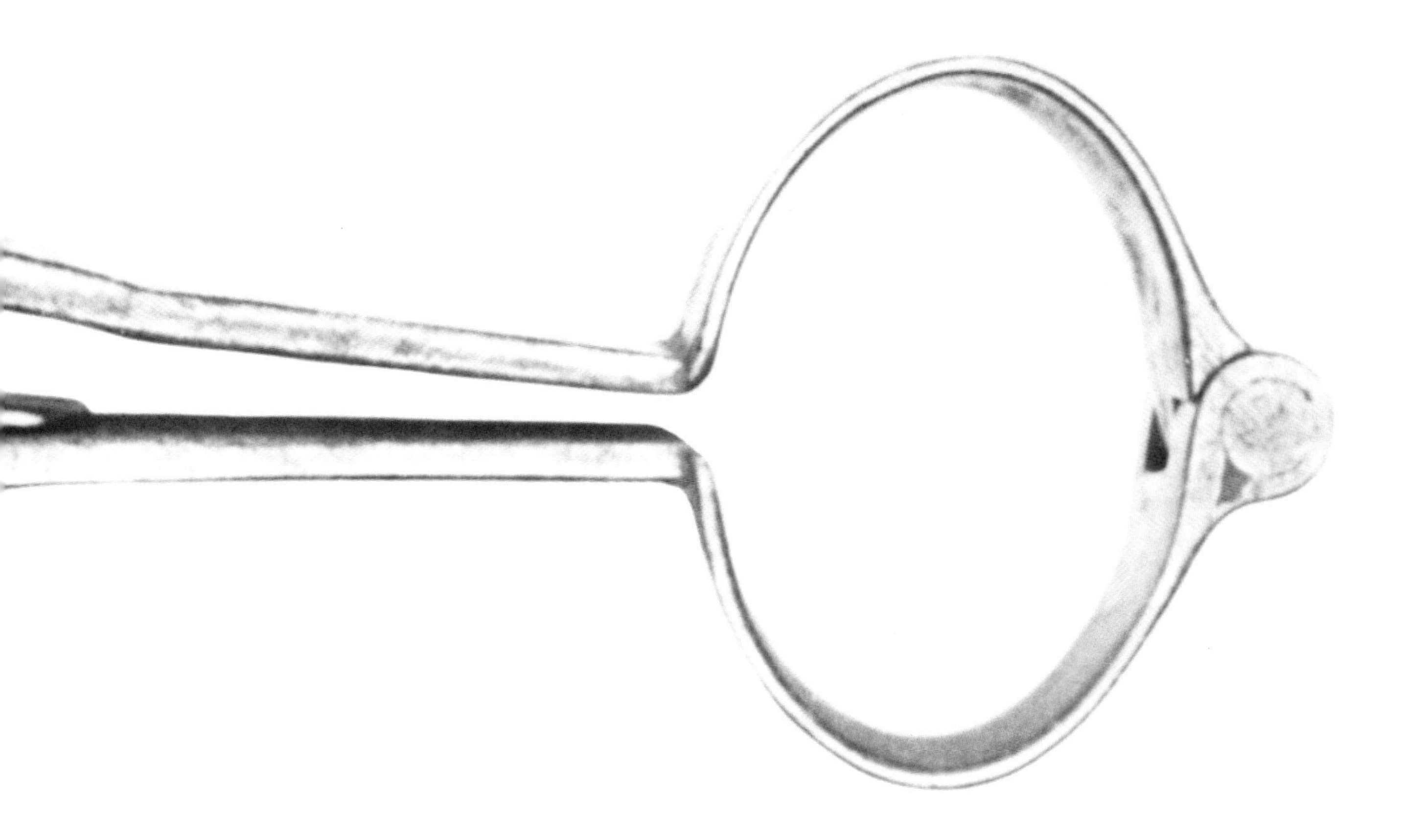

(below), each of which was connected to an iron ball weighing seventy-five pounds.

The winnowing process had been a slow one, for the Old Capitol Prison and its wooden annex, Carroll Prison, were bulging with suspects ordered locked up by Stanton. Louis J. Weichmann, a boarder in Mrs. Surratt's house, was one of those apprehended. Weeks before, he had informed the War Department of the kidnaping plot but Stanton had paid it no heed. John T. Ford, the owner of the theatre, who had been in Richmond, was imprisoned for forty days. The other two Ford brothers who had been in Washington were also arrested and jailed. All the people who were discovered to have had the slightest contact with Booth and Herold on their flight into Maryland and Virginia were put behind bars—James Pumphrey, the Washington livery stable owner from whom Booth had hired his horse; John M. Lloyd, the drunken innkeeper who had rented Mrs. Surratt's Maryland tavern in December when she had moved thirteen miles north to open a Washington boarding house and who had given Booth and Herold carbines and rope and whisky at midnight, only an hour and a half after the assassination; known Confederate sympathizers Samuel Cox and Thomas A. Jones,

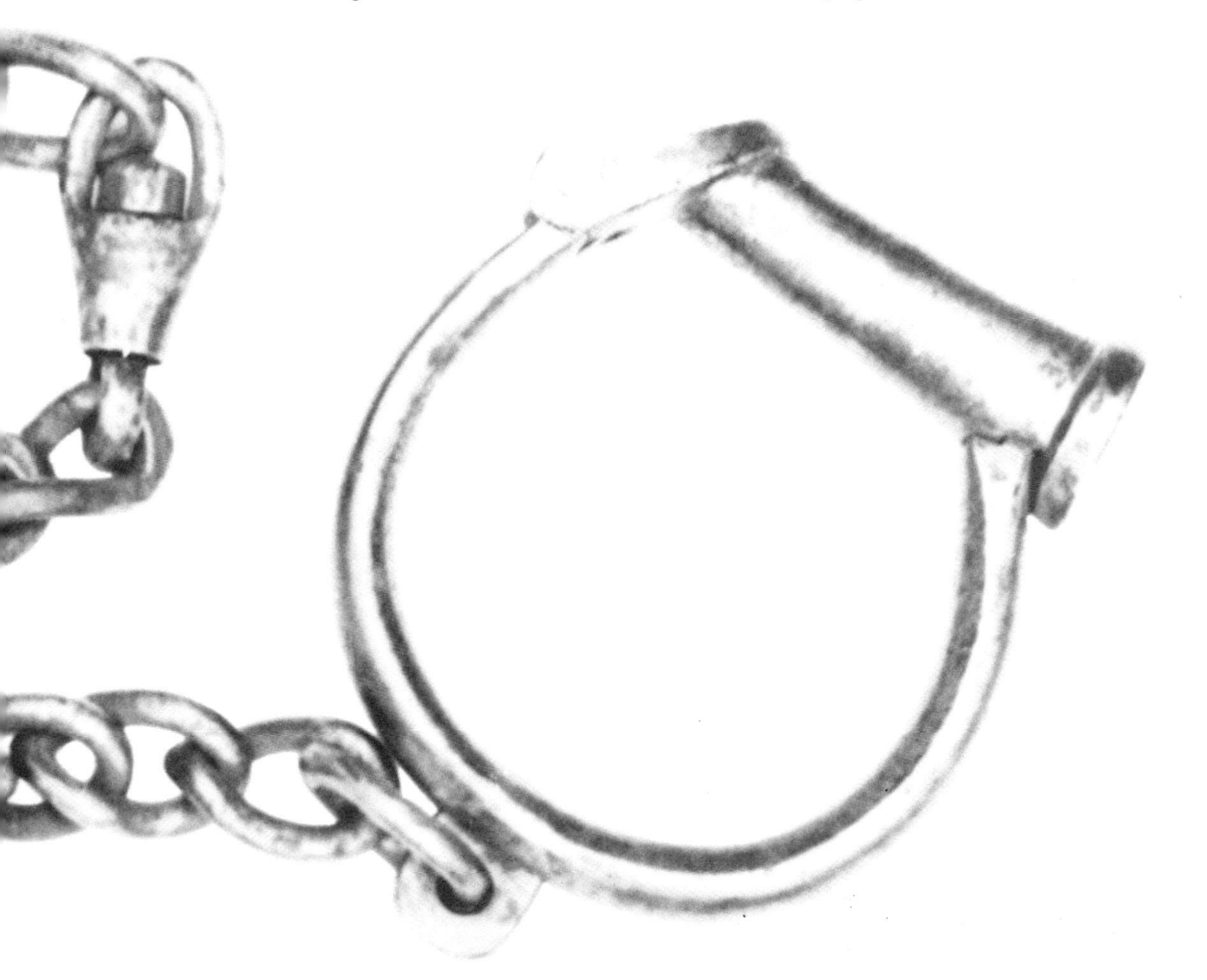

whose slaves set the government on Booth's and Herold's tracks, though it was not known that they had harbored the guilty pair for the better part of a week; one Dr. Richard Stewart, who had given them a meal but refused to have them sleep in his house; a Mrs. Quesenberry, who had also fed them on their flight; three young Confederate soldiers, Bainbridge, Jett, and Ruggles, who had helped the murderer and Herold across the Rappahannock River and let them ride with them on their horses the few miles south to the Garrett farm.

As the government dragnet reached out further and further, a Washington policeman arrested and brought back from Philadelphia a Portuguese sea captain named Celestina on information that he was deeply implicated in the assassination. Wilkes Booth's brother, the great actor Junius Brutus Booth, who was fulfilling an engagement in Cincinnati, was arrested and hurried by train to the Old Capitol Prison. Francis Tumblety, the herb doctor, who was believed to be a leader in the yellow-fever plot. and had been attending the Springfield funeral of "my dear friend President Lincoln" with as sad a face as the other mourners, was captured in St. Louis and brought back to Carroll Prison. Suspicion was at such a high pitch in Washington that even a woman who received a pass to visit a friend in the Old Capitol Prison was indignant and frantic to find herself led to a cell when she was ready to end her call.

The first of the eight finally tried for conspiracy was not picked up until three days after the assassination. Edward Spangler, the carpenter and handyman at Ford's Theatre, who had helped decorate the President's box on Good Friday afternoon, was not hard to find—there were two places to look since he slept wherever he felt like it in the theatre each night and took his meals in a boarding house several blocks away. Detectives found him at the boarding house on Monday morning and captured him and his carpet bag, which had an eighty-foot piece of rope in it, probably stolen from the theatre for his favorite sport of crab fishing. Spangler was first put in the Old Capitol Prison, but when it began to be remembered that after Booth rode crazily away on his horse down the back alley that night, Spangler had called out, "Don't say which way he went!" —he was quickly transferred to the hold of a gunboat lying off the Navy Yard, the special confinement Stanton had ordered for the ones felt to be undeniably guilty.

On that same Monday morning of April seventeenth two more of the eight who would be finally brought to trial were captured. Samuel Arnold, an old school friend of Booth's, who had been in on the original plot to kidnap Lincoln, was arrested in the store at Fortress Monroe just south of Newport News, Virginia, where he had been living and sleeping for two weeks. He had broken with Booth over the actor's bad management, as Arnold considered it, in not pulling off the kidnaping when so many good opportunities had presented themselves. He had written Booth, on March twenty-seventh, that the government was definitely suspicious of something going on and the whole enterprise was getting dangerous. And he was annoyed at Booth's insistence that he wanted to kidnap Lincoln in a *theatre* with himself glorified in the leading role, wanted to tie him up, and throw him into the arms of a conspirator who would be waiting on the stage below the box to rush him out the back door before the audience made a move. Arnold was brought back to Washington and put on the *Saugus*. Simultaneously, another old school friend of Booth's, Michael O'Laughlin, had vanished in horror at the mention of the change in plans from kidnaping to killing, but it had not been difficult to find either one of them since the government had been keeping track of them after getting wind of the kidnap plot.

On the night of that same Monday, numbers four and five—Mrs. Mary E. Surratt and Lewis Paine—were taken

This is the Old Capitol Prison and its wooden annex, Carroll Prison, where Stanton stowed everyone on the slightest suspicion of complicity in the assassination.

into custody. At about 11:30 P.M. a representative of the War Department and four or five officers arrived at Mrs. Surratt's house to arrest her, her sister, and her daughter Annie, and one young woman boarder, who were the only persons left under the Surratt roof. Just as they were about to go out of the door and into carriages, from the dark shadows outside stepped Paine, very dirty, carrying a large pickax over his shoulder. He was wearing a tight little skull cap made from the leg of a pair of underdrawers. He said he had come to ask Mrs. Surratt what time she wanted him to dig for her in the morning. Mrs. Surratt was asked if she knew this man and her answer, which counted heavily against her all during the trial to come, was "Before God, I never saw him before." All through his imprisonment Paine would blame himself for Mrs. Surratt's fate—he should never have come there and incriminated her. He had done it because he was desperately hungry by then, and tired—he had spent most of the hours since his attack on the five people in Seward's house hiding up in a cedar tree in a wood four miles northeast of Washington. Mrs. Surratt's supporters would say as the trial progressed, how could she recognize Paine masquerading as a laborer, when at her house in the past he had been alternately a Baptist minister and a gentleman invalid so frail that he had to have his meals in his room, and who had used a false mustache to confuse her further. Also, they pointed out, her eyesight was very bad indeed—she had not been able to thread a needle for years.

After a session of interrogation at General Augur's headquarters, Paine was ferried out directly to the monitor *Saugus* and secured in double irons below deck. Mrs. Surratt was put in the Old Capitol and although Annie begged tearfully to be imprisoned with her mother, she and the other two women were taken to Carroll Prison.

The sixth conspirator to finally go on trial was not captured until three days later. This was George A. Atzerodt, a German carriage painter who had ferried spies across the Potomac for money. On the assassination night Atzerodt had been too frightened to kill anyone although he was accused of agreeing to murder Vice-President Johnson. Instead he had wandered drunkenly around Washington until three o'clock in the morning, stayed in a hotel for two hours, then set off by stage and wagon to the house of his cousin, Hartman Richter, near Barnsville, Maryland. He lived there quietly for five days working in the garden, but on Thursday an informer led the soldiers to him. Both Atzerodt and Richter were arrested and taken to Washington where the cousin was imprisoned and the conspirator thrown into chains, first on the ironclad *Montauk* and then on

Inaccurate woodcut by overenthusiastic artist increased the number of suspected conspirators in this scene of their middle of

the *Saugus*.

The following day, Friday, April twenty-first, the government picked up Dr. Samuel A. Mudd, accused of setting Booth's leg at his home near Bryantown, Maryland, when the actor suddenly showed up at his house at four o'clock in the morning, five and a half hours after the assassination. After questioning, Mudd was allowed to stay on his farm over the weekend and on Monday, the twenty-fourth, four men took him by horse and buggy to Washington where, because he was a doctor and a gentleman, he was put in Carroll Prison instead of on an ironclad and clamped in regular handcuffs instead of wrist irons.

In the darkness before dawn on Thursday, April twenty-seventh, having been returned from the Garrett farm where Booth had died, David Herold was thrown into irons in the bowels of the *Montauk*. Herold made eight.

Now that the authorities had the eight people it had decided to prosecute for having conspired to kill

the night transferral to the Old Penitentiary. In fact, there were eight—seven men wearing hoods, and Mrs. Surratt, heavily veiled.

Cell block of Old Penitentiary shows second floor and part of third where conspirators were lodged.

Lincoln, President Andrew Johnson signed an executive order that a Military Commission of nine officers be named to try the alleged assassins. Johnson had acted after hearing the opinion of Attorney General James Speed that a military rather than a civil trial was proper, as the head of the United States Army and Navy had been killed at a time when the country was still partially at war, in the country's capital while it was strongly fortified against invasion. The officers were selected, seven generals and two colonels, with Major-General David Hunter as the presiding member of the commission. The Judge Advocate General Joseph Holt and two assistant judge advocates would conduct the trial.

During the late night hours of April twenty-ninth the accused were moved to the building with its high stone walls, which four would never leave—the Old Penitentiary—under a floor of which already lay the leader. Mrs. Surratt, heavily veiled, and the seven men in their suffocating canvas hoods were led through a passageway of soldiers and up the steps of the Old Penitentiary outside of which the pleasure boats going to and from Mount Vernon down the Potomac passed very near. The prisoners were lodged in cells on the second and third floors. Had they been able to stand on the Penitentiary's roof, hoods off, they could have looked northwest to the city of Washington across a stretch of river, and seen clearly the Washington monument stump, the White House, the red, many-towered Smithsonian, and the Capitol with the statue of Freedom on its dome. But there was no such excursion planned as a trip to the roof. The prisoners were in cells separated from each other by an empty cell on each side—they would have to shout to hear each other—each was guarded by four soldiers, each still wore his stiff shackles and steel anklets connected by chains to an iron ball for each foot. Each, that is, except Mrs. Surratt whose feet were merely chained together. The commission chose a courtroom which would be an easy walk from the cells, a large, upper-story room which had been freshly white-washed. Even with its four closely barred windows, it was breathless in there on hot days and there were plenty of them as the trial continued on into the burning Washington summer.

Wearing the hoods and irons Stanton ordered, the conspirators are led from gunboats into the Old Penitentiary.

The trial of the conspirators

The trial of the eight alleged assassins began on May 9th and ground on through long days of testimony heard from more than four hundred witnesses, through June 30th. In all that time not one of the prisoners was ever allowed to take the stand and say a word. Questions by the court and answers by witnesses trying to have the seven men and one woman hung, and those hoping to free them, were published daily word for word in the newspapers and the whole nation read each chapter of the to-be-continued mystery story—impatiently awaiting each new session's developments. To many it seemed as though the government was only slightly and rather grumpily interested in the eight unimportant wretches it had in its grasp and was really expending all its might in trying a group of men who were still annoyingly free—a list of names that held great fascination for they belonged to the high officials of the hated Confederacy. Of course the eight in the courtroom would be punished, but the important thing was to prove the guilt of Jefferson Davis and the group of top leaders who had been operating from the safety of Canada—where Booth and Mrs. Surratt's son John were known to have journeyed, and they just must all be found implicated in the murder plot together, somehow.

The military court was not slow in producing a bombshell. It produced two printers who had set the type for a five-day repeat notice in the Selma, Alabama, *Dispatch* starting on December 1, 1864, announcing that for one million dollars the placer of the notice would agree to kill Abraham Lincoln, William H. Seward, and Andrew Johnson by the first of March—"That will give us peace and satisfy the world that cruel tyrants cannot live in a 'land of liberty'!" The anonymous speaker would himself donate, as a starter, one thousand dollars toward the patriotic purpose of slaughtering the three villains, and the post office box number was given which would await contributions. It was never proved that Jefferson Davis, or any other top Confederates, had the slightest connection with the attention-grabbing Selma, Alabama, offer, even though Secretary Stanton, the over-all director of the trial, wanted desperately to discover evidence that would implicate the Confederate high powers in the assassination. Even so Stanton was happily positive he already had the goods on them in their efforts to start epidemics throughout the country by the introduction of deadly germs into populated areas, in their plans for setting multiple fires in the larger northern cities, for poisoning water supplies, blowing up the Union shipping, deliberately starving to death thousands of Northern prisoners—in short, "the disorganization of the North by infernal plots."

Lacking the physical presence of its most wanted criminals, the Military Commission had to get to work anyway and make do with what it had, so on May ninth, its first day of convening, it graciously adjourned to allow its eight prisoners twenty-four hours to procure counsel to defend them. As they had all been imprisoned incommunicado for a good part of three weeks, they had not been able to do much about this problem and it was extraordinary that as able a group of defenders were so quickly assembled and agreed to do their best, free of charge.

The most distinguished member of the defense was Reverdy Johnson, who had been Attorney General of the United States and Senator from Maryland, who had never met Mrs. Surratt, and now offered to be her lawyer, and he brought with him the junior lawyers of his practice, Frederick Aiken and John Clampit.

The extremely able and high-minded lawyer Thomas S. Ewing, Jr., brother-in-law of General Sherman, who had just returned from a distinguished service in the war, took on both Mudd and Spangler, though being a part of this unpopular defense was the last thing he felt like doing just then. Frederick Stone agreed to do his best for David Herold, Walter S. Cox held the futures of Arnold and O'Laughlin in his care, and a successful

The Military Commission that tried the conspirators before the Judge Advocate Joseph Holt and two assistants was made up of nine top ranking officers. In this portrait by Mathew Brady the presiding officer, Major-General David Hunter, holds a sword in the center, while Holt sits at far right.

attorney, Colonel William E. Doster, accepted a difficult client—Atzerodt. Then, because Paine was entirely friendless and without a member of his family anywhere nearby, Doster accepted him "temporarily," but had to keep him permanently as no offer to help the outstanding villain among the eight ever turned up. Doster was in no way deceived as to the hopelessness of his task—as he himself put it "this was a contest in which a few lawyers were on one side, and the whole United States on the other—a case in which, of course, the verdict was known beforehand."

Each day official members of the court and witnesses were brought from the center of Washington by ambulances. The witnesses waited in a small anteroom until they were called one by one to stand at a railed platform in the center of the room, facing the court to answer questions. All those who came from the outside world walked into the Penitentiary and up what seemed endless flights of twisting stairs squeezing past soldiers on guard every few feet, then through narrow passageways where they were seated in time to view the slow march of "the eight miserable wretches" to their appointed seats on the raised dock. The prisoners' hoods were always removed for the daily walk into the courtroom from their cells, and they took their places with a soldier between each one. Mrs. Surratt, all in black and with a heavy black veil over her head and face, sat at the far left end as the commission faced the prisoners, rather chastely, a few feet removed from the rest. She had been given an armchair, all the others were in straight chairs. As the prisoners rose each noon to file out of the courtroom for the luncheon recess, there was suddenly filling the room the harsh clank and scraping of irons, the higher ringing—almost a tinkle in comparison with the heavier chains—of Mrs. Surratt's smaller links under her skirts. Soldiers walked beside the men carrying the cannon balls which were fastened to their anklets and which they would barely have been able to pull after them across the straw matting.

There was a table in the large room for stenographers, a long one for the commission, one for the press and a small one for exhibits like Booth's riding boot which Doctor Mudd had had to split to get it off his swollen leg, his spur, Paine's knife, slouch hat, and coat, Spangler's precious length of rope for crabbing, the candle, and the compass that helped Booth and Herold cross the

Potomac. However, criminally lacking was Booth's diary which set forth in his April fourteenth entry that he had only on that very day changed his plans from kidnaping to murder. The presence of that diary, which Stanton would keep secret for two years, would certainly have saved Mrs. Surratt's life, as she was sentenced to hang on having conspired to murder.

Stanton had seen to it that the prosecution would win, and one of the aids he enlisted to help him was General Henry L. Burnett—appointed for the trial to be assistant judge advocate to Joseph Holt. Burnett said Stanton worked on assembling the evidence that would defeat the prisoners all day every day, and most nights Burnett worked with him until sunrise. When the exhausted Burnett left around three in the morning, Stanton was still bent over his desk at the War Department.

To get this head start on the eight accused conspirators Stanton used all of La Fayette C. Baker's detectives and ordered the trains of all the railroads to carry people here and there at his bidding. He sent endless peremptory telegrams and found time as well to keep throwing into prison people about whom their neighbors only "felt there was something funny." Then, too, Stanton dreamed up a wonderful rule for his side—the commission could impose any restriction it saw fit—and that was that when the prisoners got their defending lawyers, they could never see them in their cells to talk over what in their eyes they had done or not done and what should be said now. Instead they could only communicate with their attorneys in full sight of the crowded courtroom, separated by a railing and with a soldier on each side listening. It was absolutely hopeless. In sight of the commission and the press and the spellbound daily visitors, Doster's bewildering client Paine just leaned his head back against the wall day after day and said nothing—Doster knew almost nothing about him. The other prisoners leaned forward and whispered their self-justifications and their hopes, pathetically.

Lewis Paine and Mrs. Surratt were the two immensely colorful members of the accused conspirators in the dock—on whom the country's interest was centered with insatiable curiosity. Next in the strange opposite-of-a-popularity contest ranked Dr. Mudd and young David Herold. Then George Atzerodt and Edmund Spangler, the theatre handyman. And at the bottom of the eight names, so colorless and boring that people could hardly

Contemporary woodcut shows trial scene. At end of room is the raised prisoners' dock with Mrs. Surratt at extreme left. At the right are the seated commissioners. The press is at the center table and spectators at the left.

remember who they were or why they were there, were Booth's early friends, Sam Arnold and Michael O'Laughlin. Beginning in reverse order of their interest ratings, this was the way the public saw the eight wretches.

Michael O'Laughlin, a tiny man with bushy black hair and a luxuriant mustache, was the handsomest. He was labeled as having been assigned to kill Stanton, and someone had heard a rustling in the bushes outside Stanton's house on the assassination night. When the rustler emerged and drifted away, someone remembered he had been a tiny man with a fine black mustache. All during the trial he gave an impression of anxious remorse that made people a little sorry for him.

Young Sam Arnold sat next to Mrs. Surratt, or rather next to the soldier between them, and was excessively restless—constantly leaning forward and back clasping and unclasping his hands. But everyone was quite disappointed to have to admit that this one particular conspirator did not look evil at all—had a frank, open expression and looked like a nice young man.

Edward Spangler, the scene shifter, who was suspected of having cleared the back passageway off the stage for Booth to escape—perhaps having whittled

Around these faces revolve an unsolved mystery, nagging because of the men's resemblance to each other. The top face is a government photograph of an arrested suspect, on which no name was placed. The second face is that of a man standing with the group of conspirators below President Lincoln as he spoke at his second inauguration (see page 33). The third face is that of Dr. Samuel Mudd, sketched in the courtroom when he was on trial. Are these three men? Or two? Or one?

the wooden bar to place from the box door across to the mortise in the wall—who for months had been caring for Booth's horse in the alley stable—appeared to everyone to be a hard drinker whose features had been coarsened by his intemperance, and to be surly by nature. He looked terrified during the trial—often trembled visibly. Also his appearance was not endearing—his whole face was continually covered with a dingy stubble of beard.

Thirty-three-year-old German-born Atzerodt was not a favorite among the group. He had a thick accent that was hard to understand, though of course the courtroom visitors were not treated to this—on exhibition in the dock he was forbidden to say a word—but the greatest complaint was he had no neck at all. He was short, round-shouldered, and had an expression that was at the same time stupid and crafty. People said "hang-dog," "shabby," neckless—he was a poor advocate for himself. He also looked cowardly, mercenary, and as "inscrutable as some Eastern idol."

Davy Herold, the young druggist clerk with a mother and seven sisters, had no chin—as Atzerodt had no neck—practically no forehead, it slanted back so rapidly. People said his face looked like yellow wax, speckled with freckles painted thickly over cheeks and nose. He was said to be subnormal mentally—a silly boy who was easily persuaded by anyone he met to do what he had not the brains to know was wrong. Irresolute, as horribly scared as Spangler, he was thought to look like a hopeless, trapped animal, and people said it was embarrassing to look straight at someone's exposed, naked, quivering soul. His features were also too small for his face, which was contemptible and unhealthily dingy.

Thirty-two-year-old Dr. Samuel Mudd was a thin man with a mild, timid look, "entirely devoid of any nobility of character." Everyone felt he was guilty, since it was brought out that Booth had visited him in Maryland and he had met Booth in Washington—notably the day before the second inauguration when the murder had been half-planned for the following day on the East steps of the Capitol. It was beyond anyone's belief that Mudd could have set Booth's leg, have him spend a whole day in his house and not guessed this was Booth. Dr. Mudd literally convicted himself through evasiveness and a criminally faulty memory.

Mrs. Mary E. Surratt, the number two star of the occasion, muffled in black, striving to hide her person behind a palm leaf fan, her heavy black veil, her black-mittened hands, was said to be a well-preserved, pink-cheeked, pretty woman of forty-five, who fascinated the public because she had been known to be an upright, kindly Christian woman whose only sin was that she thought the Confederacy was right in its demands. She occupied a position a little apart from the others on the dock and seemed to gaze interestedly by the hour at the new straw matting that covered the courtroom floor. When her attractive daughter Annie testified, searching desperately to catch sight of her mother beyond a group of officers which hid her from view, crying out, "Where is Mother? Where is Mother?"—Mrs. Surratt made no sound from behind her mittens, her fan and her veil. But back in the cell the mother and daughter embraced and wept constantly.

The mysterious, fascinating lion of the show was Lewis Thornton Powell, alias Paine, son of a Baptist Florida minister, who had at the time of the trial six sisters and his mother and father—two brothers had been killed in the Rebel army.

Paine had no member of his family nor any friend visit him in his cell. A minister was assigned to pray with him and Paine did pray a lot, saying he believed in God and considered that killing by any method at

SAMUEL ARNOLD

EDMUND SPANGLER

MICHAEL O'LAUGHLIN

DR. SAMUEL A. MUDD

all—in battle or in a man's home by stealth—was justifiable in time of war. He also said he was guilty as charged, though he had done no wrong, and wished they would "hang him quick," and get it over with—he had no desire to live. He laughed just once, when the court made him stand up and try on the hat he had left behind on the floor of Seward's bedroom the night he attacked the Secretary. Instead of looking frightened when the hat fitted him, he had actually laughed (showing for the first time the two incongruously charming dimples in his cheeks). He never wept, never trembled, was always in control of himself—dignified, mysterious, and ever keeping his own counsel. After the day that he propelled himself headlong against the iron wall of the *Saugus* trying to batter his brains out, the soldiers chained him into almost complete immobility. And he was the despair of the prison doctors who wanted to keep him alive for the hanging. His lower bodily functions had just seemed to stop working, in spite of repeated cathartics, as though Paine had willed his body to stop living. The only pleasure of this world he still craved was a chew of tobacco, and Thomas T. Eckert of the War Department who had been sent by Stanton to Paine's cell to get him talking and implicating the others with himself and Booth, did stick a piece of tobacco through the mouth opening in Paine's padded hood. Paine was grateful, saying it was the first kindness he had received.

Paine in the courtroom was a giant of a young man, fiercely erect, beautifully developed muscularly and always wearing a dark knit pull-on shirt that exposed his bull strong neck. He leaned his head back against the wall and looked dreamily out the barred windows to the stirring trees outside. He was relaxed and seemed to be completely at ease every day—as though beyond mere man's reach—just as he alone of the conspirators slept soundly each night.

He had a thick shock of uncombed hair which hung forward over his low forehead, a fresh, beardless skin, large blue-gray eyes that met the gaze in turn of everyone in the courtroom. Some said he stared impudently—some said he scowled fiercely like a caged tiger—some that he glared at everyone, showing the whites of his eyes frighteningly as he switched his gaze right and left. He always came to court in his stocking feet for his feet had swelled so much that he could not get into his shoes.

Onlookers marveled at Paine's control of himself, even during reviling that would rouse a lesser man to some sort of intense feeling—either remorse or fighting madness. The only sign of feeling showing that ever ruffled Paine's composure was a slight pink tinge that came in his handsome complexion—and at rare times he held his breath for a long while, then let it go audibly, in a great sigh.

By the time the trial began Stanton knew exactly what witnesses should testify and they were all people who furthered the conspiracy picture. Often they were dismissed and had gone home before the defense could cross-examine them. Many were detectives and seemed to have been coached carefully in what to say. The list of perfectly available witnesses who could have illuminated the President's murder, and who were not called, seemed to go unnoticed in the daily publicizing of the memories and theories of Stanton's hand-selected list. No one seemed to notice a pattern in the tenor of what was said and when the defending lawyers protested, they were gruffly overruled by Advocate General Holt.

"Peanuts" Burroughs said that after Spangler had helped Harry Clay Ford decorate the theatre box he damned the President and Grant and said being damned was what they deserved for getting so many men killed. The actor in *Our American Cousin*, E. A. Emerson, said that Booth had whacked him over the shoulder with a cane breaking it in four pieces and saying of Lincoln—"Did you hear what that old scoundrel did the other day—he went into Davis' home in Richmond and threw his long legs over the arm of a chair and squirted tobacco juice all over the place. Someone ought to kill him." A Richmond, Virginia, blind man, Samuel P. Jones, said he had heard a man offer $10,000 for the killing of Lincoln. The little old colored woman who lived in the alley behind Ford's Theatre testified that Booth's horse had been out in the alley waiting for an hour and a half, stamping and stamping on the cobblestones, and she thought, "Whatever is the matter with that horse?" The stableman at Thirteenth and E Streets, describing Herold coming for his horse, said he had black eyebrows and "kind of a smile on his face" and made it sound incriminating. On the day that Herold's smile was described, May eighteenth, Tad Lincoln was in the courtroom in the spectators section and heard Judge Olin describe the red damask of the chair in which his father was killed as being spattered with drops of blood.

An actor from New York named Samuel Knapp Chester testified that he had rebuffed Booth in horror when asked to join the kidnaping conspiracy. Booth, Chester said, had made several trips North to plead with him, offering him $3,000 just to hold the back door of Ford's Theatre open while the President was being hustled out to a waiting carriage. Chester had refused, and Booth angrily told him he would ruin him and that he felt like doing worse. He said that when the actor John Matthews in Washington had refused to join him, he had felt very much like "sacrificing" him—Booth's refined word for killing. November 1864 was the date of the first visit to enlist Chester, and Booth came back to New York after Lincoln's March fourth second inauguration. He faced his fellow actor smilingly across the table where they were having a drink and asked him if he had changed his mind about coming to Washington and cursed him when he said he had not. There were fifty to a hundred people enlisted now and not a chance of anything going wrong, there was plenty of money and plenty of aid waiting "on the other side." The plan was still just a harmless kidnaping, no one would be hurt and the war would be over, prisoners freed and home again. Chester had put on his most dejected expression and asked Booth to think of his poor wife and mother, and that was the last he saw of him.

As the carefully government-carpentered testimony began to pile up against the conspirators, along with it came some interesting, often carefully detailed, sometimes impassioned, refutations. The prosecution had suggested that the silly boy Herold with his subnormal smile had been up to no good during the week of February thirteenth, and his sister Emma Herold hotly contested this. She remembered that Davy was home on the thirteenth because he sent her a valentine and was there the next day when it arrived in the mail, and that he was still there on Sunday the nineteenth because he met her on the stairs and tried to take a pitcher of water she was carrying from her and it spilled all over.

Just as fascinating was the refutation that Dr. Mudd had been in Washington for Lincoln's second inauguration. One Marcus P. Norton claimed that on the third of the month Mudd had rushed into his room at the National Hotel, said he must see John Wilkes Booth immediately and was directed to Booth's room. In her brother's defense Miss Mary Mudd said that she knew positively that the doctor was home at his farm on that day, as he had come to treat her for an eruption on her face that she feared was smallpox, and that he hurried to her bedroom direct from stripping tobacco all day long. He washed the tobacco gum off his hands before he examined her, right there in her room. Mary Mudd also, unfortunately for her brother, described the hat her brother usually wore as a "drab slouch hat," which fitted perfectly the hat he was supposed to have been wearing in Washington.

During the trial the doctor had succeeded in whispering to his lawyer his version of Booth's visit to him on the night he set the actor's leg, and the commission must have been pleased with its evasiveness and obvious deviation from the facts. It went like this: When Booth and Herold knocked on his door at four o'clock on the morning of Saturday, the fifteenth of April, having arrived on horseback, the doctor did not recognize Booth as the man with whom he had dickered some months before on the price for which he would sell him his farm. Booth said his name was Tyler and Herold said his was Tyson, and Booth was wearing false whiskers—which of course Mudd thought were real—and had the lower part of his face muffled in a shawl. The doctor cut off Booth's boot, set the fractured leg in a cardboard splint, and had his servant make a crutch. Booth was put in a bed upstairs where he lay till four o'clock the next afternoon when Mrs. Mudd went up to see him. She brought a tray holding cake, two oranges, and wine—Booth asked for brandy instead of wine but there was none. He complained, "My back hurts me dreadfully," and he kept his face turned to the wall. The doctor at that moment was in Bryantown visiting some patients and when he came back Tyler and Tyson had left on their horses, and Mrs. Mudd said that as Tyler came down the stairs his whiskers had become detached and almost fell off. Mrs. Mudd wondered if the askew whiskers weren't suspicious but out of fear of being left alone, she persuaded the doctor not to go back to Bryantown to report it.

During the hours when the prisoner Paine was hooded and back in his cell, Eckert was there with him, also busily working on the Mudd story. Paine told him of a meeting of the conspirators in a room that for once was not in Mrs. Surratt's house and Eckert went and found the room—poked around in a grate in a fireplace there and discovered scraps of paper on which were written details of a "kidnaping," and also, plainly, the name *Mudd.*

About this time Paine's lawyer Doster decided that the only hope of saving his troublesome client was to have him declared insane and hope that the commission would not be willing to hang a crazy man. He got hold of Dr. Nichols, superintendent of the huge government Insane Asylum up on the hill, plainly seen from the Penitentiary—just across the Anacostia, and based his suspicions of Paine's mental state to Dr. Nichols on the facts that Paine had stayed up in a treetop for three days, that he had laughed in court while trying on his hat, and that his bowels were completely deranged and only worked, according to the guards in his cell, once in every five days, and that Paine had cried "I am mad! I am mad!" as he ran down the stairs in Seward's house after attacking Major Augustus Seward. The authority on insanity gave the matter full attention and in the end said that his staying up in the tree was very close to insanity—he did not feel strongly one way or another about the paralysis of Paine's intestines—but he did point out that a person who is really mad does not ever tell people "I am mad" and that Paine was positively pretending when he said it.

As for the other star conspirator, Mary Surratt, evidence was mounting against her even though, to her lawyer and attending priests in her cell, she steadfastly protested ignorance of any knowledge of the plot which had been hatched in her boarding house. The officers

MRS. MARY SURRATT

who had arrested her said that in her living room was a framed colored picture of three young women representing "Spring, Summer and Autumn" and behind this had been discovered a photograph of John Wilkes Booth. To add to this, on top of her dresser were two bullet molds. W. M. Wannerskerch of the arresting party was asked to identify Mrs. Surratt as the woman he had taken into custody and he replied that he could not see her face. Then, the court stenographers reported, "slowly, coolly, Mrs. Surratt lifted her veil, looked steadily at him and slowly, coolly lowered the veil again." She had had to be removed from the courtroom several times because of faintness but in moments like this there was an admiration for her among the visitors —they thought her a woman of "great nerve."

It was really the two witnesses Louis J. Weichmann and John M. Lloyd the keeper of her own tavern in Maryland who had clinched Mary Surratt's conviction, as the government meant they should, and for which favor the government offered them immunity and switched them from the ranks of witnesses who were to be prosecuted to the safety of State's evidence.

Louis J. Weichmann had been an old school friend of Mrs. Surratt's son John, and she welcomed him as a second son when he came to board in her house, sitting up for him when he was out late and encouraging him in his State Department job in the Prisoners' Commissary Department. There was evidence after the trial that Weichmann had been threatened into signing a statement, written out for him, to save his own skin, that Stanton had frightened him to death by suggesting he was as guilty as the rest in the house and would have to pay the penalty, and Weichmann even summoned the courage to say to the Judge Advocate during the trial that he had confused and frightened him so much the day before that he did not know what he was saying.

But then came the day when his course was clear—Weichmann was released from prison and sent on missions for the government, even as far away as Canada. And he was completely glib when he told how on the afternoon of the fourteenth of April Booth had come to see Mrs. Surratt, had asked her to drive to her inn and tell the innkeeper Lloyd to have the shooting irons and whisky ready that very night for they would be called for. Mrs. Surratt repeatedly told her lawyer that she had gone to see Lloyd only on business concerning the inn, and that was all they had talked about—but Weichmann insisted all he said was true, and he looked so open and honest and so very sorry to have to say the words, that he was believable.

As for Lloyd, who gave the two murderers their carbines and whisky, he admitted that during his meeting with Mrs. Surratt earlier he had been drunk and could not remember what they had talked about, admitting that by midnight when the two men arrived on horseback he was "right smart in liquor" and though he felt like lying down on the sofa he could not because lying down made him feel sick and dizzy. In spite of the fact that Stanton had announced that any person found to have harbored or abetted the conspirators in their escape

GEORGE A. ATZERODT

DAVID E. HEROLD

LEWIS PAINE

would pay the death penalty, still John Lloyd, when he managed to sort out his muddled memories and remember what the government suggested to him that he had heard, was able to testify that Mrs. Surratt had asked him to have field glasses and carbines which he had hidden under the rafter ready for two men who would call for them that night.

Just as the War Department decided what certain people would testify and bribed them with a promise of immunity, it also decided just who would testify, and there were some strange omissions, and some very important faces never showed up in the courtroom.

There was, of course, the policeman John Parker who had been supposed to guard Lincoln's box door and had gone down into a front row of the dress circle to enjoy the play. He was never called upon to testify at all.

Then, too, there was a young lady closely connected with the Lincoln assassination who belonged in the witness chair at the trial but who, for reasons valid to the government, was far removed from Washington when she might have been testifying. She was Lucy Hale, Booth's fiancée. Lucy had to mourn her lost lover in silence as her prominent father, Senator from New Hampshire, used all his influence to hush up her connection with this young man, whose real self she had never known at all. Notices were placed in newspapers by her family denying that there was the slightest foundation to the engagement story, though actually Booth had received his own mother's blessing on the plans for himself and Lucy in a letter, and hoped her distinguished father would not consider an actor beneath his daughter. "You have so often been dead in love," she wrote—"A young man in love is like a child with a new toy . . . be well assured she is really and truly devoted to you." As far back as February thirteenth—and that was a long time for Booth's inconstant nature—he had been wild, for some strange reason, over this rather large, over wholesome young woman and had spent the whole night of the thirteenth writing a valentine to Lucy, using his brother Junius as a dictionary—he was searching for synonyms of the word adore. On that very night of the thirteenth Senator and Mrs. Hale were dining at the White House with President and Mrs. Lincoln. The future looked bright—Hale would be sailing soon for Spain, where he was to be the new ambassador, though he hated to leave his Lucy behind. Hale was an important person, and he was going to be able to secure an extra ticket to the inauguration ceremony on March fourth on the east steps of the Capitol—a very special ticket which would be presented, with Lucy's love, to John Wilkes Booth.

It cannot have been pleasant to learn after the murder that along with her picture in Booth's pocket when he died had been the likenesses of four actresses—and then there were the dreadful headlines in the papers announcing that Booth's mistress, one Ella Turner of Washington, had turned on the gas jet in her bedroom and tried to commit suicide. To Lucy it seemed all a dream now, but just two weeks before the assassination her "Johnny" took her to an evening's performance at Ford's Theatre and they watched the play together from Box Seven, the upper rear box on the right-hand side.

Amid the denials that Lucy had done more than meet Booth casually at an evening of dancing, John Wilkes' great actor brother Edwin was writing their sister Asia, "I have had a heart-broken letter from the poor little girl to whom he had promised so much happiness." There was also talk that Lucy had told Edwin more—that she would be willing to marry his brother at the foot of the scaffold.

As it turned out, there was no scaffold for her fiancé and Lucy was never identified as the young woman on the deck of the *Montauk* as Booth lay there just before his autopsy, who snipped off one of his black curls and had it so rudely snatched away by an irate officer. By trial time, Lucy was in Spain. It would have been unfortunate to have anyone testifying who considered that Booth had even one good quality. He must be kept all evil, all black, a fiend in human form.

Two men who had plenty to say did not testify because they successfully held their tongues and their stories were undiscovered. John Matthews, the actor, waited two years to speak out, and Thomas A. Jones, who had something much worse to hide, waited twenty. Matthews was the actor friend in *Our American Cousin* to whom, on the afternoon before the assassination, Booth handed his letter explaining what he was about to do and why.

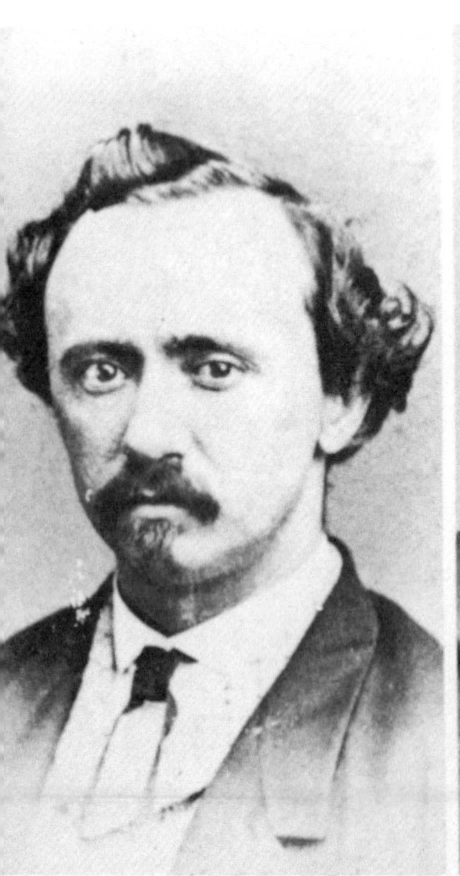

Actor friend Samuel Knapp Chester (*left*) was offered $3,000 by Booth to turn off the lights and hold open the back door at Ford's Theatre. Chester refused. John R. Ford (*right*), owner of Ford's Theatre, was imprisoned for forty days because of his longstanding close friendship with Booth.

He had asked him to mail it to the editor of the Washington *Daily Intelligencer* the following morning. That evening Matthews had played his part of the drunken lawyer Coyle and after the shooting, with the knowledge that Booth was the murderer, ran to his boarding house, opened and memorized the letter, and then burned it. If the burning had taken place a few weeks earlier, it would have been done in the Petersen House in the very room where Lincoln died, for Matthews had boarded there just before Willie Clark moved in, and Booth came there often, sprawling on the walnut spool-turned bed and smoking his pipe. Matthews and Booth were the only ones who knew of this letter, and Booth thought it had been mailed—he wrote in his diary that the government must be preventing the paper from printing it.

Jones was a Confederate sympathizer living down near the Potomac River, south of Port Tobacco. When his foster brother Sam Cox asked him to care for and feed two strangers in a thicket where Cox had hidden them, he accepted without a single longing thought for the $75,000 reward money he soon learned his charges were worth. Booth lay on the ground, his hair matted, his once dapper suit increasingly torn by briars, and his face drawn in pain, and he continued to lie there like a wounded, hunted animal for six days. Each day Booth eagerly seized the newspapers Jones brought him and put them down sadly—every line told him the same thing—instead of being a great Southern hero, his deed was considered the worst possible tragedy that could have befallen the South as well as the North and the world. Every time Jones approached the part of the woods where Booth lay in a hollow made out of leaves, he gave two sharp whistles. He pretended the food he was carrying was corn, calling loudly for his hogs to come and eat as he walked. As the searching parties came closer, Jones's heart thumped as fearfully as Herold's and Booth's, for they were his responsibility and he was in a sense living out the end of their lives with them—certainly sharing their terror. One terror was that the two horses the men had ridden down from Washington would whinny when they heard the cavalry horses nearby. There was nothing to do but lead them out to a marshy place in the woods and shoot them—leaving their bodies to sink into the bog and disappear. This did not happen as quickly as Jones had figured and his worst moments were when he saw the great carrion birds circling in the air about the carcasses—it was something that could very well make a search party curious.

Finally, as June came to an end, the trial was completed. Out of the endless sheafs of testimony, the obvious evidence, the charges, denials, insinuations, the lies, the truth, the half-lies, the half-truths, the loaded statements, the government inspired prejudice, out of the heat of the courtroom, the sight of the involuntarily silent accused persons and the valiant appeals of their lawyers, out of the still fresh memory of the murder of President Lincoln, out of the war's end and the temper of a country split, brother against brother, and finally out of the souls of nine men, had to come a decision.

John Matthews, a member of the cast of *Our American Cousin* burned letter Booth gave him to mail, never mentioned it for two years.

Thomas A. Jones, Confederate mail-runner, was jailed on suspicion of aiding Booth on the flight south. He was released for lack of evidence, but many years later admitted hiding Booth in a Maryland thicket for six days and feeding him.

Two photographs made from the same vantage point by Alexander Gardner on the morning of the execution—one showing the waiting scaffold, the other, the freshly dug graves closeby—are used here joined together to show the over-all scene which awaited the

End of a nightmare for the doomed

The nine members of the Commission met secretly on June twenty-eighth and twenty-ninth and voted the death penalty for Mrs. Surratt, Paine, Atzerodt and Herold, with a recommendation attached to the last page of their findings recommending mercy for Mrs. Surratt because of sex and age—and that her sentence be changed to life imprisonment. They voted life imprisonment for Dr. Mudd, Arnold, and O'Laughlin at hard labor, and six years of hard labor for Spangler.

President Johnson was ill and so Judge Advocate General Joseph Holt could not take him the sentences to have them reviewed and have the order for execution signed by him, until July fifth—and all those extra days the prisoners sweltered in their hoods in the hot cells, unknowing of what could be causing the delay, since the trial was over.

Johnson did not read the whole long involved findings of the commission; instead he had Holt summarize matters for him. He signed the order of execution for four and imprisonment for four, and he swore for the rest of his life that Judge Holt had never shown him the recommendation for mercy for Mrs. Surratt. Holt spent the remainder of his life telling everyone that he had seen the President read it, and that Johnson had discussed the matter with him, saying that Mrs. Surratt kept the nest that hatched the egg, and that if women were to commit such crimes as hers and go free, then men would be tempted to use women as their tools for murder and no one would be punished.

On the morning of July sixth General Winfield Scott Hancock, in charge of the military district, and General J. F. Hartranft, in charge of guarding the prisoners, walked into the cells of the four condemned to death and read them their sentences. Mrs. Surratt burst into tears

four doomed conspirators. Below is Doctor Mary E. Walker, only woman doctor in the Army, who was the sole female witness to the hanging.

—she was alone with no one to comfort her, since her daughter Annie had just left the prison. Paine was completely stoical—it was exactly what he had expected, and wanted. Herold didn't seem to realize what he was being told, but after a few minutes asked to have his sisters sent for.

Ministers were brought to the prisoners' cells to strengthen them for entrance into another world. Mrs. Surratt had two Catholic priests. Paine had a Baptist clergyman and Atzerodt, a Lutheran. Herold's sisters arrived, crying—most were grown up but two were just little girls—young "misses" the papers said. One of them brought their brother a basket of small cakes which she had to leave with General Hartranft so he could examine them and be sure no poison or knives were hidden in the basket.

The four prisoners to be executed were moved down into the ground floor row of cells so they could walk out easily the next day—and if it had not been for a part of the prison that extended forward a few feet at the south end—they could have watched the building of the gallows which began immediately, and the digging of four graves in the extremely, hard, dried-out earth of the yard. The temperature was 100° in the shade, and there was no shade in the three-acre yard, surrounded by its twenty-foot high brick wall.

The four other conspirators who were not to be hung were told nothing—they were just kept hooded in their upper story cells under heavy guard, manacled and wearing ankle shackles. It was not until the next day, after the business of hanging was over, that these remaining four, who were to enjoy the happiness of future living, were officially told of their sentences although Dr. Mudd had been sneaked the good news by his guard on the day before the execution. At first they were to have done their hard labor at the Federal Prison in Albany, but Stanton changed this to a burning, bone-dry island off Florida which had a huge fort that had been used as a prison during the war. The Dry Tortugas, Florida, would be their address.

When Annie Surratt was found and told about her mother's death sentence, from then until one o'clock the next day when the hanging took place she tried desperately to get at least an extension of three days to her mother's life—the carrying out of the sentence was so cruelly swift. It was swiftly carried out sentences for which military courts were noted—in civil courts appeals were possible—but this was exactly what Stanton and Johnson wanted. Since they had considered the prisoners guilty before the trial began, now they wanted to get the whole thing over without argument. Annie Surratt, hysterical, weeping pitifully, rushed to the White House and begged to see the President but was told he was ill and would see no one. Senator James Lane of Kansas and Preston King. Johnston's ever present most intimate friend, guarded the stairs on which Annie threw herself and made her sobbing entreaties. At last she went back to the prison, where she was allowed to sleep in the cell with her mother for that last night. Mrs. Surratt was very weak from her long imprisonment and she and Annie fainted alternately and wept in each other's arms—never slept all night—just embraced and sobbed.

The morning of the seventh was still wickedly hot, in the high nineties before eight o'clock, and already crowds were gathering outside the prison yard wall and boats were coming from Alexandria and down from Georgetown and the city of Washington and the Potomac was crowded with sightseers hoping they would catch a glimpse of the hanging—which they were never able to do. The people who had the best view were the soldiers who patrolled the top of the wall—walking safely between the ropes extending from the iron post to iron post, put there so they would not fall off into the rows of cannons below.

By the morning the gallows were built and executioner Chris Rath was constantly having it tested with two-

No relative ever visited Paine in his cell. His last hour, sketched by a *Leslie's Illustrated Weekly* artist, was, like most of his others, spent alone.

His mother and five of David Herold's seven sisters bid him an agonized good-by shortly before the execution.

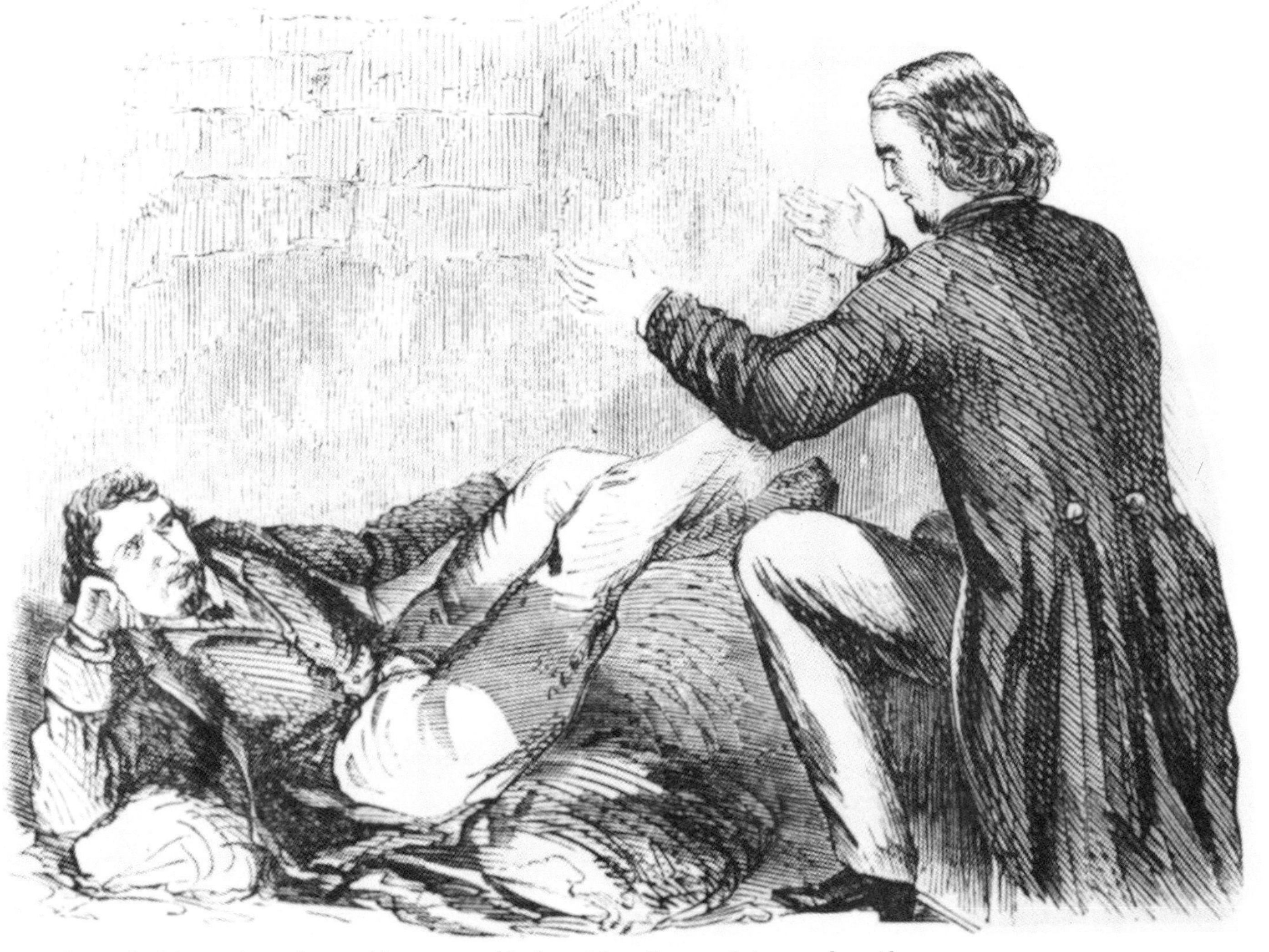

Spiritual adviser to Atzerodt urges him to repent his sins, while gallows are being tested outside.

hundred-pound weights. It was lucky he did for one side stuck and he had to make an adjustment. By 11 A.M. everything was fine—the thirteen steps leading up to the platform had been built, four nooses made of 20-strand rope, one and a half inches in circumference, were hanging neatly from their overhead crossbeam. Four chairs had been placed invitingly on the twenty-foot square platform which seemed so solid right now, but which had two ominous divisions whereby when upright timbers where knocked out from below the front portions, they would drop down and hang by their hinges and feet that had been standing there would be left with only air to stand on. Something had been added in the nearby grave area too—four rough looking wooden coffins.

Beside the military present, only one hundred tickets to civilian spectators had been issued, and everyone asking for a ticket had to be convincing that he, or she, was not there through idle and ghoulish curiosity. One she only had applied for permission to be there and actually Dr. Mary E. Walker, the only woman doctor in the Union Army, did not need a ticket as she was classed with the military present. Dr. Walker was a character greatly looked down on by her hoopskirted country-

Annie Surratt spent the last night of her mother's life in the cell with her, failed to gain her own freedom or her mother's body, buried next to the gallows in the prison yard.

Preston King (*left*), Andrew Johnson's personal adviser and closest friend, barred the President's door to Annie Surratt who had come to plead for her mother's life. James Lane (*right*), Senator from Kansas, assisted King in protecting President Johnson from frenzied Annie Surratt as she lay weeping on the White House stairs.

women as she insisted on wearing long pants under her short skirts. She shocked everyone on the hanging day by riding her horse to the penitentiary astride, like a man.

Early on the morning of the Seventh Annie Surratt had gone again to the White House to try to get to the President and beg him for mercy, but his two protectors again prevented her from climbing more than the bottom steps of the stairway. One woman did get past them, though, and she carried Annie's prayer in to Mr. Johnson in his office. The widow of Stephen A. Douglas, tremendously wrought up at the injustice being done to what she felt was an innocent woman, simply pushed and sailed past Lane and King and threw open the upstairs door. She was a very beautiful, very tall and queenly woman with a tender heart and she had hoped to accomplish a miracle, but the President was immovable.

When Annie, now beside herself with weeping as the minutes were ticking away, left to go back to the prison, a last effort was being made to save her mother. Justice Andrew Wylie of the Supreme Court of the District of

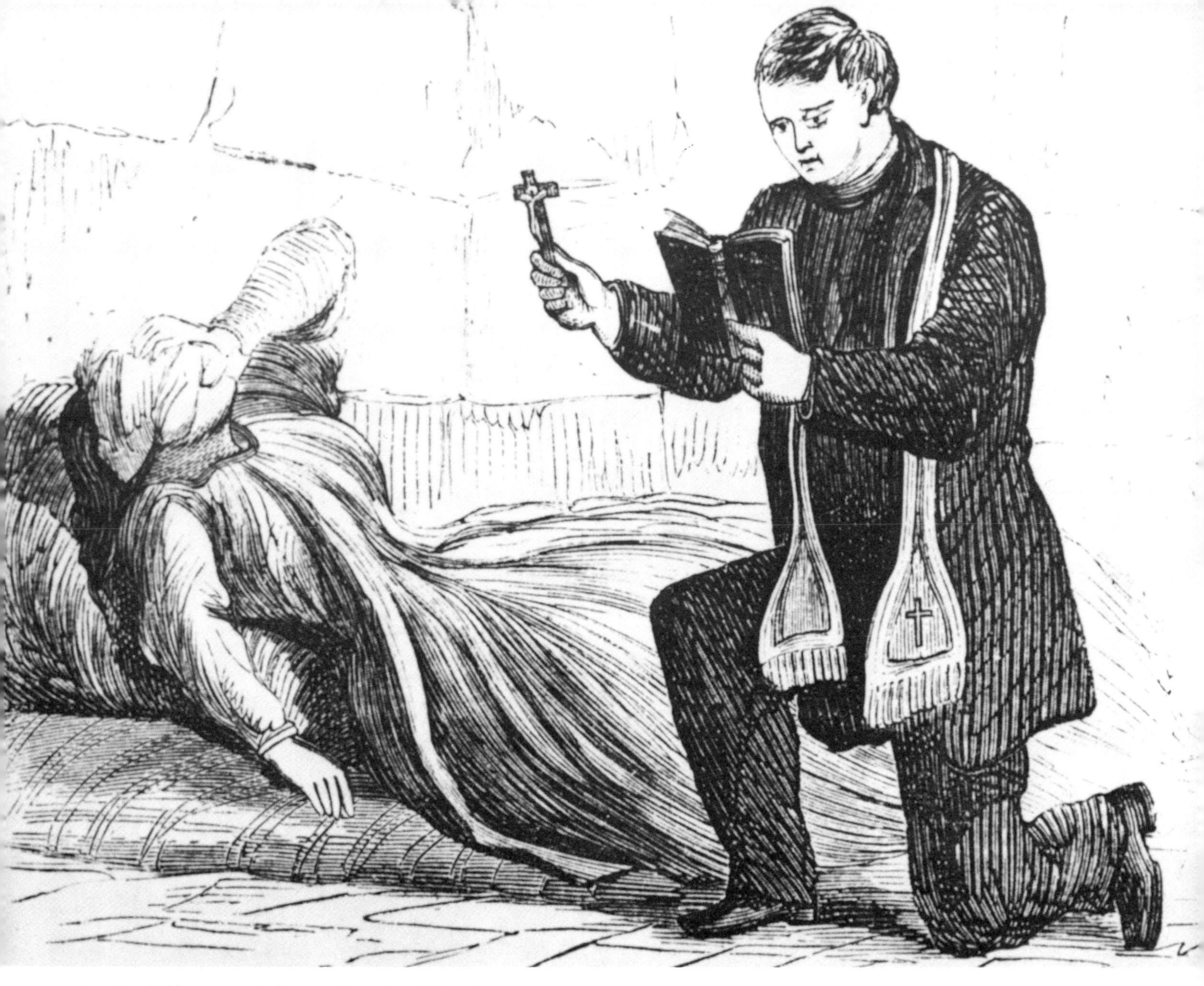

A priest holds a cross before semiconscious Mary Surratt just before the execution. Up until now she had expected a pardon to arrive from the President.

Columbia had been prevailed upon to sign a writ of habeas corpus and this was to be rushed to the prison. But Johnson had a message there first saying that he invalidated the writ as a necessary measure under the circumstances. There was now nothing for General Hancock to do except announce that the execution would take place immediately, though he still kept horsemen posted at intervals all the way from the Arsenal grounds to the White House—in case the reprieve did come.

The defense lawyers now went into the prisoners' cells and said good-by. The clergymen kept up a steady murmur of praying and now the relatives entered the cells for the last time. Earlier Annie Surratt had shrieked so loudly that she was heard all over the yard outside, but at the last people said she was so calm they thought she might have had secret word of a pardon for her mother. Atzerodt had his elderly mother crying with him; Herold his bevy of sisters; Mrs. Surratt her Annie; and Paine had no relative at all. His lawyer had sent to Florida for his Baptist minister father and if it had been a civil trial there would have been time for him to get there—but with the military commission's feverish haste to hang, it was impossible.

The procession of prisoners came out of the prison doors—first, Mrs. Surratt, supported on each side by an officer, as she seemed to sag and sway with weakness. Her guards and her lawyer said she was really more than half-dead when she was hung. She wore a black bonnet covered with a black veil and a black dress which hung limply out of style, but it would have hardly been the thing to wear hoops to this dance of death. Two priests walked ahead of her, one with a cross held over his heart, the other reaching back every few step to press his cross against Mrs. Surratt's lips. Four soldiers guarded her so that she could not escape on the journey up the thirteen steps, and when she was seated in her chair on the platform, an umbrella was held solicitously over her head to fend off the near boiling rays. Herold, Paine, and Atzerodt, each with his entourage of guards, followed.

Atzerodt had wept and prayed all night and Herold had trembled, but it was said that Paine slept excellently, and now he was the conspirator all eyes were drawn to in

wonder. He walked in, people said, as though he were a young king going to his coronation, erect and proud, and an altogether magnificent-looking young man. If only, the papers said the next day, all this could have been enlisted for good instead of evil. On the scaffold Paine thanked his guards and said what he had been saying every day since his capture, "Mrs. Surratt is innocent. She doesn't deserve to die with the rest of us." On the way through the courtyard in a sudden prankish instant he had snatched a straw hat from a bystander's head and was now wearing it with those out-of-character dimples showing beneath.

General Hartranft read the order for the execution and then all four of the condemned stood while their arms

Sitting prisoners listen to the death order being read at center of gallows as soldiers stand below ready to knock out posts and release traps.

were pinioned behind them and their legs bound. Mrs. Surratt's arms were drawn back uncomfortably and she evidently mentioned it—the binding was redone, more loosely. All four had white caps put over their heads and the nooses were adjusted around their necks. When executioner Rath personally adjusted Paine's noose, Paine noticeably stretched up his neck as though to be helpful. Rath said low to him, "I want you to die quick," and Paine replied cheerily through his white cap, "You know best." Paine stood straight and tall as a heroic statue during the ten seconds that remained—Mrs. Surratt was murmuring, "Don't let me fall"—Herold was visibly shaking as well as one could shake as trussed up as he was and Atzerodt cried out in his thick German accent just

before the drop, "Good-by, gentlemen. May we all meet in the other world!"

General Hancock clapped his hands twice and at the second clap, by arrangement, the two soldiers below and at the back of the platform rammed the supporting posts with two long poles and knocked them down. The front part of the platform swung down on its hinges and the four bodies jerked down about five feet—not enough to break Paine's bull-strong neck and he had to strangle. It took about five minutes and the crowd could see a portion of his neck which was exposed and his wrists turn purple.

Everyone thought Mrs. Surratt had died instantly. She

Hoods for the hanging are fitted and nooses adjusted on Mrs. Surratt who is still seated at the left of the platform, on Paine who stands tall and erect beside her, and on Herold and Atzerodt who both are still bare-headed.

just swung and twirled—perfectly quiet.

Herold, who had been called the silly boy all through the trial, was the most frightened on the scaffold and he stayed alive after the hanging longer than the others, trying to draw his body up repeatedly so there would not be so much weight on his neck.

People noticed that Atzerodt's stomach heaved repeatedly as he hung there, but they judged his the second earliest death after Mrs. Surratt's. When the bodies were still, Alexander Gardner, who had been taking pictures with his big camera set up in various positions around the yard, now photographed the four limp bodies.

Spectators were now asked to leave, and they went outside the prison to a crowd that was regaling itself with lemonade and cakes.

Half an hour after their hanging the dead were cut down and examined by doctors as they lay stretched out on the tops of their coffins. All were satisfactorily lifeless. Then without having their lightweight hanging-caps removed, they were placed in their coffins and buried in the four waiting graves.

As the earth was being packed and smoothed over

them, executioner Rath was already dividing the rope into suitable lengths for relics, and writing out affidavits. He sawed up the gallows into neat foot-long mementos suitable for paperweights or interesting additions to a family's mantelpiece or parlor table.

PART V

DRAWING NEARER TO THE QUIET PLACE

After Albany, Lincoln's funeral train continued West into the country he knew best—Ohio, Indiana, and finally Illinois. At each stop as the great procession drew closer and closer to home, emotions seemed to steadily heighten.

IN BUFFALO—A LETDOWN

On the day of the Washington funeral Buffalo's citizens, distracted with grief at the news of the assassination, had not been satisfied with the services at its churches. Instead the people had put on a complete mock funeral, just as though they had had the coffin and body there. They had built a magnificent catafalque, had a monster procession, given prayers, eulogies, and gone through all the motions of the real thing. Then when they got the wonderful news that their city was chosen to put on a funeral on the journey home, there was, along with the pride, a slight letdown. Buffalo had exhausted her first wild extravagance of feeling at her make-believe ceremony and now, although citizens told each other it would be a thousand times more wonderful an experience to have the real coffin, with the real body inside—somehow when

Buffalo's hearse, valanced in elegant black velvet and bearing a temple with plumes at the top, surges through the sky.

the time came, it wasn't. They used the same magnificent hearse car with its six white horses clothed in black to the hoofs. In St. James's Hall, the viewing was a model of good management. The coffin was properly up-tilted and brilliantly lighted, and sweet voices sang, "Rest, noble spirit, rest," as one hundred thousand, until eight at night, moved decorously past. But between dirges the silence was oppressive and the "utter decorum" and "remarkable order" were somehow not as much of a tribute as Philadelphia's wild straining to burst the ropes, to get near, to touch.

Among the well-mannered mourners was handsome, blue-eyed ex-President Millard Fillmore, who had opposed Lincoln's policies and campaigned in 1864 for General McClellan. In the line, too, was a solidly built, serious-faced twenty-eight-year-old bachelor lawyer who had had to stay out of the war to take care of his sisters and widowed mother. He had borrowed money to send a substitute soldier in his place—to fight in his name—which was Grover Cleveland.

CLEVELAND SOLVES THE PROBLEM—ROOM FOR ALL UNDER THE SKY

Cleveland's funeral was full of contradictions. It was both a solemn wake and a theatrical pageant of flowers. To show its admiration for this most completely native of American heroes, Lincoln, who had never been out of the United States, the city introduced an Oriental note. Proclaiming earnestly that it could sense the mourning become deeper and more passionate as the cortege moved westward, Cleveland channeled its passion into building a Chinese pagoda-type of temple in its park to view the remains. The fairy pagoda, created between dusk and dawn, set the tone of Cleveland's demonstration, and citizens listened happily to a visitor who had attended every funeral so far and told them theirs was by far the most magnificent. They turned deaf ears to a Mr. Charles L. Wilson of Chicago, who had just come from that city and said the display being planned there would stagger man's imagination and severely test his credulity. There was drama even in the rain that fell all day in the "Forest City," a name it had earned from its superb, towering trees, for Cleveland pretended it liked the rain, that the rain was "tears falling for the great, good man."

The overnight trip from Buffalo had been through lines of silent people, with continuous bells and bands and

Cleveland's six white horses back the hearse up to the outdoor viewing pavillion in Monument Square (above)

the many tableaux of thirty-six maidens dressed in white with black sashes. At Westfield at one A.M. the engine stopped for water and wood and five young ladies were allowed to bring a cross of flowers to Lincoln's coffin. Then they knelt and each in turn kissed the coffin. This took hold and from now on there were not the efforts there had been at first to kiss Lincoln's face. Kissing the coffin, with its cruel barrier of lead and wood and black material, was such a desperately futile and helpless gesture it never failed to move those who watched to tears.

The train arrived in the outskirts of Cleveland in the early hours of Friday, the twenty-eighth of April, just a full week since it had left Washington. Governor Brough and his staff and General Hooker who was now in charge of army affairs in Michigan, Ohio, Indiana, and Illinois came on board at six-thirty in the morning and rode the final way along the Lake Erie shore to the Union Station. Out of the train windows as it moved slowly into the city they could see crowds of people on the green hillsides, and high up, a maiden dressed in a flag, under an arch that said ABRAHAM LINCOLN. At exactly seven o'clock the train came to a stop at the station, and the national salute of thirty-six guns commenced firing. When the coffin was lifted to the black and white plumed, silver-starred hearse, an enormous procession set off for the Park, all bathed in Heaven's tears, which obligingly laid the dust of the broad avenue. Dust had been a problem in other cities. Now it was a glorious sight to really see the military and bands and civilian marchers moving down the long tree-lined avenue. Onlookers had flocked from all over northern Ohio, western Pennsylvania, and eastern Michigan and boatloads had come down the lake from Detroit. All females had been warned to leave their hoops for their skirts at home—the breakage of such attire in the reverent throng would be, officials said, swift and total. And yet with such uncountable throngs there was not a hint of disorder. The rain now turned to torrents, drenching the regiments that marched—the Odd Fellows, the Temperance Societies, the Laboring Mens' Union with a banner "LABOR IS THE WEALTH OF THE NATION," the Hungarian Association, the Colored Masons, the Colored Equal Rights League, the Seamen's Union which carried a full-rigged sailing ship with its flag at half-mast.

The structure in the park had been an inspiration. The size of the crowd was only limited by what all outdoors could hold, and because of the omission of the walls and doors and all inner obstructions that could squeeze a line to a standstill, the structure allowed one hundred and eighty people per minute, over ten thousand an hour, and over one hundred and fifty thousand in the allotted fifteen hours to pass by the coffin. All the other viewings had been held in the biggest buildings the cities could offer but all had been cramped and thousands outside were always disappointed. Only Cleveland had thought of an outdoor viewing that could satisfy everyone.

while long lines of viewers wait in the rain (below).

IN COLUMBUS—A FUNERAL OF FLOWERS

Approaching the State House (upper right),

The chief of the Columbus police force received a telegram from Cleveland tipping him off that a gang of pickpockets from New York who planned to work the Columbus funeral mobs would arrive in town on a certain train on Friday. The train arrived, the doors to each car were bolted while police searched every passenger. Eleven were found with their pockets bulging with skeleton keys and burglars' tools. Now just two weeks after Lincoln's death, as Columbus's funeral day—Saturday, the twenty-ninth—dawned, all eleven were safely in the Columbus jail.

The city of Columbus offered a funeral of flowers. People had roses in their hands which they tossed under the hearse's wheels and the invalid soldiers from the Soldiers' Hospital had literally covered the street near the hospital for several hundred yards with lilac blooms which the hearse wheels crushed. Many of the official train escort following in carriages behind, who had been in the lilac-drenched Petersen House throughout the death night, were more grimly reminded of the assassination's horror by this chance breath of sweet air than by the bands or black ribbon or the Columbus funeral oration they listened to at four o'clock that afternoon.

The Columbus hearse had the required black cloth and ornamental tassels, the stars and lace and curtains, and it was drawn by six white horses. There was one new feature, though, and it would have amused the martyr. On each side of the dais, plain in great block letters of silver for everyone to read, was the name "LINCOLN." Lincoln himself tried whenever possible to avoid the obvious. When in the spring of 1864 he had been asked to sign a letter presenting a sword to General Dix, Lincoln did sign his name and then he was asked to add "President of the United States." His answer, putting down his pen, was, "Well, I don't think I'll say 'This is a horse.' " Columbus constantly through the day kept saying "This is a horse." When the coffin reached the State Capitol building, it was placed on a catafalque

The seventeen-foot-long Columbus hearse was built in Chinese pagoda-style, had helpful identification neatly lettered in silver on its side.

The Columbus catafalque was the only one without columns and canopies—just a low moss and flower covered dais.

carriages and marchers in the Columbus procession move slowly to the roll of drums, the tolling of bells.

bearing the same helpful identification in large silver letters across its foot. Then, too, the city was alive with mottos in almost every window—everyone searched and chose the words of someone else to express what he himself was thinking and feeling.

The Columbus procession moved through the drapes and flowers and mottos of the city, guns firing, muffled drums beating out the dead march, soldiers' feet treading in that hesitant, nerve-rackingly slow rhythm. The long red hook-and-ladder car of the fire department carried forty-two young ladies in it singing "Great ruler of the earth and skies" and "Behold, O Lord, before Thy throne." Eight members of the Veteran Guard carried the coffin into the rotunda on their shoulders and set it down on a very imaginative and unusual catafalque. No columns, no canopy, just a low dais sitting on a black-covered platform reached by five steps. The surface of the dais was the big surprise—it was not black velvet! Instead it was a soft rising swell of moss and tender green leaves, spangled with white roses and orange blossoms. Again, when the heavy coffin sank into its soft and fragile bed, there arose the sweet scent of sacrificial flowers. Now the people in the rotunda stood transfixed as the undertaker unscrewed the top of the coffin, made a slight adjustment of the position of the body, and motioned for the viewing to begin. It was an especially silent viewing, for the first time a carpet—to deaden the shuffling and clicking of shoe leather—led up to the catafalque. When the Colored Masons and the Colored Benevolent Society came timidly into the rotunda, it was like mice approaching—not a sound.

And so it began for the eighth time—thousands upon thousands of Americans in a new city saying good-by to their fallen President. There were many who felt, watching the people's ceaseless prayer and preoccupation with the mortal remains of Abraham Lincoln, that this was the most pathetic happening in the country's history. Not so the South which already was complaining loudly that the whole thing was a vulgar exhibition, a calculated, hardhearted display of a decaying mummy, spending untold amounts of government money in an effort to inflame men's lowest passions and punish a gallant enemy. They said here was poor Edwin Booth begging for his brother's body to take home to his aged mother, but the cruel North had clawed out Johnny's entrails and thrown them to the hogs and were planning to put his head and spinal column in a museum to be scoffed at—while the blood drained out of Lincoln's body at the autopsy was "sacredly preserved" and already worshiped as a sacred relic.

The Indianapolis hearse stands ready (left) as
boughs by the wagonload are brought in to decorate the State House (above).

INDIANAPOLIS SAYS GOOD-BY TO INDIANA'S FARM-BOY

It was an eleven-hour run from Columbus to Indianapolis, from 8 P.M. to 7 A.M., and there were orders now to pass all stations at not more than five miles per hour. But at so many villages and towns the preparations were so elaborate and the people so pitifully hoping the train would stop, that it did. At Woodstock there were five hundred citizens waiting and ladies were allowed to board the hearse car and weep and strew flowers on the closed coffin. At Urbana there were three thousand people. The train stopped at St. Paris for a bouquet. At Conover three maidens sang while the population of the town stood, neatly divided into old people, middle-aged people, and children. At Richmond, Indiana, there were five thousand persons gathered and the arch the train rolled under had red, white, and blue lights hanging from it. This was a Spirit of Liberty town, and a beautiful young woman was illuminated, mourning over a mock coffin, while the real one was right there only a few yards away. Here, at 2 A.M., Governor Morton boarded the train, and it started up again, west, through Indiana, towards the capital.

A substitute coffin is brought up to the entrance of the elaborate structure specially built to lead from the street to the State House.

Abraham Lincoln had now returned to the state where he had lived from about eight years of age till he was twenty-one, where his mother had died when he was nine of the milk sickness and where he had welcomed to the family log cabin his lovely stepmother, Sally Bush Lincoln. Here he had had an ax put into his hands early, being "large for his age," and he had become an expert woodsman, fighting, as he told it himself later, "with the trees and logs and grubs" of that "unbroken wilderness there then." And from here, at nineteen, the backwoods youth had gone on his first big adventure, drifting with the current down the Mississippi on a flatboat to New Orleans. And then in 1830, driving the oxen that were carrying his family and their possessions to Illinois, he had left Indiana.

As the train pulled into the Indianapolis depot the rain, which had stopped at midnight, came down in a great solid splashing waterfall. At first it was hoped that, if the rain did stop, the procession could march in the afternoon. But the torrents of water increased in driving power minute by minute, the black decorations on every housefront hung soggy and the black dye formed dark trickles down the faces of the buildings.

Reluctantly, the giant Indianapolis procession was cancelled and the whole day instead was devoted to viewing. All the way from the station to the State House, soldiers were lined up facing each other at attention, their upright swords making two fences of steel. The hearse, marvelous with midnight-black velvet as lush as fur and silver fringe and white plumes with black trimmings, was drawn by eight white horses wearing black velvet blankets and white masks over their faces with holes cut for their eyes. Six of the horses had drawn Lincoln as President-elect four years before. At the main entrance of the State House Square was a structure that combined the ideas of many people and loudly proclaimed that too many cooks had spoiled the broth. It was a nonentity of undetermined purpose with a tremendous duplication of exhibits offered. It could not seem to decide whether it was an arch or an art gallery or a jungle-dweller's home

Legend has it that there was a photograph taken of the dead Lincoln in Indianapolis and that this lithograph by Indiana artist George Koch was made from the photograph.

REMAINS OF

ABRAHAM LINCOLN

THE GREATEST MAN OF OUR CENTURY

assassinated April 14th 1865

built on stilts to be out of the path of hungry animals. Forty feet long, twenty-four wide, it had a central passageway big enough for a carriage to roll through and two six-foot paths on either side for walking couples. The high front pillars of the building had portraits fastened to them of Gov. Morton, General Grant, General Sherman, and Admiral Farragut. On the summits of the pillars were busts of George Washington, Daniel Webster, Henry Clay and Abraham Lincoln. All four busts were crowned with wreaths of real laurel. Inside the State House were many more busts, portraits, and wreaths, and so before a gallery of the staring stone eyes of famous Americans the viewing began. The first to pay their respects were five thousand Sabbath School Scholars, the last to enter the State House were Colored Masons and hundreds of Colored Citizens who carried with them copies of the Emancipation Proclamation. They saw a coffin, if possible, heaped even more extravagantly with flowered crosses and wreaths and harps and anchors. Here, on this epic cross-country funeral expedition, an American tradition was being born, for before Lincoln's funeral it was not customary to send flowers to funerals. Now people searched in their hearts to see how they could best show their grief and the token so many decided upon was flowers. It was a brand new expression of sympathy. With the most loving intentions it was being overdone—Lincoln's biers were increasingly shaky under the contents of each city's hothouses. The colors ran heavily to red, white, and blue which would have pleased the President—he said he had never looked upon an American flag without feeling emotion. In Springfield there would be a tremendous

Topped by a silver-gilt eagle the spindly-wheeled

red heart, covered with thousands of red roses, that would ride the coffin all the way to the tomb.

The disappointed photographers who because of the continuous heavy rain had been unable to expose their negatives of the hearse carrying Lincoln's coffin to the State House were already forming makeshift plans to set up their cameras the next day and secure some kind of record for posterity. It would have to be the hearse bearing a coffin as like the dead President's as Indianapolis undertakers could provide. In a hundred years they hoped their pictures would be accepted as the real thing and nobody would ever notice that there were no shamrock designs in silver tacks on the coffin's sides.

When the procession was over the coffin was escorted back to the train with Governor Oliver Perry Morton and the whole population of Indianapolis following. Governor Morton had greeted and entertained and said good-by to Lincoln when the President-elect had passed through Indianapolis on the trip East. On that occasion Lincoln had left the city with the words, "If you, the people, are but true to yourselves and to the Constitution, there is but little harm I can do, thank God!" Now he was leaving the state of Indiana where in the silence of the forest wilderness he had heard the Baptist preacher shout the funeral service for his mother in a voice that reached neighbors a mile away. Today the great silence did not come from empty space for now a city crowded the land. This silence came from the hush of a vast multitude. And, breaking it, instead of the old parson's cry to God, there was the train's shrill whistle and the answering tongue of its bell.

hearse with its "precious cargo" stops to be photographed on an Indianapolis street corner.

AN IMPROMPTU FUNERAL AT MICHIGAN CITY

Citizens of Michigan City gather under their funeral arch.

Arches like this one stretched over their city.

With Indianapolis left behind, now all there was left was Illinois, the home state. There a mammoth funeral was planned in Chicago and then, the last, the home town funeral in Springfield. But due to an unexpected delay there was to be one more funeral, an impromptu one, right at the station of Michigan City, Indiana. The funeral train was supposed to go nonstop from Indianapolis and arrive at Chicago at 11 A.M. Monday, May first. But it was forced to wait for one hour in Michigan City for a committee of more than one hundred important men from Chicago who were coming out in the early morning to escort the train into

The citizens of Michigan City made the most of the unexpected stop. The rain had ended during the night and a brilliantly sunny May Day morning made the depot arch of evergreens and roses under which the train ran sparkle. There were mottos in among the roses, and pictures of Lincoln and flags and rosettes and black ribbons "tastily" distributed.

The three hundred weary mourners on the train were whisked off for a bountiful breakfast featuring whitefish, which was served to them in the station. Then the rule was broken about not opening the coffin except in the

the train tracks at scores of unscheduled cities and towns along the route but only Michigan City was lucky enough to get a stop.

regular cities which were putting on funerals. The townspeople were allowed to pass through the car and view Lincoln and a hurriedly arranged tiny funeral was held —prayers were said and the beautiful young maidens assembled to honor the train on its passage through sang "Old Hundred" and other hymns. Everyone wept as bitterly as if it all were taking place in the rotunda of some state capitol instead of in the little hearse car.

Lincoln had always been one to upset hard and fast rules—he hated any procedure that could not be altered on the spur of the moment for something better. His office hours were the best illustration of this—his secretaries would set the precise time of reception but the President would receive people before breakfast and after breakfast and during his lunch hour and when he was supposed to be having dinner and even in the middle of the night—"you did just right to wake me," he would say. He was the despair of all who tried to protect him from his own kind heart and willingness to drive himself. The people wanted so little, he said, and there was so little he could give—he must see them.

This Michigan City meeting with the people would have been just right with Lincoln.

IN PEACE NOBLE SOUL, PATRIOT
We Honor Him Dead who honored Us while Livin

ALMOST HOME— CHICAGO HONORS THE RAIL-SPLITTER

Lincoln was almost home now. He was in the great city of his home state, a city which had been a prairie mud-hole when he first settled in Illinois and was now aggressive, rich and crowded with three hundred thousand people. Lincoln had many ties with Chicago. He had spent a lot of time there pleading cases, and there he had argued his most important case with a skill that marked the summit of his career as a lawyer. The first bridge across the Mississippi had been built and opened for train passage on April 23, 1856, from Rock Island, Illinois, to Davenport, Iowa, against the desperate protests of steamboat factions who felt this would eventually doom shipping. On May 6, 1856, a fine side-wheel steamer less than a year old, the fastest on the river—the *Effie Afton*—was passing through the channel made possible by the lifting of the drawbridge, swerved in the strong current into one of the piers, caught fire and burned up and also ignited the drawbridge. The owner of the *Effie Afton* brought suit against the Rock Island Bridge Company, asking fifty thousand dollars and claiming that the bridge was an unlawful obstruction to navigation. Lincoln was retained to defend the bridge company and he spent months of preparation for his argument, visiting the bridge, talking to the drawbridge employees, measuring the strength of the currents at that point. He sincerely believed that if the river people won, it would postpone the development of railroads through the West and delay the essential and marvelous opening up of the country. He had had an absorbing interest in the great "Father of Waters" since his two flatboat trips to New Orleans, and he knew at first hand what he was going to advance as his argument. He saw clearly his only hope of winning was to prove that the *Effie Afton* had been inexpertly maneuvered through the opening offered. The trial took fifteen days and Lincoln's summation was masterly in logic, encyclopedic knowledge of facts, in general restraint, and incisive choice of words. It crowned his long career as a lawyer in Illinois, even though there was a hung jury and the judge dismissed the case.

It was in Chicago, too, that Lincoln's nomination for the Presidency had taken place on May 18, 1860, in the quickly constructed Republican building called "The Wigwam"—built to hold five thousand and crammed with more than ten thousand. It was there that Seward's forces were outwitted by Judge David Davis and Lin-

Thirty-six maidens in white surround the Chicago hearse as it passes through the funeral arch on its way into the city.

coln's Illinois friends, who, on the third day of the convention, when the Seward men were out parading, printed up thousands of bogus tickets and crammed the building with Lincoln men with instructions to scream their lungs out for Old Abe. And all the time the Seward men raged outside on the sidewalks for there was not a square inch of space left inside. Judge Davis spent sleepless nights cajoling delegations and promising them the moon even though Lincoln had said commit me to nothing. And when later the Judge was asked if he had not prevaricated a bit, he said, "Prevaricate! I lied like hell!" Back in Springfield, waiting quietly, Lincoln got the news by wire of what Chicago had done for him.

And it was in Chicago just before the beginning of the Lincoln-Douglas debates in 1858 that Douglas and Lincoln spoke to large audiences on successive July nights. Douglas spoke about Lincoln's position on the Dred Scott decision. "He says it is wrong, because it deprives the Negro of the benefits of that clause of the Constitution which says that citizens of one state shall enjoy all the privileges and immunities of citizens of the several states; in other words, he thinks it is wrong because it deprives the Negro of the privileges, immunities, and rights of citizenship which pertain, according to that decision, to the white man. I am free to say to you that in my opinion this government of ours is founded on the white basis. It was made by the white man, for the benefit of the white man, to be administered by white men, in such manner as they should determine . . . Illinois . . . has decided that a Negro shall not be a slave, and we have at the same time decided that he shall not vote, or serve on juries, or enjoy political privileges. I am content with that system of policy we have adopted for ourselves."

The next night Abraham Lincoln ended his lengthy and impassioned speech in Chicago with the words: "My friend has said to me that I am a poor hand at quoting Scripture. I will try it again, however. It is said in one of the admonitions of our Lord, 'As your Father in Heaven is perfect, be ye also perfect!' The Saviour, I suppose, did not expect that any human creature could

While half a million spectators choke Chicago's streets and roofs and windows and doorsteps, guards stand at attention in front of funeral car with only Willie left inside.

During the Chicago funeral the train waited on a trestle that carried the tracks out over Lake Michigan.

be as perfect as the Father in Heaven; but He said, 'As your Father in Heaven is perfect, be ye also perfect!' He set up that as a standard, and he who did most toward reaching that standard, attained the highest degree of moral perfection. So I say in relation to the principle that all men are created equal, let it be as nearly reached as we can. . . ." And then lest anyone had missed the nub of his plea, he repeated—". . . I leave you, hoping that the lamp of liberty will burn in your bosoms until there shall no longer be a doubt that men are created free and equal."

So it was into a city that had long known Lincoln and respected him greatly that his body came at 11 A.M. on Monday, May 1, 1865. It had traveled more than fifteen hundred miles to reach this point. And the hearts of the people of Chicago who awaited him were heavy.

The funeral train did not go the full distance to the Union Depot but stopped on a trestle that carried the tracks out in the lake some distance from the sandy shore, sliding in in absolute silence except for the tolling of its bell. A temporary platform had been built, with steps leading down to the ground and from there the Veteran Guard carried the coffin the short distance up the street to where a dais was waiting beneath Chicago's dramatic offering for its old friend—an unbelievably magnificent Gothic three section arch. The city had employed three distinguished architects to create the arch, to design the hearse, and to be sure that the decorations in the rotunda of the Court House were the ultimate in grandeur. Fifteen thousand dollars had been spent solely on the arch and on decorations for the courthouse—or half of what the Washington funeral cost in all. Now thirty-six beautiful maidens in white walked around the dais bearing the coffin, and each dropped a single flower on the black broadcloth surface, under which lay what everyone was passionately longing to see and yet dreading the sight of with a physical revulsion that made some weak and faint long before they reached the place of viewing.

Chicago's mammoth tribute was comparable to New York's in size and grandeur. The route of the procession ran along the elegant part of town, down Michigan Avenue first, then Lake Street, then Clark to Court House Square—avoiding the world's biggest stockyards, the McCormack Reaper works, and the flour mills. The streets along which the procession passed were filled to choking. The roofs were black with people, the windows, doorsteps, porches crowded, the branches of trees bent under human forms. There was a motto in just about every window—citizens here as in all previous cities had done their homework well in researching noble thoughts for quotation. One read: "SNATCHED FROM THE COLD AND FORMAL WORLD, AND PRESSED BY THE GREAT MOTHER TO HER GLOWING BREAST." One shop even managed to combine sorrow with a little advertising, arranging its motto against black velvet in letters made out of fifteen-hundred dollars worth of rare laces. One man who had been a member of the escorting three hundred since Washington had telegraphed ahead to have hung on the front of his house "MOURNFULLY, TENDERLY BEAR HIM TO HIS REST," because he had been so impressed with the tenderness with which, on the many repeated occasions, the Veteran Reserve Guards had lifted Lincoln's coffin up and softly set it down, conveying to the crowds in each city the concept that this was the nation's most priceless treasure.

On each side of the hearse walked six pallbearers, all old Chicago friends of Lincoln. Marching second on the left-hand side was "Long John" Wentworth, six feet six inches in height and weighing three hundred pounds. He had served in Congress at the same time as Lincoln, had started off as a Democrat but by wartime was a staunch Republican and had supported the President ably. Wentworth was known all over Illinois as a great

FURS
118
WHOLESALE

stump speaker, but people used to say he was so tall that instead of giving him a platform they had to dig a hole for him to speak from. Once at a political rally Lincoln and Long John had spent their time counting, not potential votes, but how many women in the audience were nursing babies. In 1857 Wentworth was elected mayor of Chicago and cleaned corruption out of the city. The story went that rough, gruff Long John had made a one-sentence campaign speech to a crowd from the steps of the Court House—"You damn fools, you can either vote for me or go to hell."

The procession here was just about the same as the processions of other cities. The clergy had something a little new—white crosses on their black armbands. And there was a division of Ellsworth Zouaves in baggy red pants. And there was a large group of captured Confederates who had taken the oath and were now Northern soldiers. And ten thousand school children, walking with stricken faces, with black hair ribbons and armbands and sashes and badges. One of the most shocking and upsetting things about Lincoln's death—to children—was the sight of their parents crying. Grownups just didn't cry. But now they were doing just that and had from the second of learning the dreadful news. They sobbed and real tears ran down their cheeks, and it was really true that it was as if every family in the nation had one dead beneath its roof. And the children remembered it all their lives and wrote their memories of this down, and told their descendants. Everyone remembered the exact moment he heard of the death and exactly what he was doing at that moment, and if he was a child, he especially remembered the faces of his parents, wet and unfamiliar.

In the procession there were marchers who had come to this country from Holland, groups of Belgians, French, German, Irish, and Bohemians. There were butchers and bricklayers and tailors and carpenters, all carrying banners with clumsily worded, unmistakably heartfelt messages. There was the Dramatic Profession of Chicago, walking with chins up, half defiant and half ashamed that John Wilkes Booth had been an actor too. And then, walking humbly, and actually unwanted, at the end of the four hour procession, came the "Colored Citizens." Finally the hearse arrived at the Courthouse and stood beneath the great Courthouse bell whose enormous tongue clanged so earsplittingly it could be heard to the city's farthest reaches. It was not until six o'clock in the evening that the doors were opened for viewing but then the public was admitted straight through the night and all the next day. Seven thousand people an hour peered for a swift second only down into the coffin. The light was extremely dim but the general feeling was yes, there was a tiny trace of the placid smile they had heard of from other cities. And yes, the discoloration that had started out under the right eye from the shock of the bullet wound had indeed spread over the entire face. It had been in New York that the blackness had really started to distress viewers. Lincoln looked shriveled, his coffin many sizes

The Chicago procession, equaling New York's in size and grandeur, moves through the city.

The procession comes to a halt in back of Cook County Court House.

too big for him. To many, his cheeks seemed hollow and pitted. The reporters had been positive that when the funeral train left New York there would be no more open-coffin funerals—the top would just have to be kept screwed on. But after New York, with constant care and powdering from the undertaker, Lincoln's appearance had seemed to improve. Still the violence of his death cried out in that abhorrent blackness.

Over the door at the north end of the Courthouse, by which the crowds left, was inscribed "The beauty of Israel is slain upon her high places." There was a large Jewish population in Chicago and this beautiful and evocative Hebrew lamentation proclaimed that people's grief over Lincoln's death. Coming on a Saturday morning—the Jewish Sabbath—the President's death found Jews assembled in their synagogues for their weekly services and in New York, in the Synagogue Shearith Israel, a rabbi did something that had no precedent. He recited an *Hazcarah,* or prayer for the dead, for Abraham Lincoln—the first time this had ever been done in a synagogue for someone who was not an orthodox follower of the Jewish religion. The rabbi received a good deal of criticism for thus honoring a non-Jew, but the prayer did not surprise a certain Dr. M. Wise of the Jewish Synagogue in Cincinnati. Four days after Lincoln's death, Wise announced: "Brethren, the lamented Abraham Lincoln is believed to be bone from our bone and flesh from our flesh. He was supposed to be a descendant of Hebrew parentage. He said so in my presence, and indeed, he preserved numerous features of the Hebrew race both in countenance and character."

At 8 P.M. on Tuesday the great procession re-formed and by the light of three thousand torches the eight black horses drew the hearse with Lincoln's coffin on it to the depot of the St. Louis and Alton Railroad. Now the train would start up one last time and head out over the prairie, over black earth, through high sky country, through Lincoln land, toward its final destination—Springfield and home. The people of Illinois wept. Their newspapers spoke for them. One tribute read:

> *He who writes this is weeping, he who reads it is weeping; all are weeping who knew him, loved him, trusted him, confided in him, believed in him, leaned upon him—this foremost man, this honest soul, this upright ruler, this Washington of his people, this Moses of us all; for here he comes back to us—dead! O, they have slain the beauty of our Israel!*
>
> *Hushed be the city. Hung be the heavens in black. Let the tumult of traffic cease. Let the streets be still. Let the lake rest. Let the winds be lulled, and the sun be covered up. The bells—toll them. The guns—let their melancholy boom roll out. . . . Let his body rest in peace in the midst of thy prairies. Yes, bury him at home. All lands for his renown—this land for his repose. All people for his mourners—this people for his stricken household.*

In a blurred mass the people of Chicago stream out of the Court House after viewing Lincoln.

PART VI

HE WAS HOME AT LAST

The journey was ended at last and now on the final two days of the twenty, the most moving good-by of all began to take place. For here, in Springfield, Illinois, were the old friends—the people who knew him best and loved him most. Four years before when he had left, Lincoln had known every man, woman, child, and animal in the town by name.

"HERE I HAVE LIVED A QUARTER OF A CENTURY"

The night-long trip from Chicago to Springfield was the most poignant of all the journey's separate parts, for on the welcome banners displayed at the illuminated depots along the tracks there began to appear—over and over—the word "HOME"—"COME HOME"—"BEAR HIM HOME TENDERLY"—"HOME IS THE MARTYR."

At Atlanta, Illinois, the sun came up over the prairie at five o'clock. The whole train was awake and people who thought themselves drained of emotion after the long twelve-day journey knew they would have a hard time fighting back the tears in Springfield. The funeral party looked out of the windows at the beautiful countryside that Lincoln had traveled over and loved so much, now bright with prairie flowers and blossoming fruit trees. In a few weeks the prairie would have its wild strawberries that had stained the legs of Lincoln's faithful horse, Old Bob, as he made his way through the tangle. And there were the quiet winding creeks the country lawyer and his horse had forded time and again. Where fields had been ploughed around farmhouses, the deep blackness of the earth was startling to Eastern eyes, and the arrangement of the trees in isolated small groves of hickory, oak, and sugar maple, dotting the prairie here and there, was also new and interesting.

Emotions deepened again as the town of Lincoln was reached at 7 A.M. The air was soft and fresh after last night's rain and birds were singing. This was the town that actually had been named for President Lincoln—but long ago, when he as a lawyer for his friend Colonel Latham drew up the papers incorporating land that the Colonel had bought and laid out as a town. And the colonel said he had decided to call the place Lincoln.

Here in the back parlor of his Springfield house, now draped in black for the funeral days, Lincoln had received the committee that announced he had been nominated for President.

Early on the morning of the third of May Springfield citizens begin to gather at the station to await the funeral train.

Together they had smashed and eaten a ripe watermelon to christen it.

Now the funeral party and the brakemen on the roofs of the cars caught glimpses of the roads leading to Springfield, solid inching ribbons of carriages and horses and people on foot. At ten minutes to nine the pilot engine puffed into the Chicago and Alton depot on Jefferson Street in Springfield and at nine the funeral train followed. The mass of people around the station and covering the housetops was silent and many were weeping as they had wept when they stood and heard Lincoln's farewell to Springfield that February day in 1861. "My friends"—the words seemed to echo now in that high-pitched voice so like in tone to a bugle playing taps and as peculiarly touching—"no one not in my situation, can appreciate my feelings of sadness at this parting. To this place, and the kindness of these people, I owe everything. Here I have lived a quarter of a century, and have passed from a young to an old man. Here my children have been born, and one is buried. I now leave, not knowing when, or whether ever, I may return. . . ."

Springfield had got the news of Lincoln's assassination by telegraph less than an hour after it happened. Ned Baker, editor of the *Illinois State Journal* and Ninian Edwards' son-in-law ran from his office on North Sixth Street to the house opposite where Lincoln's friend James Conkling lived, and knocked urgently. Conkling came down from bed and went back up again weeping to tell the family. The news was in every home long before dawn and people had gone out into the Square and gathered, especially in front of the two newspaper buildings, the *Journal* and the *Register*. There was a low murmur of talk and everyone seemed stunned. Before the death announcement came there was some mention of revenge and men with their lips compressed in anger rushed to a spot where someone was supposed to have said he was "glad by it," but no such person was found. After the finality of the last wire saying it was all over there was intense silence, as though the people were under a spell. For a while no one moved to go anywhere—just stood and let the tears come.

Within the hour, though, the power of motion returned and the shocked City Council met immediately and later, at noon, there was a mass meeting of citizens in the State House at which officers were elected and resolutions drawn up. The last resolution was: "Resolved, that, inasmuch as this city has for a long time been the home of the President, in which he has graced with his kindness of heart and honesty of purpose all the relations of life, it is appropriate that its 'city of the dead' should be the final resting place of all that on earth remains of him. . . ."

Fortunately for Springfield's wishes it just happened that newly elected Governor Oglesby of Illinois and Richard Yates, the wartime governor of the state who had recently become a senator, were both in Washington and had been among the President's last visitors on the afternoon of April fourteenth. Through Robert Lincoln they were now able to make a strong appeal to Mrs. Lincoln in her bedroom that Illinois claimed her husband, and he must come home, to rest among his friends and neighbors. Mary Lincoln was genuinely torn between the fact that she had quarreled with just about all her old friends and her family in Springfield and never wanted to set foot there again, and the really sincere desire she had to choose the burial place that would have been her husband's choice. Up through the day of the Washington funeral she insisted that Chicago was her first choice and that her second was the crypt that had been built for Washington beneath the rotunda of the Capitol. Her husband had promised her, she said, that after the Presidency they would make a tour of Europe and then settle in Chicago, and so she favored a quiet spot on the shore of Lake Michigan. It rather appealed to her to have the President's grave near the lapping lake waters, close to the burial spot of his old adversary, Stephen A. Douglas, who had courted her at the same time Lincoln had, and whom she gave up for the man she said even then—though it seemed a young girl's silly chatter—would be President. She had not been to Chicago since Douglas' death and did not know that his grave was desolate, with as yet, after four years, no monument to mark it—the few faded wreaths on it often lashed by the lake's waves—and that an enterprising photographer lived in a shack beside it for the purpose of catching pilgrims to the spot in reverent attitudes.

Now, as she turned her mind back to those last days

A solitary soldier, probably a member of the 48th Illinois Infantry, sits on the steps of the just completed catafalque in the Hall of Representatives of the old State Capitol.

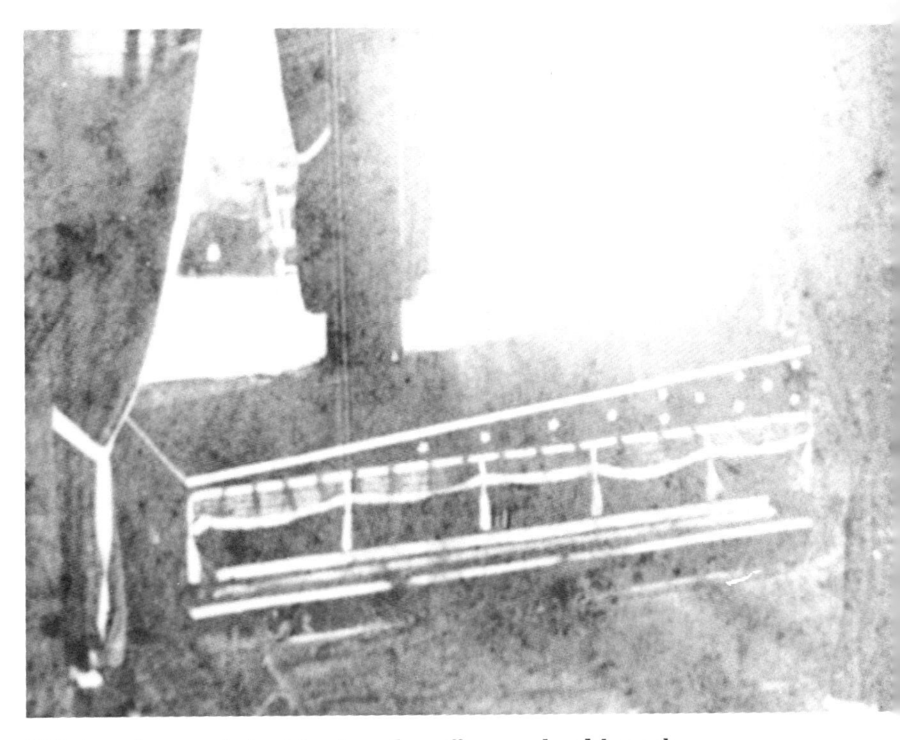

This is a close-up of the dais where the coffin was placed beneath the catafalque, one end slightly raised to make viewing easier.

of life again and again, Mrs. Lincoln wondered if her husband had had a presentiment of his death, as only a few days before he had said to her dejectedly, "You can visit Europe, but I never shall." She seemed not to know that he frequently told people how he was looking forward to living once more in Springfield. And that he had told Noah Brooks, who was to be his new secretary, that he might eventually live in California—it might offer more advantages to his two sons. And that he had told one visitor—with Tad listening delightedly—that he and Tad were going to raise onions and live on a farm in New Salem, Illinois, and have a mule, "but Mrs. Lincoln doesn't know about the onions."

"What would his choice be now?" Mary Lincoln had asked herself over and over. She remembered two things—his saying several weeks before his death that he wanted to be buried in "some quiet place" like the churchyard on the bank of the James River where spring flowers had been opening on every grave, and, how just after his nomination in 1860 he had said of the brand-new Springfield cemetery that it was one of the most beautiful spots he had ever seen. The day of the consecration of that cemetery had been blue-skied and sunny and just about everyone in Springfield had gathered at the Square and walked out the two miles to Oak Ridge in an informal procession. What they saw was a great contrast to the flat six acres within the city limits which bore the name "Hutchinson's Cemetery." Hutchinson's was run for his own profit by John Hutchinson, who made furniture in a factory equipped with steam run tools—coffins were very prominent among his offerings, for Mr. Hutchinson was an undertaker as well as cemetery owner. Lincoln not only used Hutchinson's services for the burial of three-year-old Eddie in 1850, but in 1857 he bought a "cottage bedstead" for Tad and turned in one trundle bed against the eleven-dollar bill, receiving two dollars' credit.

This woodcut shows the speedily erected tomb on the Mather property right in town where the officials of Springfield wanted Lincoln enshrined.

Hutchinson's was almost filled to capacity at the time of Oak Ridge's consecration, and the new cemetery was badly needed by the growing city. The authorities were prepared to buy Hutchinson out and transfer the bodies buried in his land to Oak Ridge. The dominant feature of this new "city of the dead" was two ridges, covered with a first growth of many kinds of forest trees, oaks outnumbering the others. In the valley between the ridges was a lovely, singing brook. At the consecration of Oak Ridge the orator of the day had been the Lincolns' long time friend, James C. Conkling, a lawyer who was considered by his many admirers to be a more brilliant public speaker than the fabled Edward Everett, and on May 24, 1860 in his long inspirational sermon on death's meaning he did not disappoint them. "How solemn, how impressive the scene! Far away from the haunts of busy life, far distant from the ceaseless rush of active enterprise, far removed from the giddy whirl of fashion and of pleasure . . ." The next words of that consecration speech must have made a more lasting impression on Lincoln than Conkling would ever suspect—"We are assembled to consecrate this ground, not to the living, but to the dead."

After a very real agony of indecision, Mary Lincoln decided that Oak Ridge was "the quiet place" and directed that the President's coffin be placed in the public receiving tomb there until she could go out herself and choose the most beautiful spot in the whole cemetery for him. Her decision was telegraphed to Springfield and the days and nights of incessant preparations began. After brief thought the city authorities decided that Oak Ridge was too far out of town and they began discussing building a temporary tomb at the intersection of two main streets or beside the Governor's Mansion. Finally they settled on the perfect location and spent fifty-three thousand dollars to buy Mrs. Thomas Mather's big stone house, set on a rise of ground in a grove of handsome trees next door to Mrs. Lincoln's sister and brother-in-law, the Ninian Edwardses. Builders were employed and worked around the clock, constructing a handsome vault and even placing urns on either side of its entrance. Six days before the funeral Mrs. Lincoln learned of the Mather tomb through "troublemakers" and sent a telegram saying that her husband was positively to be placed in the receiving tomb in Oak Ridge Cemetery. Springfield simply could not believe it and the Mather work went right on. Then on May first came another telegraphic message—"Mrs. Lincoln wishes to say in addition—that if her wishes and directions in regard to her husband's remains are not complied with she will remove them to Chicago next June." Springfield feelings ran high against Mary Lincoln. One young man named Henry Bromwell wrote his parents, "The people have

This is the public receiving tomb at Oak Ridge Cemetery, the "quiet place" where Mary Lincoln finally decided her husband would be buried.

bought the Mather grounds . . . for a burial place . . . but last night Mrs. Lincoln telegraphed that she would not let him be buried there. The people are in a rage about it and all the hard stories that were ever told about her are told over again. She has no friends here." Many felt that Mrs. Lincoln's insistence on Oak Ridge stemmed from her secret dislike of her old neighbor, Mrs. Mather, but Mrs. Lincoln kept saying it was that the Mather land was in the center of town and not the "quiet place" Mr. Lincoln wanted.

Now with Mary Lincoln's threat of moving her husband to Chicago hanging over them, even though the Mather tomb was completed and "ABRAHAM LINCOLN" was cut in marble over the entrance to the vault, the Springfield authorities decided to take no chances and at the last moment dispatched carpenters out to Oak Ridge to build a platform to the left of the public receiving tomb large enough and strong enough to hold three hundred singers and one to the right for the ministers and officials. At this point Oak Ridge's public tomb was found to be leaky and had to be hurriedly lined with "gumcloth." And a set of new doors, thick and impassable enough to protect a President's remains—were supplied at a cost to the city of Springfield of fifty-seven dollars and ninety-six cents. The three walls were hung with black velvet and evergreens and when a brick foundation was built in the center of the vault and on it placed a marble slab large enough to hold two coffins—all was in readiness.

Mrs. Lincoln still had no intention of attending even the last of the twelve funerals of her husband. She had still not left her bed, and the visits of several spiritualists whom she had received, because they said they had had messages for her from the President, had only increased her despair. Robert Lincoln cut short the cruel deception by ordering the séance conductors from the White House. He was gentle with his mother and stayed in Washington to comfort her during those first hard days, but on one thing he was adamant—he would leave without fail on a train that would get him to Springfield for the service for his father there and his interment. Tad would have to take his place in Washington for a few days and listen to his mother's complaints about how things were being done in Springfield.

The two most important buildings are made ready for the funeral.

Springfield was in a state of excitement which transcended sorrow. Every store, every house had its show of black, but the two most important buildings to be draped in mourning weeds were the home Lincoln had owned and lived in just under sixteen years, and the old State House in the center of the town square, where his body would lie for public viewing. A sixteen-year-old boy from Alton, Illinois named Edmond Beall was one of the paid carpenters who labored ceaselessly for fifteen straight days getting Springfield ready. His first assignment was to be lowered, head-first, while a rope was let out slowly, down the side of the roof of the Lincoln home. He was to fasten the lengths of the material he clutched in his hands and manage, though upside down, to fasten "droopers" or festoons of the cloth along the eaves, held up by seven rosettes. When Edmond's head hung over the edge of the roof, he found himself a few inches from the face of a lady inside the upper window. It belonged to Mrs. Lucien A. Tilton, wife of the president of the Great Western Railway. Mr. Tilton had rented the Lincoln home in 1861 for three hundred and fifty dollars a year, and bought most of the Lincoln furniture at the public sale of it in February of 1861. The Tiltons had had a busy time in the four years of their occupancy, for sixty-five thousand people had visited the home and asked to be shown through. Mrs. Tilton was rather apprehensive about what might happen on May third and fourth, but she was very kind-hearted, and she had resolved to allow each person to carry away one blade of grass or one blossom from her garden bed inside the picket fence or from the two apple trees behind the house. She now instructed Edmond to nail the rosettes separating the droopers "exactly eight feet apart." He said he couldn't quite tell about the eight feet and hung there while Mrs. Tilton went for a two-foot rule which she said had belonged to Mr. Lincoln and which she told Edmond he might keep when he was finished. Finally the droopers were perfectly spaced, the black curtains and valances adjusted at the windows across the front and the sides of the house. Thick ropes

From time to time the crowds around the Lincoln home were cleared away, a camera set up across the street, and photographs taken of various delegations of mourners. This one shows members of the official Congressional Committee which accompanied the body all the way to Springfield. Inside the fence the man on the left is Congressman Isaac Arnold of Illinois to whom Mrs. Lincoln would tell the story of her husband's request to be laid "in some quiet place."

This is how early Springfield remembered Abraham and Mary Lincoln.

of evergreens were suspended at the four corners of the house from roof to ground and an evergreen arch was constructed to span the fence posts on either side of the wooden steps of the entrance.

Mrs. Tilton in her mild worry over possible incidents during the city's overcrowding with visitors was being naïve. She would have been shaking in her high-buttoned shoes had she any prevision of the bedlam to come. Over five thousand people would arrive at her house on May third alone and ask to see everything, from the Lincoln cookstove to the Lincoln bedrooms to the carriage house out behind where Mr. Lincoln curried his horse and milked his cow, the woodshed where he stacked the kindling he chopped, the pump over the well, the privy. Long before the end of the two-day funeral celebration Mrs. Tilton, with her lawn and flowerbed and trees denuded, and people scraping the pale chocolate-colored paint from the sides of the house and prying bricks from the retaining wall for souvenirs, would beg for a soldier to keep the place from vanishing entirely.

At the other building which had played such a large part in Lincoln's life—the State House—sometimes as many as a hundred and fifty men and women—some volunteers, others paid professionals—were working at

Taken in the late 1840's these daguerreotypes hung on the wall of the family living room.

the same time, swarming all over the big stone Capitol. This building was the throbbing heart of Springfield and Lincoln had known it since the first great blocks of yellow limestone were dragged from the quarry seven miles out of town to begin building in 1837. He saw it finished finally, a building with proportions to feast the eye on—one hundred and fifty feet in length and fifty in width, two stories high. The City Council had met on April nineteenth, the day of the Washington funeral and the day all the churches in Springfield were holding Lincoln memorial services, to vote the allocation of twenty thousand dollars—exclusive of the Mather land—to be spent on the funeral in Springfield. With this magnificent sum available it seemed to many that the outside of the State House should have had richer, heavier draping, though perhaps the trouble was that so much white material was used it gave a strangely airy, cheerful look to what should have, people felt, proclaimed only anguished grief, inducing a mood of despair without that curious surge of hope that white gave. The acres of solid black they would have preferred were unobtainable by the time of this twelfth funeral, and Springfield was lucky to have as much mourning yardage on its shelves as it did have—it found by far the largest

Black and white mourning cloth, brought by the wagonload, was spiraled over the copper dome and down the columns of the old State House where Lincoln had tried more than two hundred cases.

portion in the dry-goods establishment of Lincoln's shrewd brother-in-law, Clark M. Smith, who charged three thousand, forty-nine dollars and seventy-eight cents for "drapery."

There was enough black to sheathe the entire copper dome of the State House but the columns below were twisted spirally with both white and black cloth, the white more prominent. The same thing was true of the festoons along the cornices of the building—an impression of white was given although black rosettes were numerous. There were black curtains at the windows with white streamers falling from the center top. From the window sills hung square black pieces of cloth edged in white which gave balance to the curtains above them. The great fluted columns were decorated with ropes of evergreen, cut in Michigan and brought to the Capitol by hay wagon.

The rotunda inside the State House was hung with multiple black panels—and again those airy, every-which-way white streamers. Up in the dome above the stairway were looped ropes of evergreen which a reporter said resembled nothing he could think of except an oriole's nest. Then he did think of something else and said it was "a great basket of sunshine"—again, rather an unfunereal note.

The second-floor Hall of Representatives, where Lincoln would lie in state, was in the form of a semicircle and against the flat, straight side was usually the Speaker's desk which had now been removed. In the rounded side was a gallery, supported by eleven exquisitely carved solid walnut Corinthian columns which extended up right past the gallery to the ceiling. A rising sun was shown on the ceiling, with a cloud partially covering it, representing the tragedy of the assassination. The columns were all draped with black crape and the entire cornice, running past all the columns for the complete semicircle, bore the words in big letters, white on black—SOONER THAN SURRENDER THESE PRINCIPLES, I WOULD BE ASSASSINATED ON THE SPOT. On the flat wall of the room were clouds and a partial American flag and two mottos—WASHINGTON THE FATHER; LINCOLN THE SAVIOR. Against the center of the wall stood a life-sized portrait of Washington, placed so that the first President could regard the sixteenth President closely, for the Washington portrait was exactly at the head of the catafalque which was to bear Lincoln's coffin.

The catafalque was Springfield's masterpiece. Its canopy was "Egyptian" in style, six-sided with six columns, and "half-Egyptian" suns depicted between the columns. It was twenty-four feet high and each of its sides was ten feet long. The top was black broadcloth and at the top of each of the six columns were two-foot-high black plumes with white centers costing four hundred eighteen dollars and twenty-five cents—the tallest plumes yet. Between each couple of plumes were white eagles huddled under black crape. At the tip top of the canopy was a really tall plume, much much taller than the rest. Three hundred yards of black goods and three hundred yards of silver fringe were worked into this catafalque. The inside roof of the canopy was blue, spangled with three hundred silver stars which cost four hundred seventy-four dollars and twenty-five cents at Chatterton's Jewelry Store on the Square where Lincoln had bought the broad gold wedding ring he gave Mary Todd, with the inscription "LOVE IS ETERNAL."

It was in this hall, where his coffin would lie, that Lincoln gave his famous "house divided against itself" speech, which all his friends in Springfield said was premature in its prediction regarding slavery, was against the prevailing temper of the country, and would end his political career. If that were true, he said, he would like to go down with his name linked to truth. Even then, he could not be the passive onlooker who kept silent and safe. He was willing to risk and involve himself in the crusade for right against wrong, and he inspired others, troubled and uncertain, to join him. "A house divided against itself cannot stand. I believe this government cannot endure permanently half-slave and half-free. I do not expect the Union to be dissolved. I do not expect the house to fall, but I do expect it will cease to be divided."

This was said at the Republican State Convention held at Springfield on June 16, 1858, and Abraham Lincoln did not "go down." There were cheers throughout the speech, and when he closed, the hall rang with applause.

All three of the law offices Lincoln had occupied during his career were close by the State House—always on one of the four sides of the Square—and it had become as natural as breathing for him to run up the steps of that familiar yellow building to consult the library there on an endless variety of subjects—what the precedent was in a pig-stealing case, the rights of competing river ferrymen, damages from prairie fires, enforcement of gambling debts, divorce, the drawing up of wills, taxation problems, the rights of guardianship, definition of terms in libel and slander cases, foreclosure of mortgages, land boundaries, patents, what the punishment for atrocious assault should be—everything that had to do with the daily lives of people. Lincoln's first case with his first partner, John T. Stuart, concerned an occurrence routinely familiar to any backwoodsman. He defended a man whose accuser said "had struck, beat, bruised, and knocked him down; plucked, pulled and torn large quantities of hair from his head, and with great violence, forced, pushed, thrust, and gouged his fingers in plaintiff's eyes."

The State House became Lincoln's home away from home. Early in his career when only a small number of people turned up to hear him make a scheduled political speech inside the building, Lincoln got a drum and stood beating it outside on the steps until a crowd gathered to see what was up and stayed willingly—there was a power and fascination in his reasoning even then and a freshness in his choice of words.

Lincoln's last use of the building was during the summer of 1860 when he was the Republican nominee for the Presidency. The governor lent Lincoln his office, a long narrow room in the southeast corner of the second floor, and here the nominee answered his mail and met all callers while the campaign was being conducted. For the mail he had the help of a clerk named John Nicolay, lent to Lincoln by his friend Ozias Hatch, the Secretary of State, whose office was in the northwest corner of the first floor. When the letters came too thick and fast, John Hay, just out of Brown University, who was studying law in his uncle's office, was offered as an assistant letter writer—free—his uncle would support him.

The callers that streamed in to that office were of every kind and Lincoln talked to them all, from the venerable farmer who came to warn him when he got to Washington not to eat anything "but what your old woman cooks for you," to important Eastern visitors like Salmon P. Chase who had his eye on the Cabinet. John Bunn, who with his brother Jacob had raised the ten thousand dollars for the Lincoln campaign, came hurrying to Lincoln after meeting Chase on the great stairway landing. He said he hoped Lincoln would not choose Chase for a cabinet member. "He thinks he is a great deal bigger than you are." Lincoln answered, "If you know any other men who think they are bigger than I am, I want to put them all in my Cabinet."

This was the building, holding within itself uncountable memories of the prairie lawyer, that now was to hold his body too, one last time.

After viewing the body visitors drifted from one Lincoln landmark to another

The first place any visitor to Springfield on that Wednesday of May third went was straight to the State House for the viewing. Long before the imposing procession arrived from the station, interminable motionless lines had stretched away from the north gate. Now there would be a delay, though, for upstairs the undertakers had opened the coffin. Even they were shocked. Thomas Lynch was courtesy undertaker for this occasion, invited to assist Dr. Charles D. Brown, Lincoln's embalmer. The doors of the room had been locked and the two specialists were alone when Dr. Brown, in great distress, said he had no idea how to remedy the totally black condition of Lincoln's face. According to Lynch's account, "I asked to have the body turned over to me, and the other undertaker readily consented. Making my way with difficulty through the crowds which thronged the corridors of the State House, I called at a neighboring drugstore and procured a rouge chalk and amber, with such brushes as I needed, and returned to the room.

"I at once set about coloring the President's features, placing the materials on very thick so as to completely hide the discoloration of the skin. In half an hour I had finished my task and the doors were thrown open to the public."

The crowds were admitted shortly after 10 A.M. and they walked six abreast upstairs to the Hall of Representatives, were sorted out by guards so they arrived at the four steps of the catafalque two abreast, walking along beside the coffin approaching Lincoln's face and then across the room to the exit, down the stairs, and outside again where they were asked if they cared to make a donation to the Lincoln Monument Fund.

In Springfield hardly anyone shed tears while making the trip past the coffin—they were too shocked by what they saw. But outside on the streets they broke down and wept. Everyone asked everyone else what he had thought of the remains, and most people felt they had a duty, out of a queer loyalty to Lincoln's memory, to

To view Lincoln's body the people of Springfield lined up around the square and entered the State House grounds through this specially built arch.

lie. They said for the most part he looked peaceful and as if merely asleep. Children especially would forever remember the sight, or hear their friends tell of it and remember it in that way, and many of them that evening went to their rooms alone and made entries in their diaries like this one of a young Springfield girl named Anna Ridgely.

"Crowds of people went to see it, men women and children gazed upon the decaying corpse. I am thankful I did not go for I know the image would have remained in my mind. Janey [her sister] went with the Philharmonic Society to sing and sat where she could not but look upon the body for an hour. The room was close and the gas lighted, the air was scented with evergreen which was placed all around the room and the poor child came near fainting. She was so nervous when she came home I feared she would not sleep."

After viewing, people had nothing to do on Wednesday except drift from point to point in the town where natives told them Lincoln had lived or worked or done some particular thing, soaking up lore to pass on to their children and their children's children. The most obvious thing to do first was to walk over to Eighth and Jackson Streets to visit the Lincoln home. They walked through a town mostly made up of frame houses, each with two or three trees for shade, neat lawns and gardens that were just now a mass of color. And everywhere were lilac bushes in bloom. The air was heavy with their scent and there were many people who would say in later years when asked their memories, "I never smell lilacs without thinking of that day."

The easiest way to reach the Lincoln home was to walk two blocks south from the State House to Market Street, turn left and walk a block east, past Dr. William Wallace's house. Lincoln's doctor was only two short blocks away from the Lincolns—easy to reach on a moment's notice as when Mrs. Lincoln had her frequent blinding headaches. It was Dr. Wallace who had operated on Robert for crossed eyes, on Tad for a cleft palate, and taken care of Willie when he had a long hard case of scarlet fever in the summer of 1860. Dr. Wallace had added ties to the Lincolns, for he was married to one of Mrs. Lincoln's three sisters, Frances. Relations between Mary Lincoln and Frances were cool because no "thank you" had ever been said for the President's appointment of Wallace as a district paymaster, and because of the Wallace family's unwillingness to send their daughter East to the White House to be her aunt's companion. Frances knew that enough would be demanded of such a companion to make her a servant, except in name. Even so, relations between Mary Lincoln and Frances were better than Mrs. Lincoln's relations with her other sisters. Elizabeth Todd had married Ninian Edwards, the elegant son of a

Only a handful of Springfield citizens wept when they viewed Lincoln—they were too shocked at what they saw. But once having left the State House and outside on the street again, they broke down and cried. In the picture on the left the Negro leaning on his cane toward the head of the line is the Reverend Henry Brown who was asked to lead Lincoln's horse in the funeral procession.

former governor of Illinois, and though she was the only sister, Mary said, who had expressed any pleasure at the Lincolns' rise in the world, still who could ever forget how Ninian and Elizabeth back in 1841 had opposed her engagement, pointing out that Abraham Lincoln was far beneath a Todd of Lexington, Kentucky—in fact, "white trash." The third sister—and she was the one whom Mary Lincoln felt most bitterly about—was Anna, married to the very successful Springfield merchant, Clark M. Smith. Smith was head of a store on the Square which sold groceries, fancy dry goods, boots, and shoes. In the fall of 1861 Anna made the remark that Mary was behaving in the White House as though she thought she was the main character in "Queen Victoria's Court," and Mary Lincoln never forgave her—Anna, she said, had a viper's tongue and was too low a person to warrant notice.

Lincoln's doctor, William S. Wallace, for whom Willie was named, was also a brother-in-law, married to Mrs. Lincoln's sister, Frances.

One block farther east from the Wallace house and one block south to Jackson Street and there was the Lincoln home. What had been a five-block walk for the out-of-town visitor on May 3, 1865, was never that long for Lincoln, for he had short cuts, across lots and behind peoples' houses in a straight line—they were used to looking out of their windows and seeing him "stalking and stilting it" on his long legs, as his law partner Billy Herndon described it. He often ran an errand for Mrs. Lincoln to the market, returning with a remarkably small piece of meat—Herndon considered that Mrs. Lincoln kept a stingy table.

On the third of May Mrs. Tilton estimated that people approached the Lincoln home at the rate of two hundred every five minutes. She let them into the house and showed them the parlors, back and front, with a portrait of Mr. Lincoln hanging from the ceiling between the two rooms and festoons of black cloth everywhere. She showed them, too, the tall Lincoln desk in the family sitting room to the right of the front door where Mr. Lincoln had sat in February four years before and cleaned out all the drawers—throwing letters he did not mean to keep on the floor, where some were picked up and preserved by neighbors on the long chance that they might be worth something someday.

Two of the greatest attractions at the Lincoln house

Two more delegations of mourners line up in front of the Lincoln home to have their portraits taken.

NINIAN EDWARDS, the aristocratic son of an Illinois governor who married one of Mary Lincoln's three sisters, is shown here first as a young man with his son Charlie and then alone years later at the time of the funeral.

ELIZABETH TODD EDWARDS was Ninian's wife and although together they tried to discourage the Lincoln marriage, the wedding finally took place in their parlor.

JOSIE REMANN, always one of Lincoln's favorites. As a tiny neighborhood child Lincoln used to carry her about on his shoulders. Grown up, Josie married Ninian Edwards' son, Albert, and so became a niece of Lincoln's by marriage.

HENRY REMANN, shown here first wearing little Eddie Lincoln's clothes which were given to him after Eddie's death, grew up to be Willie's best friend and corresponded faithfully with him in the White House.

on May the third were the Lincoln horse, Old Bob, aged sixteen, and Lincoln's dog, Fido. They had both been brought back for the day. Old Bob, so named to distinguish him from young Bob—Robert Lincoln—was an endearing animal with his sway back and rounded belly. "A splendid old horse of dark bay color with swelling nostrils and eyes of an eagle," one slightly over-romantic visitor described him. Lincoln had given Old Bob to a Springfield friend before leaving for Washington. The horse had taken part in the victory parade after Lee's surrender, and all the tiny flags stuck in his red, white, and blue blanket had been seized by relic hunters.

Suddenly Old Bob was big business. It was said two speculators had bought him for five hundred dollars and were planning to take him through the country on exhibition. A special funeral blanket was being prepared for him, and he was to walk in the procession directly behind the hearse, led by the Reverend Henry Brown, a Negro preacher who had done odd jobs for the Lincoln family for many years. Brown was now living in Quincy, Illinois, but he had been told of the honor that would be his and he planned to be there. In the meantime Old Bob had to be protected. People were already begging for hairs from his tail.

This is Lincoln's horse, named Old Bob to distinguish him from young Bob Lincoln. In the right hand picture the Rev. Henry Brown, who had done odd jobs for the Lincolns, stands by Old Bob in his funeral blanket, ready to take up their position in the procession directly behind the hearse.

When Mrs. Tilton was asked where Old Bob had lived with the Lincolns, she showed them the carriage house out behind. It was a small, low wooden building with one undivided space inside in which used to be crowded a two-seater buggy, a cow, hay and grain, as well as Old Bob.

Young John Roll, who had been given Fido when Tad and Willie left for Washington, had brought the small nondescript yellow dog back to the Lincoln house, too. In the old days Fido had rolled on the floor with Mr. Lincoln and his boys, always ending the fun in a breathless pinwheel chase after his own tail. And this put Lincoln in mind of the conundrum: "If you call a tail a leg, how many legs does a dog have?" He caught his small sons with this one. "Five? No, you're wrong. Calling a tail a leg don't make it a leg."

Up through the spring of 1860 Fido led a carefree life. But everything had changed on May eighteenth, the day Lincoln was nominated. That evening at the Lincoln home, hurrahing men and women and children had pushed through the front door into the parlor and out the kitchen way. At this hour Fido usually lay asleep on the floor, but that night there could have been no thought of sleep. There was nothing for a dog to do but crawl to the old horsehair sofa and hide under it, trembling the way he did during summer storms. The morning after the nomination Fido trotted along behind Lincoln as he walked as usual to market with basket on arm, but the walk was interrupted every few feet by people who made the candidate stop and talk. This day Lincoln was too preoccupied to let Fido, as he sometimes did, carry a parcel in his mouth. There was

Clark M. Smith, a successful Springfield merchant, was married to Mrs. Lincoln's sister, Anna, and of all her relatives it was Anna whom Mrs. Lincoln felt most bitterly about.

James C. Conkling, one of Lincoln's oldest friends, had been the orator for the consecration of Oak Ridge Cemetery in 1860.

no chance today for a call on Billy the Barber, with the usual lounging around after a shave or haircut to swap stories while Fido waited outside in unhurried communion with the other animals attending their masters.

After Lincoln was elected he gave his two sons a sad piece of news. It would be better, he said, for Fido not to come to Washington. A train filled to capacity and lurching and speeding across the country at thirty miles per hour would be no place for a dog. In vain did Tad plead, "I could take care of him, Pa."

The problem was what to do with their old friend and pet. Lincoln wanted a good home for Fido and it should be with children he already knew so the little dog would not feel deserted. There were so many children Lincoln had romped and talked with over the years. He had put up rope swings for them, let them sit on his tall shoulders when there was a circus parade, played marbles with them, told them stories about bear hunts or the Indian war he was in when he saw people who had been scalped, and about the river pirates he had fought on the Mississippi when they tried to steal his flatboat. There was Henry Remann and his sister Josephine. Mr. Lincoln was Henry's ideal, and when Springfield's most famous citizen went to Preston Butler's studio on the square in the summer of 1860 to have his picture taken, Henry followed and had an ambrotype made of himself standing beside the same table draped with the same flowered cloth, his hand resting beside the same studio property book. As for Josie, once Lincoln had run all the way to the railroad station with her trunk when the hackman forgot to come for it and he found the little girl crying out in front of her house. There

Isaac Diller was the son of the owner of Lincoln's drugstore and one of Willie Lincoln's best friends.

America Bush Logan and Mary Nash Stuart were the wives of Lincoln's first two law partners. Mrs. Stuart was one of Mary Lincoln's few remaining close friends in Springfield.

was Johnny Kaine, to whom Lincoln had given a twenty-five cent donation for a new pump for the juvenile fire brigade and agreed that the name "Deluge" was far superior to "Gusher" or "Spouter." There were the three Dubois boys, Fred and Jess and Link, Lincoln's namesake, the only human namesake he had so far—but there was that fine bull calf down in Southern Illinois. One dark night all three boys had hidden behind a fence and knocked off Mr. Lincoln's stovepipe hat with a stick as he went by. Then they all shouted and jumped on him and clung to his hands, and he dragged them up the street to a store and treated them to cake and nuts. There was little Isaac Diller, a year younger than Tad. Isaac's father was the owner of Diller's drugstore where the Lincolns got their castor oil and soap, cologne, cough medicine, candy vanilla, hair balsam, calomel and restorative. On a hot summer day Lincoln like to go there to sit at the fountain, a recent novelty, holding a glass of fruit-flavored soda water alternately to Tad's and to Willie's thirsty mouths. Fido was very much at home there, and a drugstore dog would have the best of care should he be taken sick.

But, all in all, perhaps the Roll family was best. John Linden Roll and Frank Roll, gentle, serious children, were about the same ages as Willie and Tad. Fido had always made a fuss over them, licking their hands and running halfway home with them when they left after playing with him. Moreover, their father, John Eddy Roll, was Lincoln's oldest friend in Springfield. John Eddy Roll liked to recollect the day when the traveling magician came to town and asked for someone's hat to cook an omelet in and Abe hesitated, as he said, not out of fear for his battered hat but out of respect for the eggs. Abe looked more like a scarecrow in those days than a future President.

In the end the Rolls were chosen. Fido got good care from his new masters. They had been left explicit instructions—the Roll boys had promised never to leave Fido tied up in the backyard alone and he was not to be scolded for wet or muddy or dusty paws. He was to be allowed inside whenever he scratched on the door and be allowed in the dining room at dinner time because he was used to be given tastes by everyone around the table.

On the sad day that young John Roll brought Fido back to meet the hundreds of out-of-town visitors, the little wagging-tailed dog was in high spirits. "The Lincoln Dog" caught everyone's fancy immediately as being an important historical character, and he was taken to the photographer Ingmire on the Square, where he was not the most patient sitter and his nose did a double-take. But card photographs for the parlor albums of the country were speedily on sale.

Lincoln's little yellow dog Fido, left behind in Springfield when the family moved to Washington, was brought back to the Lincoln home by his new master to meet the out-of-town funeral visitors.

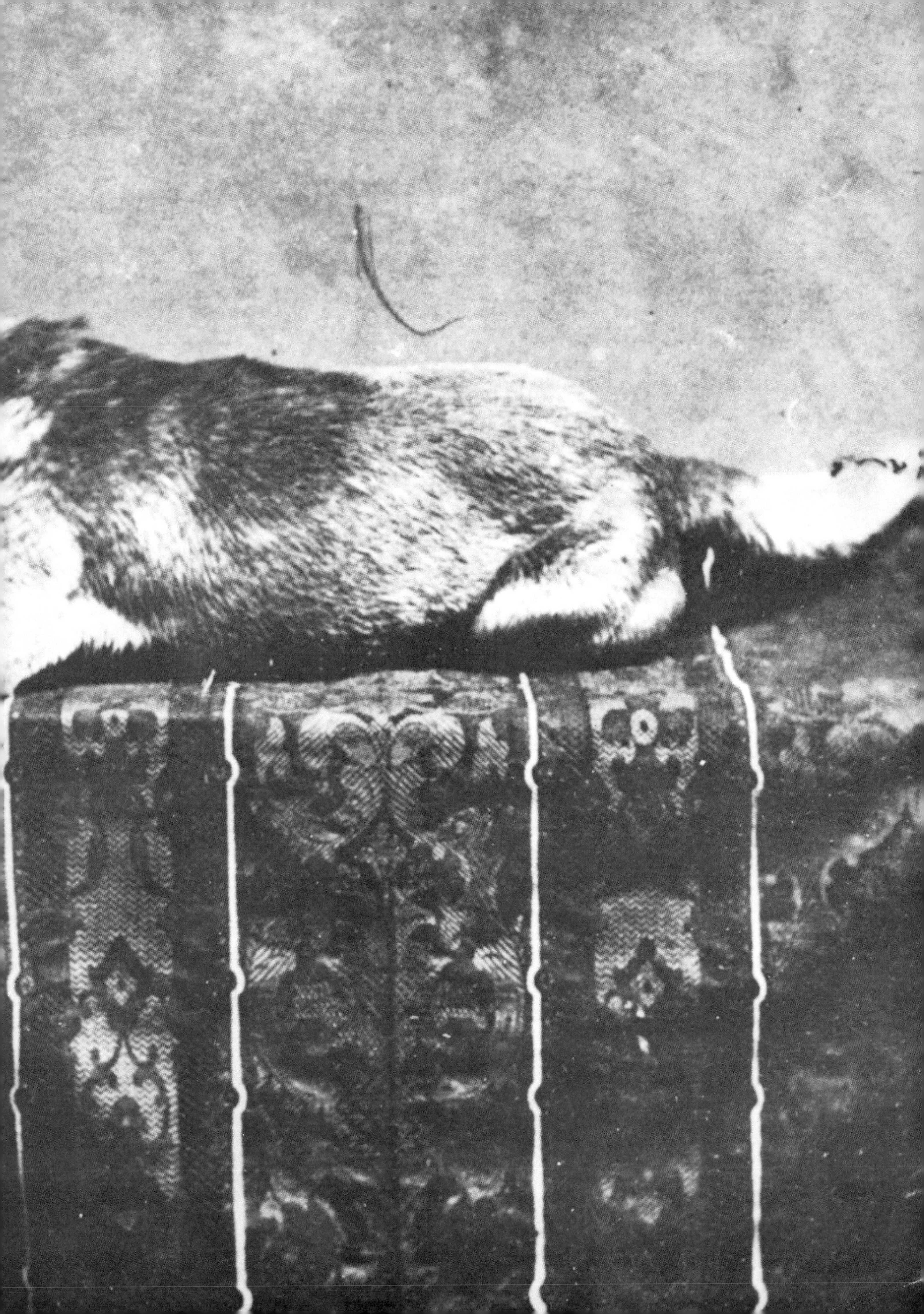

Lincoln's three law offices were among the landmarks.

The trains were coming into Springfield every few minutes with box cars full of visitors, disgorging them into streets that seemed too crowded to take more. The crowds asked questions of the hometown people and then made their way to whatever landmarks they were told were bound up in Lincoln's life.

The First Presbyterian Church was draped in mourning and so was the Lincoln pew inside, for which Lincoln paid twenty-six dollars a year, a pew so shallow it seemed impossible that he ever sat there and managed to stow away his grasshopper legs.

On the east side of the Square stood the Springfield Marine and Fire Insurance Company. This was Lincoln's bank and here he deposited his earnings from his law practice and drew on his account to pay for the charge accounts Mrs. Lincoln ran up at shops around the Square, for his political trips, for Robert's expensive tuition and board at the fancy eastern school in Exeter, New Hampshire, where he was studying to get into Harvard—having failed his examinations after his preparation in the Springfield private school for which Lincoln had paid twenty-five dollars a year. When Lincoln left Springfield to become President of the United States he was worth fifteen thousand dollars. When he died, the government had paid such a major part of the family's expenses in the White House that he had saved the main part of his twenty-five-thousand-a-year salary—had kept putting it into government bonds and Treasury notes and gained ten thousand dollars in interest. His net estate in April 1865 amounted to eighty-three-thousand, three-hundred-and-forty-two dollars and seventy cents, exclusive of his home in Springfield which was assessed at thirty-five-hundred dollars.

People were interested in where, around the Square, Lincoln's law offices had been during his three law partnerships which stretched over twenty-four years. They found them; those of Stuart and Lincoln and Lincoln and Herndon on Fifty Street north of the State House, and that of Logan and Lincoln on the southeast corner of the Square.

John T. Stuart, Lincoln's first law partner, was a major in the Black Hawk War in which Lincoln was a captain. After that Stuart and Lincoln were two of the "Long Nine"—nine representatives of Sangamon County, all above six feet tall, in the Legislature at Vandalia. Stuart suggested to Lincoln that he study law, lent him books, coached him and formed a firm with him which lasted from April 1837 to April 1841.

In the beginning Lincoln walked or rode horseback—when he could borrow a horse—the distance from New Salem to Springfield, got the books at Stuart's big, fashionable house, was given words of counsel and directions of how and what to study, and went back again each time to New Salem—and later to Vandalia where he was in the legislature—to study. Lincoln was admitted to the bar in 1836. The kind of examination that was given in those days by a friendly elder lawyer needed just seven words—"In what direction does the Mississippi flow?"

In 1839 Stuart won a seat, beating Stephen A. Douglas, in the Congress in Washington and left for the Capital. After that Lincoln was on his own—doing his best with the cases that came to his firm—dividing the fees of five, ten, twenty, and twenty-five dollars religiously—and he was also serving his fourth term in the state legislature. He was a coming man.

Stuart, who was a first cousin of Mary Lincoln, was much too interested in politics during his association with Lincoln to give the younger man much training. It was a casual kind of practice and it was not till he

LINCOLN'S LAW PARTNERS AND HIS LAST LAW OFFICE

John T. Stuart (*left*) persuaded Lincoln to become a lawyer and took him on as his partner in 1837. When Stuart was elected to Congress in 1839 and left for Washington, Lincoln carried on with the Stuart-Lincoln firm, riding the circuit and tending to Springfield business until in 1841 he joined the brilliant Stephen T. Logan (*center*). His last law partner was William H. Herndon (*right*). Their office was in the second-floor rear of the building, shown here as it looked on the day of the Springfield funeral.

HE LIVES IN THE HEARTS OF HIS PEOPLE

MILLER
10

BELTING
CUTLERY

Four and a half years before, during the summer of 1860, the Republican rally had passed the Lincoln home. The nominee stood at the doorway, towering above the crowd, dressed in a cool white suit. Mrs. Lincoln in bonnet and best dress was a prominent sight in the left-hand downstairs window while on the second floor in the second window from the left leaning over the sill was Willie who was just recovering from a long siege of scarlet fever. Out in the street in a long

formed a two-year partnership with the brilliant, thorough Stephen T. Logan that Lincoln really had first-rate instruction and experience.

Logan first saw Lincoln after the Black Hawk War when he was trying to be elected to the State Legislature. "I saw Lincoln," said Logan, "before he went up into the stand to make his speech. He was a very tall and gawky and rough-looking fellow then—his pantaloons didn't meet his shoes by six inches. But after he began speaking I became very much interested in him."

Logan said Lincoln was very useful to him "in getting the goodwill of juries. Lincoln seemed to put himself at once on an equality with everybody."

Lincoln's third law partner, William H. Herndon, was eager to tell all who would listen about his famous friend and how he had said to let the partnership sign hang and he would be back. One climbed up a narrow flight of stairs from the entrance on the Square to a small back room with two windows that opened on a tar-coated roof just beneath them. On hot summer days, and it was hot on May third, a strong smell of tar filled the office. A battered table, two bookcases, and a few

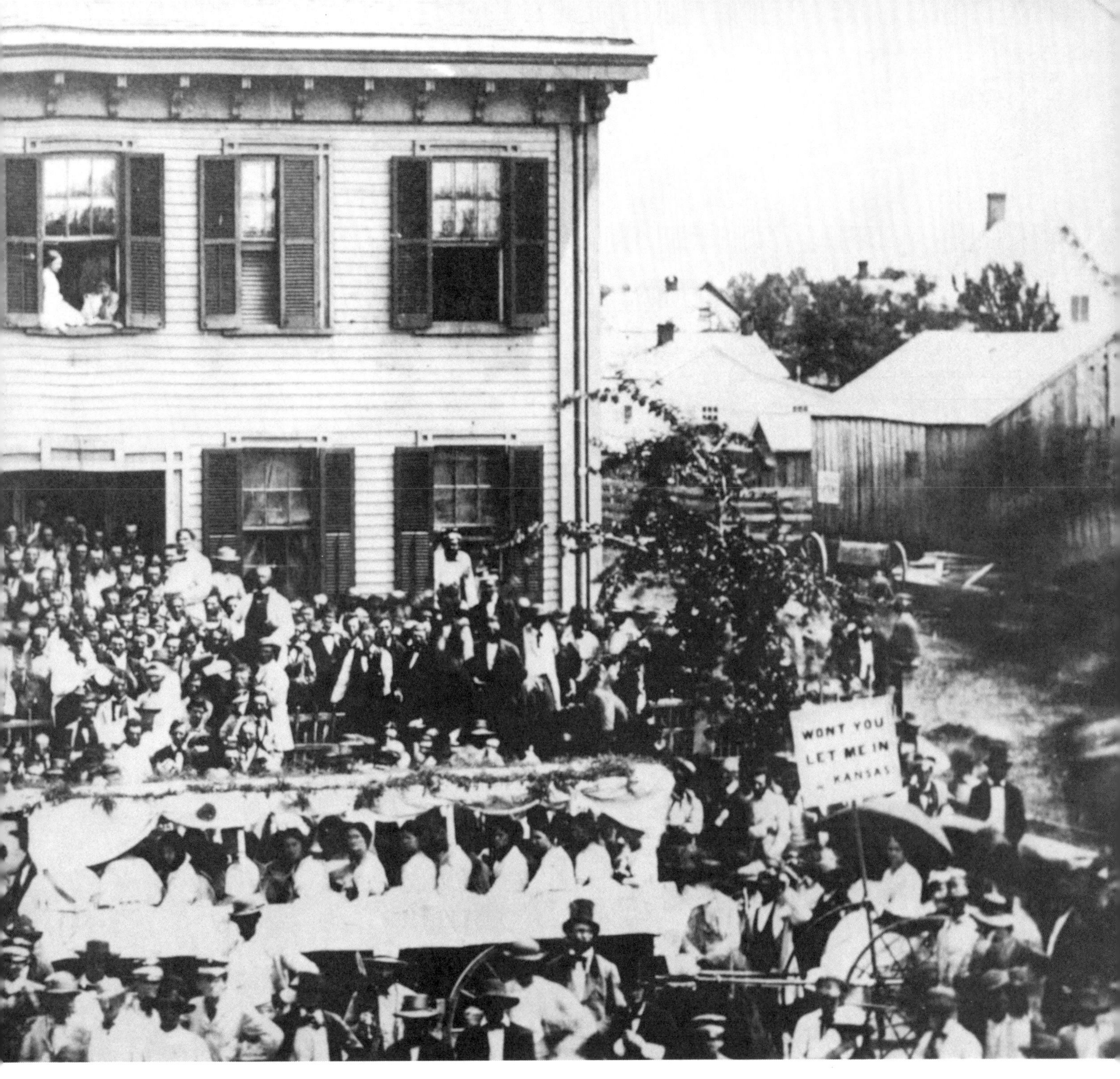

covered wagon sat thirty-three white-clad maidens representing the States of the Union, and behind was a single young girl in a buggy with the sign "Won't you let me in?" There was not a person in the crowd who did not have a firm, unchangeable point of view on whether Kansas was to come in to the sisterhood as a slave state or a free state.

chairs were the same furniture that had been here in Mr. Lincoln's time. Books belonging to Lincoln were still on the shelves and Herndon announced that Lincoln had given them all to him before he left for Washington. Herndon had a bundle of miscellaneous papers of Lincoln's tied together which he liked to show visitors—with the direction on a slip of paper—"When you can't find it anywhere else, look in this."

When Lincoln said good-by to Herndon in 1861 he asked him, "Billy, how long have we been together?" Herndon answered, "Over sixteen years."

Lincoln continued, "We've never had a cross word during all that time, have we?"

"No, indeed."

Lincoln had ended, "Give our clients to understand that the election of President makes no change in the firm of Lincoln and Herndon; for if I live I'm coming back in due time and then we'll resume practice as if nothing had ever happened."

Yet on May fourth, when the funeral procession lined up in the streets with both Stuart and Logan among the twelve old and intimate friends serving as pallbearers,

Herndon was missing from that small intimate group. The reason was his feud with Mrs. Lincoln, who had not even allowed him to enter the door of their house. She regarded him as a drunkard whom Lincoln had taken on only through pity to do routine office work that would have been only drudgery for her husband's brilliant mind. For his part, Herndon never hesitated to tell visitors that Mrs. Lincoln was the "female wild cat of the age," that Lincoln's life with her was "hell on earth" and that Lincoln had confessed to her his heart was forever on the grave of another woman—Anne Rutledge, the lovely young innkeeper's daughter he had known in New Salem—and this was why she tortured him.

As for the Lincoln children, Herndon recounted how Lincoln brought Willie and Tad to the office and they scattered papers, bent pen points, put their fingers in ink and drew pictures on the desk and walls—all with nothing but smiles from their father. Words failed voluble Billy Herndon on one subject only—those small monsters, the Lincoln children.

When the three law offices had been visited there was the Globe Tavern, a reminder of the young lawyer's modest beginnings. Lincoln had gone there on his wedding night after being married in the Edwards' house by the light of three sperm-oil lamps with cut-glass prisms hanging from their globes. The Tavern had been the Lincolns' home—at four dollars a week—for the two of them until after Robert was born in the summer of the next year. It was a very simple little inn used by two stage lines passing through Springfield to put up passengers and horses and their drivers. The huge bell on top of the two-story wooden structure clanged every time a stage arrived, for the stable men out behind to come and help. The bell had bothered Mary Lincoln's nerves, and they had moved to a temporary house until they bought for fifteen hundred dollars a pretty little cottage of one and a half stories from Dr. Charles Dresser, the Episcopal minister who had married them.

A block away from the crowd lined up to view the remains, just a little northeast of the Tavern, was the Chenery House, the hotel the Lincolns had moved to just before taking the train to Washington in February 1861, after they had auctioned and sold a good part of the furniture in the house. It was new, had gas fixtures in all its one hundred and thirty rooms and the family stayed there until February eleventh. On that morning Mr. Lincoln had come down to the hotel entrance hall, tied ropes around his and Mrs. Lincoln's and the boys' trunks, refusing help, then tacked hotel cards on each, unprinted sides up, on which he had written "A. LINCOLN, WHITE HOUSE, D.C."

Not far east of the State House, between Sixth and Seventh on Adams was Billy's barber shop Lincoln had visited regularly and where Lincoln had had his last haircut before leaving for Washington. The colored barber William Florville had become a good friend. Billy was three years older than Lincoln, had been born in Haiti and had come to Illinois in 1831. On his way to Springfield, and out of funds, he had met a man in New Salem wearing a red shirt and carrying an ax on his shoulder—Abraham Lincoln. Lincoln had taken Billy to the Rutledge Tavern and had rounded up enough shaves so that Billy could continue on his way. When Billy opened his barber shop in Springfield in 1832 it was the only one there.

As Florville remembered it after Lincoln was President, it was not Diller's drug store that had been Lincoln's so-called club house where he swapped stories—the location was his barber shop. Billy claimed Lincoln could be found there almost every evening animatedly discussing the state of the nation with "the boys."

Lincoln was Billy's lawyer and advised him in the buying of real estate at which he eventually became very successful. Billy wrote his advertisements in rhyme for the newspapers, called himself the Barber King of the Village and charged fifteen cents for a haircut. He said the hardest thing he ever had to do was say good-by to President Lincoln as he left his shop after the last haircut—and the first trimming of his brand new beard.

On the day before the funeral as visitors swarmed over Springfield, Billy was making up his mind on a very difficult subject. He had received an invitation to walk in the grand procession tomorrow with some of Lincoln's close friends. Finally he decided to refuse, to walk instead with the other Negroes of Springfield, even though they were given the last position at the tag end of everybody. He wanted to be among the people, said Billy "who felt Lincoln's loss most truly."

Springfield was, statistically, a city of twelve thousand, capital of the state, a prairie town. But on the eve of the funeral of its best-loved son, it was also a city of memories. People could remember seeing him carrying a little girl on his shoulders, or cramping himself into his little church pew or kneeling to plant the elm tree out in front of his house. They could remember him bent over the horse trough in the public square sailing the model of a boat invention, a river vessel with bellows on its sides by which it could lift itself over shoals. They could remember him flying off in all directions playing handball in an alley just off the Square, using balls made of raveled old stockings rolled into tight wads and covered with buckskin, the seams handsewn. They could remember Lincoln at an evening social with all the women in the room grouped about him listening to him talk. He always drew them irresistibly with his first word. Returning from one especially gala evening, his only remark had been, "Didn't those women look clean?" All the little memories, now treasured, of their fallen friend, before he was the nation's leader, filled the minds of the citizens of Springfield that day and night. And then suddenly it was the morning of May fourth the final day of the memorable, heartbreaking twenty.

This is Lincoln's barber, William Florville, who was affectionately known in town as Billy the Barber. His shop was one of Lincoln's favorite haunts, where the prairie lawyer used to regale his friends with his latest jokes and stories.

The day of the Springfield funeral— the last of the twenty.

The morning of the fourth of May was a scorcher, the kind of day when people in a sizzling midwest town usually stay home in rooms with the shades drawn, drink lemonade, and fan themselves. All night long there had been the steady tramp of people coming up the big staircase in the State House and across the Hall to the catafalque. Thirty-six guns were fired at dawn and after that a single gun every ten minutes until the procession began to move. At first people seemed to be just wandering, but as the morning progressed fragments of the procession began to find their arranged meeting places around the Square and in the adjoining streets. Out in the Square groups admired the fire department with its red shirts and modern hook-and-ladder equipment and steam pump engines imported from Philadelphia. In front of a nearby stable the gold, silver and crystal hearse, borrowed from St. Louis, that would transport Lincoln to the cemetery stood glittering in the sun. The six black horses that would pull it whisked their tails impatiently as grooms carried their coats and shined the silver on their harnesses. Springfield had decided that no hearse car constructed in a rush would be fine enough for the occasion, and had accepted the offer of the mayor of St. Louis for the use of St. Louis's magnificent structure that had been built in Philadelphia at a cost of six thousand dollars.

At 10 A.M. the doors to the Hall of Representatives in the State House where the coffin lay were closed and the undertaker and embalmer "reverently cleansed the face and dress" and renewed some of the trimmings of the coffin. A rosebud attached to a geranium leaf from a woman in Buffalo was found nestling over Lincoln's heart. The Veteran Sergeants carried the coffin out, down the stairs, and through the rotunda to the colossal hearse which now stood waiting at the north entrance. As the box was tenderly slid in place, a choir of two hundred and fifty singers on the Capitol steps burst forth with "Children of the Heavenly King, As ye journey sweetly sing" and twenty-one guns were fired. Now the soldiers drawn up on Washington Street began to move forward with Major General Joseph Hooker at their head, and the final funeral procession began its ritual

The triumphantly elegant hearse Springfield used in its funeral procession was lent for the occasion by the city of St. Louis.

march, the drumbeats as insistent and maddening as ever.

General Hooker was the most eyecatching figure in town that day, tall, handsome, and superlatively self-assured. "Fighting Joe" he was called, although his short career as commander of the Army of the Potomac ended in inaction and disaster. Hooker was third in the series of generals Lincoln had tried out in his search for someone who could win, a search which had ended with Grant. The President had given Hooker the appointment in spite of the fact that Lincoln knew he was insubordinate and arrogantly vain, but with the appointment had come a letter.

> *General, I have placed you at the head of the Army of the Potomac. Of course I have done this upon what appear to me to be sufficient reasons. And yet I think it best for you to know that there are some things in regard to which I am not quite satisfied with you. I believe you to be a brave and a skillful soldier, which, of course, I like. I also believe you do not mix politics with your profession, in which you are right. You have confidence in yourself, which is a valuable, if not an indispensable quality. You are ambitious, which, within reasonable bounds, does good rather than harm. But I think that during Gen. Burnside's command of the Army, you have taken counsel of your ambition, and thwarted him as much as you could, in which you did a great wrong to the country, and to a most meritorious and honorable brother officer. . . . The government will support you to*

On the funeral morning a carriage moved down Springfield's square which was paved with boards. The building with its columns decorated in barber-pole fashion for the funeral is the Sangamon County Courthouse.

Major-General Joseph Hooker, in charge of the military portions of all the funerals from Cleveland on, led the last procession of them all.

To the right of the imposing Sangamon County Courthouse is Lincoln's bank, the Marine Fire and Insurance Company, and the sliver of a building just to its right is Lincoln's drugstore—Diller's.

the utmost of its ability, which is neither more nor less than it has done and will do for all commanders. I much fear that the spirit which you have aided to infuse into the Army, of criticising their Commander, and withholding confidence from him, will now turn upon you. . . .

And now, beware of rashness—Beware of rashness, but with energy and sleepless vigilence, go forward, and give us victories.

Yours very truly,

A. Lincoln

Hooker said when he read the letter, "He talks to me like a father. I shall not answer it until I have won him a great victory." He drilled and trained and perfected his army, organizing his men so that they were able to present great display parades that were the wonder of onlookers. Then in his first battle, at Chancellorsville in May of 1863, he gave Lincoln a sad defeat. Some said that Hooker was drunk, some said that a heavy piece of wood in a collapsing building had stunned him. On June twenty-eighth Lincoln gave General George G. Meade command of the Army of the Potomac.

By order of Secretary of War Stanton, General Hooker had been in charge of the military portions of the Lincoln funerals since Cleveland. The day before, on the short march from the Springfield station to the State House, Hooker had deferred to a home-town general and native son, Brigadier-General John Cook, who had been mayor of Springfield in the mid 1850's, then sheriff of Sangamon County.

Even so Hooker, a blue-eyed, curly-haired blond with a dramatic presence and a beet-red face, managed to steal the show. Just before the procession moved Hooker caught sight of a pickpocket at work and he charged the man and kicked him so powerfully that, according to witnesses, the thief landed "ten or fifteen feet away."

Today Hooker was in command and now he began to lead the procession on its zigzag route from the State House, past the Lincoln house, past the Governor's Mansion, out into the country road leading to Oak Ridge Cemetery. At Market Street there was a conflict. Brigadier-General John Cook gave the command to wheel left which would have led everybody straight to the Mather tomb two blocks west, but straightway came Hooker's firm counter order, to proceed up Fourth Street.

Behind Hooker came the soldiers, including a regiment of a thousand soldiers made up of the entire 146th Illinois Infantry which had been drilling five hours a day for the last two weeks at Camp Cook near Springfield just so they would march smartly in the Lincoln funeral procession here. They were wearing new uniforms, tops of dark blue, trousers lighter blue with red stripes down the sides, and they had brand-new rifles

Elizabeth Todd Grimsley, a first cousin of Mrs. Lincoln's and one of the few relatives she really loved, rode in the procession alongside Robert.

with shiny bayonets, all carefully held in reversed position.

Following the soldiers the hearse came, drawn by six black horses, now adorned with enormous black plumes attached to their foreheads. Six pallbearers walked on either side. Considering the heat and the distance, it seemed folly for the older men chosen as pallbearers to walk as they did beside the hearse all the way to the cemetery. Elijah Iles had been born in 1796, and Charles R. Matheny had laid out the first plan of Springfield when it was unbroken prairie land. Stephen T. Logan, one of the younger men, was sixty-five and James Lamb, father of one of Mary Lincoln's bridesmaids, had also been born in 1800. Erastus Wright had been a pioneer school teacher, a favorite of the young because he owned an elk which he rode and drove in harness. Gustave Koerner had been Lincoln's minister to Spain, he had also been president of the 1858 Republican Convention in the State House when Lincoln had given his "house divided" speech. Koerner said he had been surprised to be a pallbearer, and had only learned of it by reading his name listed in the paper. He considered Lincoln the "justest" man he ever knew.

Charles R. Matheny had stood up with Lincoln at his marriage in the Edwards' house in 1842 and delighted to tell that as Dr. Charles Dresser, the Episcopal minister, instructed Lincoln to repeat after him "With all my wordly goods I thee endow" the rough, tough old judge present broke out with "Lord Jesus Christ, Lincoln, God Almighty—the Statute fixes all that!" Judge Browne,

The funeral procession passed a block away from the Globe Tavern where the Lincolns first lived after their marriage and where Robert was born. To the right of the two chimneys is the bell which so annoyed Mrs. Lincoln when it clanged to announce arriving stage coaches.

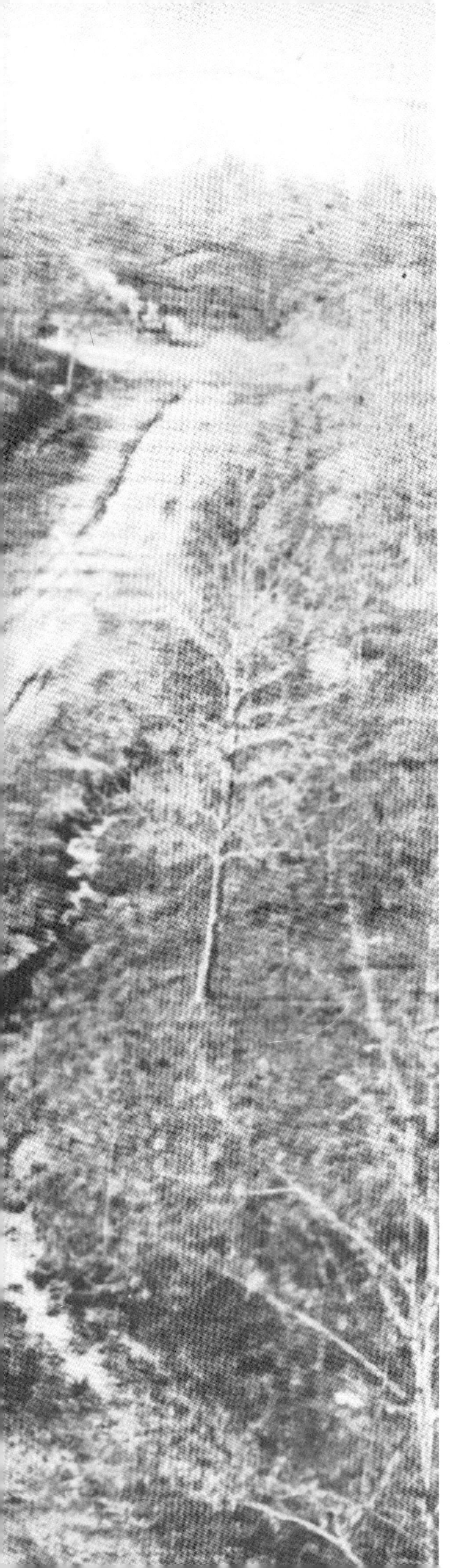

used to tying the marriage knot with a few businesslike words in a courthouse, was amazed at a church service which allowed a young man with no possessions whatever to present them to his bride.

Immediately after the hearse came Old Bob, almost hidden under his mourning blanket with silver fringe. Then the Guard of Honor made up of high navy and army officers, followed by relatives and family friends. Robert Lincoln, looking tired from his long train trip and stonily sad, rode in a carriage with a cousin, Elizabeth Todd Grimsley, who had spent six months visiting the Lincolns in the White House and who loved them all dearly. The feeling was mutual. In fact almost alone out of all those present, Mrs. Lincoln loved Lizzie. The telegraph had brought the word that Mrs. Lincoln was "enduring agonies of distress in anticipation of the burial of her husband," and now Lizzie's eyes were red from crying. Here she was about to say good-by forever not only to the President but also to Willie, the gentle boy that she had advised during her White House stay not ever to pick out a tune on the piano on the Sabbath, since as his father's son he must be an example to others. The people of Springfield had urged the President to appoint Lizzie their postmaster, but Lincoln had demurred, saying "They will think I have given all the positions to my family." Other than Robert, Lincoln's only blood relative present that day was his cousin, John Hanks, who had come to represent old Sarah Bush Lincoln, the President's stepmother, back to her Goosenest Prairie cabin. She was too infirm to make the

The long procession entered the "quiet place" where Lincoln was to be entombed through this arch of evergreen boughs (*above*) and wound down this dirt road (*left*) through the lonely isolated wilderness of Oak Ridge Cemetery.

journey and it was the consensus of opinion among those closest to her that since the moment news of Lincoln's death reached her "she never had no heart after that to be chirp and peart like she used to be." Lincoln had been devoted to this cousin who now walked unrecognized in the crowd.

After the relatives and friends came the Congressional delegation, foreign ministers, governors of the states, "citizens at large," and last of all "colored persons," among whom walked Billy the barber. Billy had made a true sacrifice in walking with "those who cared most," for later in the day when the services at the tomb were over, the tail of the procession had not yet reached the cemetery's entrance.

The largest marching spectacle the West had ever seen seemed to be in no hurry as it passed through Springfield, through the oppressive heat and the overpowering scent of lilac, winding its way out onto the country road that led to the cemetery two miles away. As it made a turn a block from the house of Ninian Edwards' brother Benjamin, the gathering on the porch had a splendid view. A long table with enough food for three hundred guests had been set up. One young lady remarked in surprise, "It was a fine display but it was not solemn at all." From a block away the firemen and their shiny red wagons and pump engines and the marching soldiers looked gay—when you couldn't see the people's expressions close up—and the hearse with its lavish gold and silver decorations, its frumpery and tinsel, resembled a circus calliope. From time to

Many of the spectators arrived early for good positions and scattered themselves over the hillside behind the receiving tomb.

time along the country road, bands broke out with dirges and there were four newly composed "Lincoln's Funeral Marches," and when the music was silent all that could be heard was the unbroken, ominous, muffled roll of the drums. As in all other cities it was the hypnotic, endless beat of wooden sticks against taut animal skin that conjured up such an unbearably repetitive sound—like the fevered pulsing inside oneself of one's own blood—beat—beat—beat—it went on, never faster, never slower and rub-dubbed people's nerves raw. It was that muffling by the black cloths shrouding the drums that made every thump dreamlike, but it was a terrifying dream—a few resonant ear-splitting rolls with no muffling would have cleared the air and set people free again. There was no escape and throats contracted in convulsive small gasps—the beginnings of sobs sometimes fought back, sometimes given in to as the only relief. Finally the procession wound under the evergreen arch at the cemetery's entrance and down through the little valley between the two ridges with their trees just leafing out, along the brook, to where the receiving tomb, half embedded in the hillside, stood with both its iron gates and its heavy new vault doors open in welcome. On the left was the big platform the carpenters had built for the three hundred singers, on the right the smaller platform for the clergy and the official who would read the second inaugural address.

With no delay the President's coffin was carried from the hearse and laid on the marble slab inside the vault. As soon as the hearse and horses moved away and let

the people come in close, it was seen that there were two coffins on the slab—"The littlest one for me, the biggest one for father," as Willie had so touchingly written in Three Bears style of beds and washbowls and towels in his letter about his Chicago trip with his father many years before. Willie had been brought to the vault first and had been waiting.

People were standing and sitting behind the tomb on the hillside and along the valley in front of it, with the brook dividing the crowd as it rushed merrily by, swollen by the spring rains. Robert Lincoln stood at the tomb's entrance, with Lizzie Grimsley on one side of him and Ward Hill Lamon, Lincoln's flamboyant friend and bodyguard on the other. Lincoln had given in to Lamon's pleas and against his better judgment issued a blanket pass for him to travel south and trade in captured cotton. Thus the Marshal of the District of Columbia who had long been dissatisfied with the low fees he received for making arrests had been given hope of making a quick fortune. Lamon loved luxury—loved his carriage lined with red satin back in Washington, his fancily appointed home where his wife Puss never had to do any housework. Now with the President's death his financial future looked black indeed. Lamon had stayed right close beside Lincoln's body all the way west, skipping meals and acting as though he must still fight off assassination attempts, alternating between helpless weeping and helpless raging at fate which had prevented him from being in the box at Ford's Theatre to save his friend. Now he cried unashamedly.

Chosen over every other minister in the United States for this historic occasion, Bishop Matthew Simpson of the Methodist Church delivered the funeral oration.

Another old friend of Lincoln's who stood close to Robert in front of the open tomb was Judge David Davis. In the 1850's a young lawyer with an introduction to Lincoln had come to Danville, Illinois, and was told Lincoln was upstairs in Judge Davis's room. There he found two men in nightshirts having a wild pillow fight: "One a low heavy-set man who leaned against the bed and puffed like a lizzard"; the other "looked seven feet tall" encased in a long yellow nightgown which reached to the floor showing "two of the largest feet . . . it had been my privilege to see."

Lincoln was one of the few allowed to tease the ponderous judge about overweight. His huge stomach which shook like jelly and resembled St. Nick's, was an object of fascination to the Lincoln boys. Lincoln once twitted his fat friend about using a mounting block to reach the saddle of his horse. The judge retreated from the block, put his foot in the stirrup and managed such a cannonball leap that he landed on the ground on the far side of his steed. This was the kind of friendship that existed in those circuit days between the self-made lawyer and the college-bred judge. Lincoln was practically allowed to hold a separate court in the courtroom, convulsing the other lawyers with his stories, though one time Davis pounded the gavel and told him one or the other of them would have to close up court. Afterwards he went to the lawyer Lincoln had been talking to and said, "What was that story Lincoln was telling?" David Davis was largely responsible for Lincoln's nomination in 1860—cajoling, persuading, making bargains and promises where Lincoln had said to make none, at the Republican Convention.

After the election friends constantly told Lincoln how much he owed to Davis and urged him to reward him. It was not until October of 1862, when Justice McLean of the Supreme Court died, that Lincoln appointed Davis to the vacant seat. Things were strangely changed between the two men. Davis said, when he went to Lincoln to tell him what to do on certain matters, Lincoln was friendly, but would sit with his head down, eyes on the floor, saying nothing. Never once did he ask for Davis's advice on anything. Assigned to the Eighth Federal District and sitting in Springfield again, Judge Davis had come east immediately on hearing the news of the assassination and in answer to Robert Lincoln's telegraphed request, he had worked on packing up the Presidential papers and on Mrs. Lincoln's finances, then returned to Illinois for the final services. "I shall never," he said, "become reconciled to Lincoln's death or the manner of it." Now as he stood with his friend's son before the open tomb, the massive Justice of the Supreme Court, wilting and sweating in the heat, was a pathetic figure, strangely isolated in the crowd's midst.

Standing alongside Robert Lincoln at the funeral was the President's old friend—tall, striking, 320-pound David Davis, the judge of the circuit in which Lincoln had practiced and the man most responsible for his nomination.

Abraham Lincoln was enormously proud of his great height which gave him an immediate advantage over other men wherever he went. He humorously stood back to back with other tall men, holding a book over their two heads to see in which direction it

Memories of their neighbor and leader came flooding back.

As for Robert, he was the object of everyone's sympathy, for the prayers about to be offered would beseech that the mantle of his father might fall upon him. It was all too evident that he was his mother's son—a Todd through and through—and that just about the only physical inheritance he possessed from his father was the dimple in his chin. Of late years this interesting feature of Lincoln's face had been hidden by his beard but his old friends and most especially his barber remembered it well.

Robert, to his sorrow, had scarcely seen his father to speak to for ten minutes at a time during the war years, but from now on he would turn increasingly to the early memories of his boyhood here in this town, when they went together for all-day rambles out on the prairie. One unforgettable moment was the time Robert had been nipped by a strange dog that had foamed at the mouth. His father had been so terrified that lockjaw might develop that he had journeyed with his son all the way to Indiana where there was a famous "mad-

slanted. He loved to guess other tall men's heights and rarely went far wrong. Here he is shown visiting General George B. McClellan —sixth from the left—at Antietam during the fall of 1862. The photographer was Mathew Brady.

stone." The country people felt it had magical properties when merely laid on the wound to draw out the poison, and Lincoln had great belief in "the people's" trusted remedies. Robert had been looking forward to seeing a great deal of his father now that the war was over, and he hoped to win for himself the same kind of love the President showered on Tad. To Robert his loss would be as crushing every day of his long life as it was now. And of the assassination he would say, "I thought the interminable agony of that night would never end" and "I felt utterly desperate, hardly able to realize the truth."

Now as the service began with hymns and Bible readings and the entreaty that the Lord "remember Thy servant Abraham," the people clustered about the tomb, and sitting huddled under their umbrellas or shading the sun from their eyes with their hands, they knew that this was really and truly good-by. Memories came flooding back again about myriad little things that their neighbor and President had been to them. They remembered what he looked like, that ungainly gaunt giant of a man with the dark, channeled, sad face that could light up with radiance, slightly stooped in the shoulders, with long arms, huge hands, a body of cord and muscle and sinew. This was not a casual age and a chief executive was expected to expose only his face and, within limits, his hands to the public. Thus President Lincoln had remained perpetually hidden within his long-coated two-sizes-too-big black suit. Few people had seen even his lower extremities though there was a story that at Antietam he had walked to a brook, pulled off his boots saying that his feet were hot, and waded, and that he was wearing no socks. John Hay, his secretary, had seen him in his nightshirt, which was so long he looped it up behind. Not much of the startling physique could have come into view as Hay merely remarked that Mr. Lincoln reminded him of an ostrich. Even when he rode horseback, to and from his country cottage out at the Soldiers' Home, he jogged along in the same formal black-crow costume which he wore for everything—a military review, an inaugural ceremony, or church. When he played ball with Postmaster General Blair's grandchildren, he did not strip to his undershirt as he would have done in freer days in the West. The children would never forget how the President's long coat-tails flew out behind him as he ran.

Back in Illinois people remembered the young Lincoln as a spectacular earthy giant whose muscular strength was so famed that he himself thought at the beginning of the New Salem years that the best use he could put his life to was to become a blacksmith. The emaciated, saint-like figure he became at the war's end with the image of Father Abraham presented a change so radical that not one cell seemed to remain of the original human structure.

A rolypoly boy had turned into a fast-growing youth with plenty of beef on his bones, and in his twenties he had weighed two hundred pounds—the deep pink of health showed under his skin and his animal vitality and power were almost like an electric shock. Abe Lincoln was more than eight inches taller than the average male in the United States and wherever he went, this marvelous height worked for him even before he proved he could whack an ax farther into a log than any other contestant. He was a winner of foot-races, could go forty-one feet in three hops, and no wrestler could force him down with his back to the earth. He was most of all a champion weight-lifter. He loaded the most corpulent hogs for market by picking them up in his arms, and

The hands of Abraham Lincoln in his thirties shown here were still the hands of a farmer and a woodchopper—muscular, almost muscle bound from years of physical labor. The hands of Lincoln the President of the United States underwent a miraculous transformation, strangely parallel with the development of the man's mind and character. The coarse flesh vanished and the fingers appeared graceful and sensitive—hands refined by their habit of life, now turned to work with the pen, not the hoe and the ax.

he once carried a neighbor's six-hundred-pound chicken house to a new location on a farm. All this strenuous exercise and rough fun became things of the past with the move to Washington as the nation's head. As late as 1858, Lincoln remarked wistfully, perhaps longing to try his winning Indian hug once again, that he had never been dusted, laid on his back in a wrestle and he believed the same to be true of George Washington. "Do you know," he added, "that if George were loafing around here now, I should not mind having a tussle with him. I think one of the plain men of Illinois would hold his end against the aristocrat of old Virginia."

No one who had been exposed to them would soon forget the Lincoln looks from his twenties on, when the deep pink in his cheeks abruptly blanched and the new young man began to be called Old Abe. Especially someone like Billy Herndon who now stood in front of the receiving tomb, his ears ringing with the choir's well-rehearsed bass and tenor, alto and soaring soprano. He had always diagnosed his partner's swift aging as due to lung trouble—he required no proof in his one man opinion—he just threw the tidbit out as an attention-getter—Lincoln was consumptive. And Herndon had read up on the tendencies of consumptives.

> *His eyebrows cropped out,* [*was the way Billy thought of his friend*] *like a huge jutting rock out of the brow of a hill; his face was long narrow, sallow and cadaverous, flesh shrunk, shriveled, wrinkled, and dry, having on his face a few hairs here and there; his cheeks were leathery and saffron-colored; his ears were large and ran out nearly at right angles from the sides of his head, caused by heavy hats in which he carried . . . his bank book, his letters, and his memoranda generally, and partly by nature; his lower lip was thick and on the top very red, hanging undercurved or downcurved, the red of his lips being a good sign of a tendency to consumption, if it was not on him, biting the life out of him; his neck was neat and trim and did not show much of the animal, though consumptives are quite passionate, goaty; his head was well balanced on his shoulders, his little grey eyes in the right place . . . he was odd, angular, homely, but when those little grey eyes and face were lighted up by the inward soul on fires of emotion, defending the liberties of man or proclaiming the truths of the Declaration of Independence, or defending justice and the eternal right, then it was that all those apparently ugly or homely features sprang into organs of beauty, or sank themselves into the sea of his inspiration that on such occasions flooded up his manly face. Sometimes it did appear to me that Lincoln was just fresh from the hands of his Creator.*

As the service continued, there were memories, too, in the minds of the people who had come all the way from Washington. The memory of Lincoln standing straight and tall in the White House East Room receiving Indians who sat on the carpet before him in paint and feather war bonnets, courteously trying to make himself understood in broken English: "Where live now? When go home?"

Lincoln's feet were long and narrow, with extraordinarily exaggerated big toes, the other four on each foot reducing markedly in size until a very small toe was reached. By modern measurement Mr. Lincoln would wear a size 14 shoe. Although as President his shoes were made to order for him, he never could find any pair of boots that was perfectly comfortable, and visitors to the White House more often than not reported him to be wearing old slippers. One horrified governor of a Southern state said he had been barefoot during an interview.

The memory of Lincoln being met at Alexandria one day by an escort of soldiers and hearing one woman call to another that it was Jeff Davis—he had been captured. Lincoln addressed her delightedly, "Oh Yes! They have got me at last!"

The memory of Lincoln seated with a company of soldiers, sharing their midday beans and hardtack. "Well, that food suits me better than anything I get at the White House."

The memory of Lincoln on board the *River Queen* with Admiral Porter on his way to visit the surrendered city of Richmond. The first night was uncomfortable as the berth was much too short for the President. During the next day Porter had it lengthened six inches and said nothing. The next morning Lincoln greeted him, beaming. "I shrank six inches last night!"

In hundreds of minds right now hundreds of simple, gentle pictures such as these flashed for a moment before the occasion drew to its deepest solemnity.

Suddenly there were all the memories of Lincoln's extraordinary mind

Now at Oak Hill Cemetery the Reverend A. C. Hubbard began to read Lincoln's Second Inaugural Address, and suddenly there were all the memories of Lincoln's incredible mind. No one was hearing the address for the first time, but everyone was listening with new ears. Used as a summation, at the final scene of a life, this poem that was only technically prose and that spoke with such pathetic beauty to the best self of every man present, asked a question. With the great President so inseparable today from the long ago backwoods child all the world knew of, it was impossible not to see in imagination the black haired baby boy joyously riding a stick horse beside his wilderness cabin. Or the better-known twelve-year-old, gravely figuring his sums on the wooden fire shovel by the hearth, encouraged by the stepmother whose signature was two crossed lines. Bridging the span of years, no one could help being compellingly and incredulously curious. How had Lincoln learned to write the way he did? They were such simple words, merely clothing the speaker's thought, they were perfect for their purpose.

To Lincoln the thrilling privilege that went with the Presidency was the chance to talk familiarily with the great men of his time and pick up straight from them the nuggets that each had mined. Mining and miners were romantic to Lincoln, and he called himself a miner, too, a miner of that elusive above-ground gold, weightless and beyond price. It was a shining prize for a man still laboring hourly to gain sufficient learning to do the job for which he was responsible.

They all came to his office in the White House—authors like Hawthorne and Emerson, preachers like Henry Ward Beecher, learned and famous professors, statesmen, physicians, actors, practicing spiritualists, artists, scientists, inventors, visiting foreigners, and top officers of the Army and Navy. The President held his own with his callers, often to their surprise, always bringing the subject around to the special field of their knowledge—relying on his remarkable memory which was a storehouse of everything he had read and heard in his life, to make one sensible contribution on the visitor's subject, and then plunging, as if his life depended on it, into asking questions.

With the doctors Lincoln had a sure fire topic. Anesthesia was new—only known since 1848—and yet the President had already practiced it on himself. In the office of an astonished dentist of Washington, where he had gone to have a tooth pulled, he reached into his pocket for a bottle, held it to his nose, inhaled deeply, then said "Ready," and enjoyed a painless extraction.

Lincoln especially held his own with the men of science and the inventors. He came to Washington with two inventions of his own behind him, his bellows to lift boats off river shoals, and a new method of steering a wagon whereby the axle was rigid and the front wheels free-moving.

Lincoln came to the Capital with these and other daring ideas, and he was prepared to discuss them boldly, putting down any sense of inferiority that would naturally arise in learned company. He was convinced future generations would find some way to tame and harness for its use earth's greatest motive power, the wind. He thought man would make a servant of water too. Lincoln had worked in a saw mill and seen water working in a small way. But he had watched the thundering falls at Niagara, and had been propelled by the mighty currents of the Mississippi. His conception of the new power from this element was now immense.

He saw the gigantic molten fireball, earth's sun, with strength to lift the water of rain and lakes and rivers and oceans and hold it ready for another descent. What to ask of the sun? Lincoln expected pure magic from steam, that long ago in Egypt had first been used in a children's toy, with no practical purpose. In 1846 he had seen the first feebly powered prairie car, in Illinois, equipped with a sail as well as steam, breaking down after eight miles and its passengers walking home. Now he envisioned a great system of railroads veining the country, with trains shooting along at one hundred miles an hour, binding the people together and allowing edibles of different climates and products of different sections to be exchanged with rapidity

His special interest was the steam plough, and with it he would ciltivate farms measured in miles, with a snorting iron substitute for the flesh and blood horse pulling cohorts of diversified earth-turning equipment.

Farming would become a new science. In 1862 Lincoln helped it on its way by changing the Bureau of Agriculture, which had existed mainly to hand out seeds and slips of exotic plants to the more powerful poli-

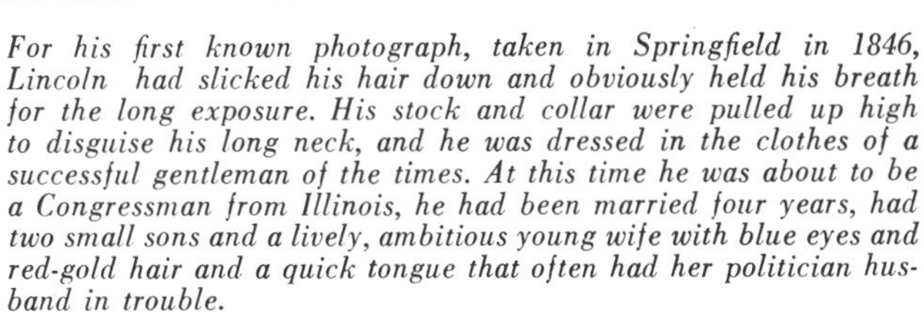

For his first known photograph, taken in Springfield in 1846, Lincoln had slicked his hair down and obviously held his breath for the long exposure. His stock and collar were pulled up high to disguise his long neck, and he was dressed in the clothes of a successful gentleman of the times. At this time he was about to be a Congressman from Illinois, he had been married four years, had two small sons and a lively, ambitious young wife with blue eyes and red-gold hair and a quick tongue that often had her politician husband in trouble.

Eleven years later the sitter was not ready to acquiesce in all the photographer's demands. He asserted his own individuality and at the last minute ran his hands through his hair, making it stand up in wild disorder—remarking that his friends would never recognize him if his hair was not in a "bad tousle." He was then campaigning for the Senate against Stephen A. Douglas. Lincoln used to tell with amusement that newsboys offered this particular photograph for sale with the remark, "Here's your likeness of Old Abe. Will look a good deal better when he gets his hair combed."

ticians, into a full-fledged Department—he spoke of it as the "People's Department."

Lincoln was powerfully drawn to a study of the heavens. He speculated on what man might some day discover concerning limitless space, so gemmed with other planets and stars. He had come to the conclusion that there was an order and purpose in the whole "and a Creator, who intended some noble end for man, his noblest work." Evenings in Washington when he could get away from his office the President would drive to the Naval Observatory on the Potomac's edge, and peer through the great telescope there. He marveled that distances could be accurately computed and wondered what would be discoved with more powerful telescopes in centuries to come.

For a man who numbered his schooling in months to find himself suddenly heading the list of the members ex-officio of the Smithsonian Institution was breathtak-

In May 1858 Lincoln was attending court in Beardstown, Ill. and a few minutes before this picture was taken he had won his case—his client "Duff" Armstrong who was accused of murder had been acquitted. Back in his New Salem days young Lincoln had been befriended by the Armstrongs and now he agreed to defend their son whom the state claimed had got into a drunken brawl and killed a man. A witness said he had seen the murder clearly because the moon had been shining directly overhead and brightly on the scene. Lincoln discredited him by producing an 1857 almanac which showed conclusively there had been no overhead moon at the time. Since the witness had been found so fallible, Lincoln begged for the boy's life and one who listened said, "I have never seen such mastery exhibited over the feelings and emotions of men . . ."

Here in this daguerreotype taken in Chicago July 11, 1858, Lincoln's high cheekbones are accentuated, his cheeks almost cavernous, and he looks the tough politician who can take care of himself. Only the day before he had spoken in Chicago to answer a speech of Douglas's. Douglas had attacked Lincoln powerfully and he had said, "I am opposed to taking any step that recognizes the negro man . . . as the equal of the white man." The next evening Lincoln answered, "It is one of the admonitions of our Lord, 'As your Father in Heaven is perfect, be ye also perfect' . . . So I say to in relation to the principle that all men are created equal, let it be as nearly reached as we can."

ing. Dr. Joseph Henry, the learned Secretary of the Smithsonian was Lincoln's good friend early in the administration and the two men discussed everything, from climatology and the weather reports the Institution received from all the country, to such questions as the use of balloons and the future of guided flights in the air. The President had been the first to urge Dr. Henry to see the aeronaut, Thaddeus T. C. Lowe, and talk over his plan for the use of balloons in war. Dr. Henry had written Lowe in regard to the flight he wanted to make across the Atlantic, that he had no faith in any of the proposed plans for navigating the atmosphere by artificial propulsion. A balloon, he felt, with man's present knowledge, could only drift with the great currents of the atmosphere and there was no motive power yet known that could accompany the thing and cause its great surface to resist and cut through the wind. But Lincoln had faith in the future of travel by air and as a

This ambrotype was taken in Macomb, Illinois, on August 26, 1858, five days after the first debate with Senator Stephen A. Douglas. Here again the photographer had asked Lincoln to "fix up" but he had said no—"It would not be much of a likeness if I fixed up any." In that first debate with Douglas Lincoln had said that he never had maintained that a Negro was his equal in color. "But in the right to eat the bread, without the leave of anybody else, which his own hand earns, he is my equal and the equal of Judge Douglas, and the equal of every living man."

This ambrotype was taken during the heat of the Senate campaign in Pittsfield, Illinois, October 1, 1858, six days before the fifth debate with Douglas in Galesburg, Ill. The picture plainly shows the seams and wrinkles that were evident in Lincoln's face even as a young man—as well as the deeply serious, almost sad expression of his eyes whenever he was photographed. Lincoln had just said he did not believe the extinction of slavery could possibly be sudden. "I do not suppose that in the most peaceful way ultimate extinction would occur in less than a hundred years *at least. . . .*

beginning he had Lowe installed as aeronaut for the Army of the Potomac to spy out the enemy's fortifications and troop movements. Before long Lowe had organized seven thousand ascensions. Sitting in the White House, Lincoln made history when he received the first telegraphic communication from an airship aloft.

Interspersed with the lively discussions of air travel, the Capital's men of science were wondering whether it might be possible to capture the electricity that flashed across the skies in the lightening of storms and somehow use it to lessen the work of men and animals. The President was deeply interesed in the laying of the Atlantic cable, and he had plans to stretch wires up and down the country's coasts along the Pacific as well as the Atlantic. He had communicated with the Czar of Russia about laying a telegraphic cable clear across to his country, with wires fanning out from Russia all over Europe. Lincoln talked with Cyrus Field on the whole

Now we see the transformation of the face of the prairie lawyer-politician into the face of President Lincoln—statesman and martyr. Taken just before he left for Washington and his first inauguration, this is Lincoln's face as his fellow townspeople saw it on the evening of February 6, 1861, as seven hundred crowded into the parlor of the Lincoln home in turn to press his hand, look up into his eyes which wore this tender expression. He had been sitting alone writing his inaugural address, pleading that the people remain one country. "Physically speaking, we cannot separate. We cannot remove our respective sections from each other, nor build an impassable wall between them."

Two years later with the country deep in civil war, Lincoln sat for an amateur photographer and employee of the Treasury Department. The Presidency had already taken all the youth from his face, and here we can plainly see how Lincoln's left eye wandered upward when he was tired. This was the year of the calamity of Chancellorsville, of the siege of Vicksburg, of Gettysburg. Even though he had not yet found the great leader who would press the war to its conclusion, Lincoln could write that summer, "Peace does not appear so distant as it did. I hope it will come soon, and come to stay; and so come as to be worth the keeping in all future time. It will then have been proved that, among free men, there can be no successful appeal from the ballot to the bullet; and that they who take such appeal are sure to lose their case, and pay the cost."

future of rapid communications around the world and what unbelievably far-reaching changes this would bring.

Lincoln consulted with John Ericsson who was working tirelessly on armor-plated ships which were to be a new, undreamed of era in navy warfare, with iron monsters with hooked beaks in their prows attacking and disemboweling each other. They also studied the possiblity of propelling boats under the water's surface—the whole subject of submarine travel and exploration was on the verge of becoming practicable. The President kept his finger in everything. When told that the newly invented *Monitor* could have her machinery drowned if an enemy poured water into her turret, he sent a message that she had better not go "skylarking" up to Norfolk.

Tirelessly Lincoln tried out new gunpowder and new guns, asking to see their "inwardness" and expressing a wish that someone would invent a gun that would shoot around corners. He went down to the flats beside the Washington Monument and shot at a target with

On November 15, 1863, Lincoln visited Alexander Gardner's Gallery. This is one of the rare photographs that finds the President looking directly and intently at you, and it has a curious, immediate impact of closeness to the man. Three days later, depressed because Tad was sick and Mrs. Lincoln hysterical, the President left for Gettysburg, the following day to make the short, eloquent, moving address that would become one of the great documents of mankind. . . . "that we here highly resolve that these dead shall not have died in vain; that the nation, under God, shall have a new birth of freedom; and that government of the people, by the people, for the people, shall not perish from the earth."

To keep this engagement for a sitting at Brady's studio Lincoln had to walk there—after waiting for some time at the front portico for his carriage which never showed up. This was on February 9, 1864, a month before the appointment of General Grant to the full command of the Federal forces. The night before this photograph was taken Lincoln had gone to the theatre to see Laura Keene in Sea of Ice. *The day after the sitting the President's private stables caught fire and the Lincoln horses and his dead son Willie's pony were burned to death. Lincoln had leapt over a hedge and flung open the stable doors to try to get the animals out. Later, watching the still smoldering stables from the East Room, he wept.*

Christopher Spencer, the inventor of the Spencer Repeating Rifle. The President also studied bullets and knew their varying shapes—most especially the cruel Minié balls, conical and propelled in a twisting motion that flew like arrows and were constructed to burst inside the flesh they penetrated.

The President was a passionate believer in the democratic society. "It is not merely for today," he said, "but for all time to come that we should perpetuate, for our children's children this great free government," and "I happen, temporarily to occupy this big White House. I am a living witness that any of your children may look to come here, as my father's child has."

In this eulogy of Henry Clay, Lincoln seemed to be describing his own method of obtaining an education in a free democratic country. "Mr. Clay's education was comparatively limited" but "from time to time he added something to his education during the greater part of his whole life—it teaches us that in this country, one can scarcely be so poor, but that if he *will*, he *can* acquire sufficient education to get through the world respectably."

Abraham Lincoln's guiding desire, expressed in early manhood and carried through to his last day, was to leave the world a little better for his having lived in it. There came a time when he saw clearly how he would do this. He would pass on to future generations not scientific discoveries, but certain truths he had come upon that were timeless in their application to man's needs. The President never confided in anyone what he knew before his death. It was his skill with written words, part acquired and part God-given, that was to give permanence to his beliefs and secure his immortality.

He was a profound student of history, making use of what he considered man's greatest invention, the written word—"enabling us to converse with the dead, the absent, and the yet unborn." He had conversed with the dead by reading history with concentration and perspective, and the fact that he was a student of the past freed his mind to range far ahead of his own lifetime and explore the wonders to come.

Though he would speak ostensibly to the country and his generation, more and more he found he wanted to communicate with the unborn, the hope of the great family of man. His whole being was turned with passionate anticipation toward the glories of a coming civilization and "man's vast future." He figured that there were those alive with him who would see the United States supporting a population of two hundred and fifty million. He felt, like a prophet of old, driven to reach these people.

Though Lincoln would have repudiated the word genius, he was quite conscious of a strange, exhilarating power to compose—actually to orchestrate the elements in the English language to create a heart-melting and powerful symphony.

He embarked on his writing with an extraordinary instrument at his service—his mind. Both he and his friend Joshua Speed describe it almost identically. Said Speed: "His mind was like polished steel, a mark once made upon it was never erased. His memory of events, of facts, dates, faces and names surprised everyone." Said Lincoln: "My mind is like a piece of steel—very hard to scratch anything on it, almost impossible after you get it there to rub it out." Noah Brooks said: "Everything, if it tickled his fancy fastened itself onto his memory," and General Viele said Lincoln could repeat "almost word for word anything he had read."

Lincoln wrote very, very slowly, dipping his pen in the inkwell and waiting long periods before using it, perhaps looking out the window at his jumping goats, Tad's particular pets, or up at the ceiling where a spider was spinning a web, but thinking, laboriously, searching for the right words. He would sit and read the dictionary for hours complaining to Nicolay that the exact words for his ideas just didn't exist. All during the war he worked patiently at writing his own letters and speeches. If someone told him he had split an infinitive he would say good-naturedly: "Oh you think I'd better turn those two little fellows end to end?" But when he was saying something important, he took no advice.

Toward the end of 1864 Lincoln received a handsome Bible from the Negro people of Baltimore and thanked them extemporaneously, adding, "in letters and documents sent from this office—I have expressed myself better than I now can." He had driven himself relentlessly to set down with his pen his words to posterity. He had worked out a style that was his and his alone, trying always for brevity and clearness, always searching for the simple and exactly right word. There was a distinctive cadence to what he wrote and a transparent honesty and he could make the kind of man he was shine through his messages. He had the ability to translate suddenly everyday commonplace things into matters that took on a spiritual quality—gave the reader hope and a philosophy.

As the reading of the Second Inaugural Address drew to a close, the people listened in silence to the familiar words as they rang out over the wild cemetery grounds.

> *With malice toward none; with charity for all; with firmness in the right, as God gives us to see the right, let us strive on to finish the work we are in: to bind up the nation's wounds; to care for him who shall have borne the battle, and for his widow, and his orphan; to do all which may achieve and cherish a just and lasting peace among ourselves, and with all nations.*

Bishop Matthew Simpson of the Methodist Church rose to give his funeral oration. The Bishop's voice was shrill and harsh and people found it unpleasant—but this was forgotten as the speaker's tremendous earnestness was felt. The people stood rapt as he said:

> *More people have gazed on the face of the departed than ever looked upon the face of any other departed man. More have looked upon the procession for 1600 miles or more—by night and by day—by sunlight, dawn, twilight and by torchlight than ever before watched the progress of a procession.*

We ask why this wonderful mourning—this great procession? The great cause of the mourning is to be

On April 10, 1865, Lincoln sat for his last portraits. This was the only print that the photographer, Alexander Gardner, made from a negative that had been cracked—the last exposure of the final sitting. Gardner threw the negative away—the original print is in the Meserve Collection. Two weeks after this was taken, in City Hall in New York still another photograph was made, but in it the President's weary, loving eyes were closed. Abraham Lincoln had died never knowing how many friends he had.

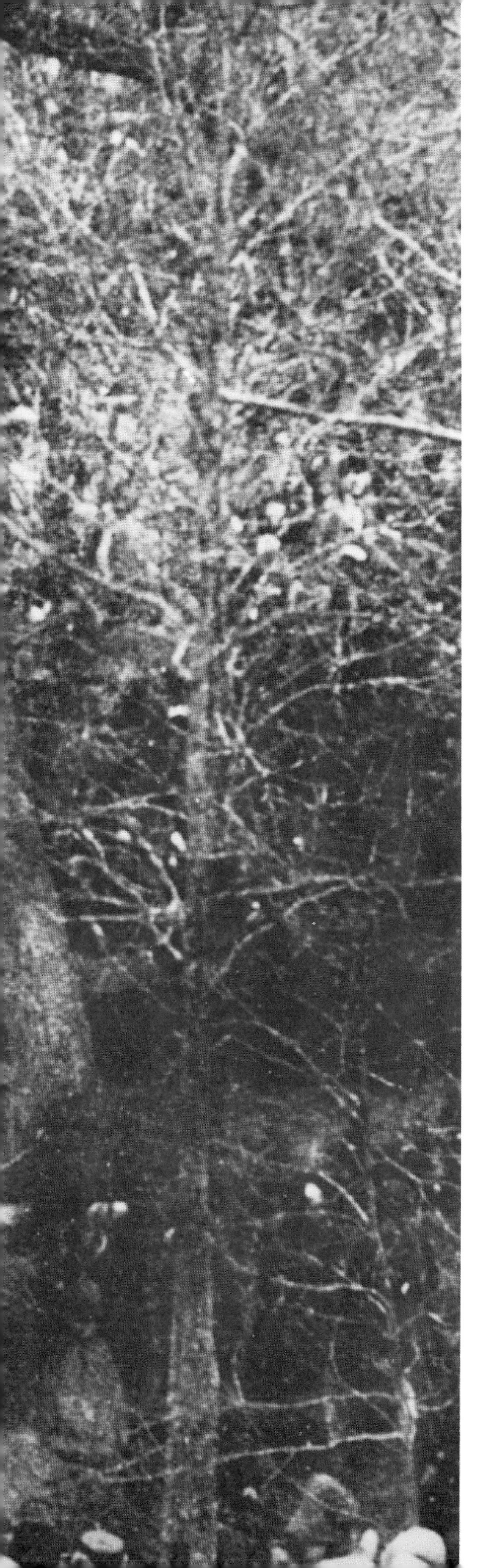

found in the man himself. Mr. Lincoln was no ordinary man . . .

In his domestic life he was exceedingly kind and affectionate. . . . During his presidential term he lost his second son Willie. To an officer of the army he said not long since: 'Do you ever find yourself talking to the dead?' and added—'Since Willie's death, I catch myself every day involuntarily talking with him as if he were with me.' On his widow, who is unable to be here, I need only invoke the blessing of Almighty God that she may be comforted and sustained. For his son who has witnessed the exercises of this hour, all that I can desire is that the mantle of his father may fall upon him.

Now in his high, grating, impassioned voice, Bishop Simpson began his decription of the President the world knew:

He made all men feel a sense of himself—a recognition of individuality—a self-relying power. They saw in him a man who they believed would do what is right, regardless of all consequences. It was this moral feeling that gave him the greatest hold on the people, and made his utterances almost oracular.

Simpson spoke so eloquently that people applauded parts of his sermon, and forgot his rasping voice and his strangely unfinished clerical robes held together at the seams with big basting stitches. Possibly the Bishop's luggage had been misplaced, but it was obvious that some Springfield housewife had run up this voluminous makeshift garment in a few moments' time.

When the Bishop was done, a hymn was sung, and then Dr. Gurley, who had been the officiating clergyman at the Washington funeral, delivered the benediction. This was followed by the funeral hymn that Dr. Gurley had composed for this last service—"Rest, Noble Martyr! Rest in peace." Black-edged cards with the printed words had been distributed and most people mouthed the lines—not trusting voices they knew would quaver and fail. The crowd did better with the doxology—all present joining in as the last thing they could do. While they watched, the gates of iron and the heavy doors of the tomb were closed and locked, shutting out the sight of the two coffins with their offerings of Springfield garden flowers arranged in vases and brought from the homes of friends. Aside from a big red-rose valentine heart there was nothing set and wired. All offerings were garden-gathered.

The crowds with umbrellas up to keep off the burning sun press in closely as Lincoln's coffin is placed in the receiving tomb alongside Willie's which is waiting there.

The key to the tomb was handed to Robert Lincoln who gave it to his cousin, John Todd Stuart. People began to stir in the heat, put down their umbrellas, talk quietly to one another, come down off the hill.

It was over now, the long and unprecedented pilgrimage of a nation to the tomb of a hero and a saint and a plain friend. The lakes of tears had been spent, the mountains of flowers had buried him over and over along the way—he who could not even get a flower to grow in his little Springfield yard. The continuous music from hundreds of bands and choral groups had sung him to his rest—he who was so tone-deaf that he could barely distinguish "Dixie" from "The Star-Spangled Banner." He had come seventeen hundred miles back to his own black earth. A million Americans had looked upon his face. Thirty million more had attended religious services, or sung or posed or merely stood and watched that train, that long black box go by. Twelve cities had competed one with another over whose funeral trappings were most fitting and elaborate. Great teams of horses, black as night or white as snow, had pulled him through the streets. Fantastic hearses had made his rides royal. Strong engines had moved him westward over the rails he loved and fought for. Millions of yards of mourning cloth had turned the great cities and their people black. Sun, rain-sky, the moon, torchlight had lit his path across the country. And now he was home. The exhibition of a nation's grief was closed. Abraham Lincoln had once said of George Washington: "Let us believe, as in the days of our youth, that Washington was spotless. It makes human nature better to believe that one human being was perfect—that human perfection is possible."

Now in one swift second of time Abraham Lincoln was himself destined to be perfect, in his countryman's eyes, no matter what they had felt before. And in a little over two weeks time the manner of his death was beginning to be accepted as the only possible thing—it was unthinkable that he should have lived into old age and merely faded away. His going seemed suddenly inevitable—the final requirement—the sacrifice named in Booth's diary.

Later that day back in Springfield a crowd went to stand in front of the governor's mansion and listen to the band of a St. Louis regiment which had come to march in the funeral procession serenade the governor. It was the first quick-time, happy music heard in Springfield in almost three weeks.

And that afternoon a girl went to a neighbor's house where a group was gathering. There was laughter there, joy and fun. It was just not possible, people were beginning to live again, already. But it was what Lincoln meant when he said after the death of his three-year-old son—"Mary, we must live."

Strewn with flowers from Springfield gardens the two coffins—"the littlest one for me, the biggest one for father"—stand side by side just before the heavy iron gates are swung closed.

ACKNOWLEDGMENTS

Although the concept for *Twenty Days* and the authors' collaboration on it began a full five years ago, the study of Abraham Lincoln the man and the brutal, stupid, heart-breaking act of his assassination being a family commitment, with the early findings a heritage, reaches back so many years before that—in particular for the more ancient half of this writing team—that many of the first and greatest helpers are not living in this year 1965. We wish they could see the completion of their and the authors' labors. At least, in grateful memory, eight names shall lead the list of those persons to whom we are in debt for generous, untiring aid.

Frederick Hill Meserve comes first—contributing most, through closeness of blood and complete identity of interest. His passion for the faces out of the American past, his pioneering work in seeking out, collecting, identifying and preserving the tens of thousands of photographs that tell that early story of this land and its people, his thoroughness, his diligence, his dedication—all have been an inspiration that has spanned generations. One of us his daughter, the other his grandson, will be forever in his debt, and were he alive today, though he had looked at the photographs of Lincoln in his collection so many thousands of times, he would examine them again in our book, murmuring as always, "Priceless! Priceless!"

Philip Bradish Kunhardt, Sr., husband of one of us, father of the other, was an expert on the land and rivers of Illinois and the geography of all our researching trips. For years he read Lincoln books exclusively on his commuting trains and thrived on them. He was ever our most constructive critic, our most devoted backer, our greatest inspiration, even to his last days upon this earth.

Robert Lee Kincaid, President of Lincoln Memorial University at Harrogate, Tennessee, who in boyhood knew the feel of a log cabin's dirt floor between his own toes, was as impassioned and determined about the accomplishment of our undertaking as though it were his own. "You must tell this story," he wrote over and over. "Bit by bit you can put it together like a builder erecting an edifice. At the beginning the job seems too big, but as it takes form you will find excitement and exhilaration in your efforts."

Harry E. Pratt, of Springfield, Illinois, State Historian of Illinois, and his wife, Marion Bonzi Pratt, an Illinois archivist and an editor of the Rutgers University ten-volume *Collected Works of Abraham Lincoln*, gave frequent invitations to come and talk under their roof. That meant sharing their inexhaustible and incomparable knowledge not only of the facts, seemingly almost hour by hour, of Lincoln's life, but also their thoughtful conclusions on that life's meaning to the world. This dedicated husband-and-wife team of scholars considered it no trouble to set up cots in their dining room or book-crammed study, though in the end there was never any need for the furniture of sleep, as the chorus of excited, exploratory, adventurous conversation went on straight through each night.

William H. Townsend, of Lexington, Kentucky—Mary Lincoln's home town—was a distinguished lawyer, an inimitable raconteur, a writer with a flair. He was also a collector, a Lincoln scholar, and a kind respondent to pleas for assistance. It helped to be taken up to the attic in the Townsend house, which stood almost exactly where Mary Lincoln had gone to school, to see Lincoln's small nail-studded traveling trunk, the short brown hairs of the calfskin worn in patches from stagecoach travel. It helped to be taken by Mr. Townsend through Henry Clay's home, "Ashland," where Lincoln first met his hero and was so disappointed in him—and to watch him surreptitiously dig up from behind the Todd family house a brick which Lincoln "must surely have stepped upon" and present it in courtly manner to his guests. Most profitable of all was the ride to a country mansion to meet an old lady—Mrs. Lincoln's great-niece, who babbled proudly about "Aunt Mary." "Listen to her, look at her, you'll get a firsthand look at Mrs. Abraham Lincoln," Mr. Townsend said. It was true—there was the strange iron-strong femininity, there was the hair curling in beguiling tendrils at the nape of the neck, the same porcelain-white skin, the startling blue eyes, the deep-South accent.

We remember Frederick Meserve's friend Carl Schaefer, of Cleveland, Ohio, a generous contributor to all that furthered knowledge of Lincoln. Old newspapers containing accounts of Lincoln's funerals westward and long-treasured photographs of the motionless crowds, the catafalques, the ceremonial trappings of death were soon winging their way to us. Carl Schaefer was a sensitive man who literally worshiped this fallen President of so long ago. Each April

14th, overcome by the memory of the tragedy, he would journey to Washington to stand in the Petersen House, on the exact spot where Lincoln died, at exactly 7:22 on the morning of the 15th—and he would grieve anew.

The last of our eight who shall be first is Churchill Newcomb, a 1923 Harvard graduate of Southern-aristocracy ancestry who like ourselves was actively engaged in tracking down elusive facts concerning the Lincoln murder plot. He believed it to be far-flung, immensely complex, enlisting large numbers of conspirators whose names we might never know unless we galvanized ourselves to act with all possible speed to seek out all-but-vanished clues. Working on a book of his own, he was following a dozen trails at once, and for a period of months a few years ago there came almost incoherent, excited telephone calls, and his brilliant and eagerly questing letters with the words spattered across the paper at breakneck pace as the mind outran the hand. He was sharing his findings, his guesses, his firm beliefs. Then one day as he sat writing at his desk in Virginia, possibly at that moment puzzling over the madman who murdered Lincoln, a madman came into Newcomb's house and murdered him.

Of our living collaborators, there is one who almost weekly sent us bits of information and wise advice which have added immeasurably to what we were striving for. This peerless friend is Miss Josephine Cobb, famed iconographic expert of the National Archives—Lincoln scholar herself. Though she is too young in years for one to fully believe it, she was Frederick Meserve's helpful source of information on their mutual interest—photography of the Civil War years. He regarded her with affection and read her findings with respect. Miss Cobb took us on as we became knowledgeable enough to speak her language, and her meticulous research, channeled for our sakes into the spring months of 1865 (she gave us no inconsiderable number of her valuable evenings) led us to turn to her instinctively when in need, doubt or plain despair. We found her calm, cheerful and unchangingly enthusiastic about our project, even when we broke the news that our book would have no footnotes and no bibliography, with a view to having it read by "people" as opposed to a few Lincoln specialists.

Three other major supporters whose kindness and graciously given aid have been tremendously appreciated are: Mrs. Josephine Allen, of the Government's Lincoln Museum, housed in the old Ford's Theatre in Washington, D.C., up to the recent start of that building's restoration, and of the Petersen House where Lincoln died, just opposite on 10th Street; Fred Schwengel, former Congressman from Iowa, now president of the Capitol Society of Washington, D.C.; R. Gerald McMurtry, editor of *Lincoln Lore* and director of the Lincoln Collection at the Lincoln National Life Foundation of Fort Wayne, Indiana.

Mrs. Allen tirelessly searched among the Lincoln treasures and assassination relics owned by the Lincoln Museum, sending us endless and fascinating photographs to choose from, and where no photographs existed, she spent hours posing the appalling mementos in her care and then had a photographer make the pictures just for us. Through her courtesy it has been possible to walk through the upstairs rooms of the Petersen House and see just how the boarders lived and where they gathered as Lincoln died downstairs. Standing with Josephine Allen in the Petersen House back yard, sharing her absorption in the history of that plot of earth, it is almost possible to smell blooming lilacs, though none are planted there now.

Fred Schwengel, when a member of the House of Representatives, worked with single-mindedness and tact to open doors for us which would otherwise have remained closed and would have severely restricted the scope of our findings. A deeply respected leader in the Lincoln field, his energy is boundless, and he has imaginative and extensive plans for the future.

Gerald McMurtry has lectured on Lincoln in countries around the world and seen the universality of Lincoln's hold on men's souls. At Lincoln Memorial University he taught the first full year's college course on the subject—Abraham Lincoln. In Fort Wayne he opened his Foundation's varied holdings, to the enrichment of *Twenty Days*, exhibiting relics such as the bloodstained piece of material cut from Laura Keene's costume of that April 14th evening and the various separate swatches of bloodstained towels which reached him from varied sources. If any man can come near knowing everything that will ever be known about Abraham Lincoln, Gerald McMurtry is that man and the unselfish giving of his findings to us is appreciated.

We are under obligations to others who have helped in many different ways and their names shall be listed here alphabetically, with their contributions known only to the authors who thank them with grateful hearts for their gifts of time, their specialized knowledge, and encouragement. Our publishers are unable to allow us the space we would need, for instance, to describe the inspiration and aid given by Carl Sandburg, who once spent a week with our family. He then thought his greatest contribution might well be his urging us to nail up on the wall of our workroom a gigantic poster, shouting three gigantic words—"WRITE IT NOW!"—a piece of advice which Harper & Row—witness to our many broken deadlines and protestations that we must know more, and still more, before writing—realizes was never taken, though it was brooded upon.

We salute these benefactors:

James N. Adams, of Springfield, Illinois, associate editor of the *Journal* of the Illinois State Historical Society. *Paul M. Angle*, for the past twenty years to March 1, 1965, director of the Chicago Historical Society. *Commander Philip R. Baker*, of Pasadena, California, great-grandson of Mrs. Ninian Edwards, Mrs. Lincoln's sister. *Kenneth A. Bernard*, Professor of History at Boston University. *George L. Cashman*, curator of the Lincoln Tomb, Springfield, Illinois. *Herbert R. Collins*, of the Division of Political History, the Smithsonian Institution. *Miss Norma Cuthbert*, of the Henry E. Huntington Library, San Marino, California. *Edith Kunhardt Davis*, of New York, daughter of one of the authors and sister of the other. *Miss Margaret A. Flint*, assistant Illinois State Historian, of Springfield, Illinois. *Carl Haverlin*, of Northridge, California, Lincoln scholar, collector, poet. *Clarence L. Hay*, of New York. *Oliver Jensen*, editor, *American Heritage*. *David C. Mearns*, Chief of the Manuscript Division of the Library of Congress. *Ralph G. Newman*, owner of the Abraham Lincoln Book Shop in Chicago, and chairman of the Illinois Commission, New York World's Fair. *Miss Helen Purtle*, of the Medical Museum, Armed Forces Institute of Pathology, Washington, D. C. *Lawrance W. Rathbun*, of Concord, New Hampshire. *Robert L. Reynolds*, managing editor of *American Heritage* magazine. *Miss Gail Ridgwell*, of *Life* magazine. *James I. Robertson, Jr.*, associate professor of history at the University of Montana. *Dr. Francis S. Ronalds*, of the National Park Service, curator of Washington's Headquarters' Museum and Library at Morristown, New Jersey. *Carl Sandburg*, of Flat Rock, North Carolina. *Miss Margaret Scriven*, of the Chicago Historical Society. *Wayne C. Temple*, editor of the *Lincoln Herald*, Lincoln Memorial University of Harrogate, Tennessee. *Colonel Randle B. Truett*, Chief of History Branch of the National Capital Region. *Justin G. Turner*, of Los Angeles, California, lawyer, collector, author.

In addition, in expressing our gratitude for help given us in the making of this book we want especially to thank the staffs of a number of institutions for extraordinary service cheerfully given, as through the years we studied and all but devoured their rare books, manuscripts, photostats, microfilms and photographs. We owe much to the Library of Congress and the National Archives in Washington, D.C., to the Chicago Historical Society, the Historical Society of Pennsylvania, the Henry E. Huntington Library of San Marino, California, the Widener Library of Harvard University in Cambridge, Massachusetts, the Historical and Philosophical Society of Ohio in Cincinnati, the New York Public Library, the New York Historical Society, the Illinois State Historical Library in Springfield, Brown University in Providence, Rhode Island, Boston University, and Lincoln Memorial University in Harrogate, Tennessee.

Our thanks go to Charles Dahlmeyer, a fine photographer of Morristown, New Jersey, who over the years made prints from thousands of our original Brady negatives—a task which requires skill and patience. Many of these fine prints appear in *Twenty Days* and were developed in Dahlmeyer Studios with care beyond the call of duty.

Last but certainly not less gratefully, we name Brendan F. Mulvey, identified on the copyright page as our art director, who has devoted endless hours to planning with us the unusual and, we feel, dramatic welding of text with pictures. His interest and real dedication went much further than the mechanics of fitting words and pictures onto pages, and it became routine for the three of us to see dawn come as we worked together trying different combinations, sizes, exciting visual patterns—discarding, then trying again. Our art director has always spoken of it as "our book," and with reason.

INDEX

Reference numbers in **bold face** *indicate illustrations*

PICTURE CREDITS

All photographs in this book are from the Meserve Collection in New York, with the following exceptions:

P. 9: photo by Abbie Rowe, courtesy National Park Service.

P. 18, left: Widener Library, Harvard University.

Pp. 24–25, bottom: Lincoln Museum, Washington, D.C.

P. 29, top and bottom: Lincoln Museum, Washington, D.C.

Pp. 40–41: The Library of Congress.

P. 42, bottom: The Library of Congress.

P. 44, left: Illinois State Historical Library, Springfield, Illinois.

Pp. 44–45, center: Illinois State Historical Library, Springfield, Illinois.

P. 45, right: *Frank Leslie's Illustrated Newspaper* (Meserve Collection).

P. 47: Lincoln Museum, Washington, D.C.

P. 49: Lincoln Museum, Washington, D.C.

P. 52, bottom: Lincoln Museum, Washington, D.C.

P. 60: Lincoln National Life Foundation, Fort Wayne, Indiana.

Pp. 64–65 (death scene): National Library of Medicine, Washington, D.C.

P. 73: Dr. John E. Washington, Washington, D.C.

P. 81: From the private collection of Clarence Hay.

P. 88: Lincoln Museum, Washington, D.C.

P. 89: Lincoln National Life Foundation, Fort Wayne, Indiana.

P. 92, top right (Dr. Crane), and bottom row, second from left (Dr. Curtis): National Library of Medicine, Washington, D.C.

Pp. 92–93 (probe and bullet): Armed Forces Institute of Pathology, Washington, D.C.

P. 94: Armed Forces Institute of Pathology, Washington, D.C.

P. 95: Armed Forces Institute of Pathology, Washington, D.C.

P. 100, both pictures, and p. 99, left: Mrs. J. Marvin Smith, Greensboro, North Carolina. Mrs. Smith is the granddaughter of Alphonso Donn, doorkeeper at the White House during the Lincoln Administration, to whom Mrs. Lincoln gave the frock coat, the trousers, the vest, a large portion of the cravat, and the overcoat the President wore to Ford Theatre the night he was shot.

P. 101, center: The Smithsonian Institution.

P. 101, right: Lincoln Memorial University, Harrogate, Tennessee.

Pp. 102–103: Mrs. Luther Osterhoudt, Brooklyn, New York.

P. 104, top center and right (bloodied towel pieces): Lincoln National Life Foundation, Fort Wayne, Indiana.

P. 104, bottom left (gloves): Illinois State Historical Library, Springfield, Illinois.

P. 104, bottom right (letter): New York Historical Society.

P. 106: New York Historical Society.

P. 109, center (coins): Chicago Historical Society.

Pp. 122–123: *Harper's Weekly* (Meserve Collection).

P. 125: Lincoln Museum, Washington, D.C.

Pp. 128–129: *Harper's Weekly* (Meserve Collection).

P. 135: Illinois State Historical Library, Springfield, Illinois.

P. 143: Chicago Historical Society.

Pp. 152–153: *Frank Leslie's Illustrated Weekly* (Meserve Collection).

Pp. 154–155, top left: David T. Valentine, *Obsequies of Abraham Lincoln in the City of New York*, New York, 1866 (Meserve Collection).

Pp. 156–157: New York Historical Society.

P. 159, right: New York Historical Society.

P. 160, right: Chicago Historical Society.

Pp. 162–163 (both pictures): Illinois State Historical Library, Springfield, Illinois.

P. 164: Mrs. Elizabeth Springer Harrison, Irvington, Virginia. A contemporary print of the same picture was sent to the authors by Herbert B. Osborn, Salem, Massachusetts, with permission to publish.

P. 172: Albany Institute of History and Art, Albany, New York.

P. 175: The Smithsonian Institution.

Pp. 176–177: *Frank Leslie's Illustrated Newspaper* (Meserve Collection).

P. 181, top right: Lincoln National Life Foundation, Fort Wayne, Indiana.

P. 181, bottom right: La Fayette C. Baker, *History of the United States Secret Service*, 1867 (Meserve Collection).

P. 182: *Frank Leslie's Illustrated Newspaper* (Meserve Collection).

P. 183: La Fayette C. Baker, *History of the United States Secret Service*, 1867 (Meserve Collection).

Pp. 184–185: The Smithsonian Institution.

Pp. 186–187 (both pictures): The Smithsonian Institution.

Pp. 190–191: *Frank Leslie's Illustrated Newspaper* (Meserve Collection).

P. 192: Lincoln Museum, Washington, D.C.

P. 193: *Harper's Weekly* (Meserve Collection).

P. 196 (courtroom): *Frank Leslie's Illustrated Newspaper* (Meserve Collection).

P. 198, right (Dr. Mudd): Lincoln Museum, Washington, D.C.

Pp. 206–207 (three pictures): *Frank Leslie's Illustrated Newspaper* (Meserve Collection).
P. 209: *Frank Leslie's Illustrated Newspaper* (Meserve Collection).
P. 220, top: Cleveland Public Library.
Pp. 222–223 (all three pictures): Lincoln National Life Foundation, Fort Wayne, Indiana.
P. 226: Lincoln National Life Foundation, Fort Wayne, Indiana.
Pp. 228–229: Lincoln National Life Foundation, Fort Wayne, Indiana.
Pp. 230–231 (both pictures): Lincoln National Life Foundation, Fort Wayne, Indiana.
P. 232: The Library of Congress.
Pp. 234–235, top: Chicago Historical Society.
P. 234, bottom: Lincoln Museum, Washington, D.C.
P. 236: Mr. Justin G. Turner, Los Angeles, California.
Pp. 238–239: Chicago Historical Society.
P. 247 (both pictures): Illinois State Historical Library, Springfield, Illinois.
P. 248: *Frank Leslie's Illustrated Newspaper* (Meserve Collection).
P. 249: Illinois State Historical Library, Springfield, Illinois.
P. 252: The Library of Congress.
P. 253: The Library of Congress.
P. 260: Illinois State Historical Library, Springfield, Illinois.
P. 261, bottom: Illinois State Historical Library, Springfield, Illinois.
P. 262, top left: Mrs. Milton A. Loucks, Gloversville, New York.
P. 262, top right and bottom right (two pictures): Illinois State Historical Library, Springfield, Illinois.
P. 264: Illinois State Historical Library, Springfield, Illinois.
P. 266 (all three pictures): Illinois State Historical Library, Springfield, Illinois.
P. 267, center (Mrs. Logan): Illinois State Historical Library, Springfield, Illinois.
P. 270, center (Mr. Logan): Illinois State Historical Library, Springfield Illinois.
P. 274: Illinois State Historical Library, Springfield, Illinois.
P. 278: Illinois State Historical Library, Springfield, Illinois.
P. 280: Illinois State Historical Library, Springfield, Illinois.
Pp. 282–283, center: Illinois State Historical Library, Springfield, Illinois.
Pp. 284–285: Ilinois State Historical Library, Springfield, Illinois.
P. 290: The Library of Congress.
P. 293: The Library of Congress.
P. 303: Illinois State Historical Library, Springfield, Illinois.